FIVE-POINT PLAY

FIVE-POINT PLAY

Duke's Journey to the 2001 National Championship

by Mike Krzyzewski

with Donald T. Phillips

WARNER BOOKS

NEW YORK   BOSTON

Warner Books

Time Warner Book Group
1271 Avenue of the Americas, New York, NY 10020
Visit our Web site at www.twbookmark.com.

Printed in the United States of America

First Edition: November 2001

10   9   8   7   6   5   4   3   2

ISBN: 0-446-53060-3

LCCN: 2001095990

Dedicated to the

2001 Duke basketball team

Contents

Foreword

by Shane Battier

With about 10 seconds to go in the 2001 national championship game and our opponent, Arizona, letting the clock run out, I crouched down and said a little prayer of thanks for all our blessings. Then the clock hit zero and I had the most unbelievable sensation rush through my body, my mind, and my soul. The victory celebration with my teammates was an unforgettable experience—a beautiful moment.

We had talked about winning championships at Duke all the time—so much so that it almost became an intangible thing. Well, at that moment, it became tangible. Everything we did during the year—all the practices, all the hard work, all the things we said to each other—suddenly made sense. I finally understood what being a champion was all about. And that was almost as cool as winning.

Between my sophomore and junior years, several players left the program early to pursue careers in the NBA. Coach K never wavered, though. In his commanding voice and optimistic tone, he told us that we were going to be okay—that no matter what happened, we were still going to be Duke, that we were going to play at a high level, and that we were going to win. Because I believed in him, I took what I had learned during my first two years and stepped forward to keep the program strong. So did my team-mates, Chris Carrawell and Nate James.

During my junior year, we won the Atlantic Coast Conference regular season, we won the ACC tournament, and we made it all the way to the Sweet 16 in the NCAA tournament. That was a pretty good achievement for a team with a lot of very young players. But it was in my senior year that everything came together. Our young players had a full year under their belts. We had gained experience as a team. And our play improved and our confidence grew as the season progressed. It was apparent to everybody that something very special was in the making.

The book you are about to read chronicles my senior year—Duke's 2001 national championship season. While the basketball specifics are interesting in their own right, they are only peripheral to a much more important story. The truth is that basketball was only the vehicle for a remarkable journey filled with human emotions, peaks and valleys, major adversity, courage, love, and, ultimately, triumph. In this book, Coach provides a behind-the-scenes look at how he forges a successful team environment. He shows how many of our wins on the court were really the result of connections off the court—fashioned during moments of privacy with individual players. And he reveals, with specific examples, his coaching philosophy that success is not as much about the *X*'s and *O*'s as it is about human relationships.

My own personal relationship with Coach was anything but one-way. He listened to what I had to say. He was sensitive to my opinions and to my feelings. We discussed things in detail. At times we joked, and at other times, we were extremely serious. There wasn't a day in my career at Duke that I didn't look him in the eye and believe what he said to me. He asked me to be one of the leaders of our team and an extension of himself out on the basketball court—and that's what I tried to do.

When I was younger, Coach actually had more confidence in me than I had in myself. He kept telling me that I was going to be a great player, a champion—and that I could achieve every dream I ever had. After awhile, with that kind of encouragement, I started to believe it myself. During my senior year, I placed four gold cards on the wall of my apartment. Each card listed a goal I hoped to achieve: Win the national championship, be First-Team All-America, win the Player of the Year Award, and be Academic All-America. I achieved all those goals. A lot of my individual success is owed to the support my parents provided, to my teammates, and to my own inner work ethic. But I also know in my heart that, if it had not been for the friendship and coaching of Mike Krzyzewski, none of it would have been possible.

It's very rare, especially in an athletic world that is so focused on winning games, to find a man who both inspires and demands adherence to higher principles. With Coach, it's not just about winning games. It's about performing with class and integrity. It's about having fun along the way. It's about knowing who you are. And it's about continually improving yourself.

During the season, I watched my teammates improve to a level that some of them did not know they could reach. That's another of Coach's strengths. He sees each individual player for who he is and he finds a way to bring out the best in everybody. Then he coaches us all how to be part of a successful team. In turn, that teaches us how to be successful in life.

I count my blessings to have had the opportunity to spend four years at Duke with Coach. During that time, I not only became a champion, I became a man. So read along now, and see how Coach took a group of young players, elevated them to the next level, and made them all champions.

During the season,

Your team should be led with exuberance and excitement.

You should live the journey.

You should live it right.

You should live it together.

You should live it shared.

You should try to make one another better.

You should get on one another if somebody's not doing their part.

You should hug one another when they are.

You should be disappointed in a loss and exhilarated in a win.

It's all about the journey.

—Mike Krzyzewski

Prologue

On March 29, 1999, Duke lost the NCAA national championship game to the University of Connecticut by three points. We had a very strong team that year—led by three-time All-America Trajan Langdon and the national player of the year, Elton Brand. We'd sailed through the regular season and won the Atlantic Coast Conference title and then cruised through the postseason with championships in both the ACC tournament and NCAA East Regional. Nearly everybody was picking us to win it all. And why not? We were 37–1 and our average margin of victory was over 20 points per game. We did manage to beat a great Michigan State team in the Final Four semifinal, but a national championship was not to be.

Immediately after the season ended, I underwent hip replacement surgery. During those first few days recuperating in my hospital room, I began to think about the upcoming season and how I would regroup our team with three seniors departing (including Trajan Langdon). At this point I invited Elton Brand and his mom to come over for a chat. There had been a great deal of speculation about Elton, a sophomore, leaving school early to pursue a career in the NBA, and I simply needed to know if he was going to be part of next year's team or not. However, I could tell as soon as he walked into the room that he wanted to leave. Elton's eyes gave him away. So I told him that if leaving was best for him and for his mother, then I'd be fine with it, and so would Duke University.

While I was prepared for the possibility that Elton Brand might jump to the NBA early, I was not prepared for what happened next. Over the following few weeks, two more members of the team, William Avery and Corey Maggette, announced that they, too, would go pro early, and one player, Chris Burgess, decided to transfer to the University of Utah. Clearly, I was taken aback. I lost some sleep and became a bit disengaged. For a while, I think I was actually in shock. In 25 years of coaching, nothing had ever happened to me like this before—nothing even close. At this point, the pain in my hip seemed inconsequential as I realized that we were faced with not three, but *seven* members of our team leaving.

"What now?" I wondered.

In short order, Chris Carrawell, Nate James, and Shane Battier—the three key players who *were* returning, came over to my house for a meeting. They assured me in no uncertain terms that they all would be back and that I was not to lose any more sleep over the matter. And I told them we were going to be good regardless of the team members we lost. In fact, with the outstanding new recruits we had coming in, I believed the potential was there to have a good team. But it would take a lot of work from those three.

"Do you believe we can do that?" I asked them.

"Coach," said Chris Carrawell, "I believe it because you said it."

That meeting was the beginning of a two-year journey that would culminate in Duke's winning the 2001 NCAA basketball championship. In the midst of adversity, the four of us came together, inspired each other, and bonded together in a common cause.

It takes time to build trust. It took me awhile to build it to the level that Chris, Nate, and Shane showed that day at my house. But now we would have to start all over with a new group of guys. And if we were to be successful, I knew I would need much more help from our assistant coaches and from the remaining players.

That next season, we won the ACC regular-season title, won

the ACC tournament, and made it to the Sweet 16 of the East Regional. As a matter of fact, our team was actually ranked Number 1 in the national polls going into the NCAA tournament. Unfortunately, we met up with a very tough Florida team that ended our season in Syracuse, New York.

But the second year is the real story. During the 2001 season, we tried more motivational things than with any team I've ever had. We never used our adversity as an excuse for not being excellent. And almost miraculously, there were no attitude problems with the players. It seemed as though we lived in a protective bubble in which jealousy, envy, and selfishness weren't allowed—something I'd never before experienced to that degree in a team. While I always sought to reach that level of trust, no coach could ever hope to achieve it alone. The truth is that the players themselves created this No Jealousy Zone. And from the beginning, Shane Battier and Nate James set the example. They were unbelievable. The last month of the season was the most amazing in my coaching career. Many incredible things happened. When one player had a bad game, another stepped forward to pick up the slack. There were highs, lows, injuries, and out-of-body experiences. There was also adversity, courage, defeat, and victory. You name it, it was all there.

There's no doubt that our ability to hit the three-point shot carried us to the national championship. As a matter of fact, we broke the record for most three-point shots attempted in one season. But the real secret of this season's success was our five-point play—which we symbolized with a fist. There are five fundamental points that can help make a team great: communication, trust, collective responsibility, caring, and pride. I like to think of each as a separate finger of THE FIST. Any one individually is important. But all of them together are formidable.

So often in leadership, you hear about the group believing in the leader. Well, this group believed in the leader. And the leader believed in them. But the real story here is that they believed in each other. The season's journey was like a storybook. I'm glad I was in the book, but I wasn't the main character. This team had tremendous heart and great courage. They gave their hearts to me, and I gave mine to them. But more important, they gave their hearts to each other. More than anything else, that's what brought us the success we achieved. That is what won us the national championship.

Preseason

A few moments after my wife, Mickie, and I walked into the Lahaina Civic Center in Maui, Shane Battier and Jason Williams spotted us and waved. They were in the middle of a summer practice session as part of the U.S. Select Team chosen to help the 2000 U.S. Olympic men's basketball team prepare for competition. We had just arrived in Hawaii at the invitation of the National Basketball Association to attend a reunion of the 1992 Olympic "Dream Team"—on which I had served as an assistant coach.

After a break in the action, Shane and Jason jogged over to greet us. "*Hi Coach. Hi Mrs. K,*" they said almost in unison.

"Hi guys. How's it going?"

"*Great. When did you get here?*" asked Shane.

"Our plane landed about an hour ago," I said. "We thought we'd come over, check things out, and see if you wanted to have lunch with us."

"*You mean you came here first?*" asked Jason.

"Of course," Mickie replied. "We've got plenty of time to spend with those NBA stars. You two are our top priority."

Every preseason, I identify at least one or two individuals who will be the heart of our team. Invariably, they'll be the ones who will lift everybody else to a higher level of performance and achievement. In 1986, it was Johnny Dawkins and Mark Alarie. In 1994, it was

Grant Hill. In 1996, Chris Collins. In 1998, Steve Wojciechowski and Trajan Langdon.

This year, it was clear to me that Shane and Jason were going to be the two key guys. They already had a good relationship, but on a different level. Shane was one of the leaders on the court last year and Jason was an inexperienced freshman. But because they were both going to be leaders this year, it was imperative for them to relate differently to each other.

I viewed it as my responsibility to start them on the path to that new relationship—and also let them know they could count on me. The best players need the support of the head coach because being the leaders on a team can be lonely. Who do *they* turn to in moments of doubt? I had to deepen my relationship with Shane and Jason, and this seemed like the perfect opportunity to do so.

Later that afternoon, we met for a casual lunch in the restaurant next to our hotel. We were outside, a cool breeze was blowing, and the iced tea tasted sweet. All in all, it was the perfect setting for a no-pressure, amiable conversation with my wife and two of the main guys on our basketball team. We laughed, joked, and talked about our families until, eventually, the discussion turned to the upcoming season.

"I hope you both realize that this year you will have to be very close on the court. We have a fairly young team and the guys will need both of you to lead. You two should know that you can depend on one another at the highest level. Your relationship should be mature. Not that you'll never get on one another, but for the most part, you guys should be calming influences as we develop our team."

I asked them how they felt about the situation they were in and how they felt about the team overall, and I asked for their perspectives on each individual player. It was a good discussion and I learned a lot about how they think and what they believe. Then, knowing that Shane has a tendency to wear himself out, I decided to address a key issue with him right off the bat.

"You're going to have a lot of pressure on you this year, Shane. You'll probably be the preseason pick for Player of the Year. So you shouldn't come in and be running at 100 miles an hour. You should run at 80 miles an hour and work your way up to 100. Also, you'll need to rely on Jason more so you don't become the worrywart for the entire team—which would diminish your performance. We'll need you to be healthy both mentally and physically.

Then I turned to Jason. "Jason, can you help Shane?"

"*Yeah, I can help,*" he replied.

"Good," I said. "But you know there'll be pressure on you this year, too—mostly to go pro."

Jason, who had just returned from Brazil where he led the World Junior Team to a silver medal, was definitely NBA material. But I knew he still had a lot of improvement to go before he became the great professional basketball player I knew he was going to be.

"How have you liked playing against the pros here in Maui?" I asked.

"*Oh, it's great, a lot of fun.*"

"Well, it can be intoxicating. But don't get caught up in all that. Remember these guys aren't at the top of their game right now. You still have a lot of improvement to make. We'll watch your progress this season and keep talking about it. And don't forget that your plan is to graduate."

"*Right, I won't. Besides, my mom won't let me forget.*"

After awhile, Jason excused himself to go to the restroom. "How's Jason doing," I asked Shane.

"*Well, he's the best player here. No doubt about it.*"

"You should tell him that. Do you feel comfortable telling him that?"

"*Yes.*"

"Then tell him. The two of you should be joined at the hip. You know he wants your approval. He respects and admires you. If you tell him, it will help him."

"*Okay, Coach,*" replied Shane. "*I'll tell him.*"

After the guys took off, I looked at Mickie and said, "Well, *he's* rock solid."

"You mean Jason and the way he's playing?"

"Well, yes, Jason's doing great. But I was actually referring to Shane. Did you hear how honestly he responded about his teammate—the one who, no doubt, will give him the most competition for attention this year? Shane could just as easily have said something noncommittal about Jason and talked about himself. But he didn't; he simply stated that Jason was the best player there. That's our senior leader, Mickie. Honest. No jealousy. Rock solid. I hope he can spread that to the rest of the team."

At this point, we had completed our first major step of the year. We had determined that the heart of our team was going to be these two young men. And, as always, I was going to lead with the heart.

*   *   *   *   *

During the summer, other players also were busy preparing for the upcoming season. Actually, preparation for the 2001 season began in March 2000—only a few days after we lost to Florida in the Sweet 16 round of the NCAA tournament. Nate James, for instance, our rising fifth-year senior, was in the gym right away working out, shooting, watching tape—and he continued to do so nearly all summer. He was determined to graduate from Duke with a championship ring on his finger. Many of the other players followed his lead in the off-season.

Mike Dunleavy went home to fully recuperate from the mononucleosis that had sidelined him for part of last season. Toward the end of the summer, he worked out with the NBA's Portland Trail Blazers—which were coached by his dad, Mike Dunleavy Sr. Casey Sanders traveled to Europe to play on a touring all-star team. Carlos Boozer headed in the other direction—paying his own way to Hawaii where he attended the Pete Newell Big Man's Basketball Camp. And our three freshmen, Chris Duhon, Reggie Love, and Andre Sweet, stayed in Durham to take classes and, in the process, became fast friends. Not only did they study together, they played full-court one-on-one games nearly the entire summer. They were in unbelievable shape when the fall semester started.

Also that summer, Carlos Boozer's parents moved down from Juneau, Alaska, and Chris Duhon's mother moved up from Slidell, Louisiana. All our players enjoy wonderful support from their parents. And that's the way it should be. One of the things I look for when I recruit a player is parental support and mutual respect. And perhaps because I had such a close relationship with my mom, I especially home in on those kids with a special mother-son connection. It seems to provide a particularly strong foundation for character, courage, and the capacity for learning and growth.

In the off-season, I like to work in my garden. If I take something from good soil and replant it in even richer soil, it seems to grow great. It's kind of like that with our players. All of them come from good homes to join our Duke basketball family. As individuals, they arrive with a certain amount of intelligence, confidence, and unselfishness. Their parents plant them with me and say, "Coach, here's my son. I'm going to support you." And I try to create a fertile environment to grow the individuals into one collective team—into a beautiful garden.

Here's how I saw our players as the year began.

The Players

Shane Battier
Senior, 6′ 8″, 220 lbs.

Born leader; potentially a great, great leader. A responsibility vacuum cleaner. Wants to be The Rock for everybody. Not afraid for everybody to be good while he's good. Enjoys the success of his teammates. Maturity and thought processes are way beyond his years. He does need to have somebody ask, "Are you okay?" But you have to do that privately. Sometimes I have to counsel him about not over-committing himself. Have to be careful not to wear him out; can't have the maître d' sweep the floor every night. Tremendous will to win.

Carlos Boozer
Sophomore, 6′ 9″, 270 lbs.

Has a big heart. Understands he needs a team to make him the very best. Very coachable; doesn't make excuses. Craves instruction. Methodical; needs to develop a habit of doing things at a quicker pace; sometimes too laid-back for his own good. Sometimes gets bogged down in the process. Has not yet learned to function at full capacity; he wants to, but hasn't developed a habit for doing that. Has tremendous potential that must be developed.

Andy Borman
Sophomore, 6' 1", 181 lbs.

Starter on soccer team. Always dreamed of being a Duke basketball player; works hard to make his dream a reality; living his dream. My nephew; Mickie's sister's son; not on the team because he's my nephew; on the team because he works his rear off. Teammates like him; works hard to pump them up; comic relief for the team.

Andre Buckner
Sophomore, 5' 10", 170 lbs.

Has a smile that fills his face and lights up a room. Very likeable. Quiet around me; but around his teammates, he's animated. Comic relief for the guys. Sometimes physically can't compete because he gets asthma-type attacks. Can pressure the ball very well.

Ryan Caldbeck
Senior, 6' 3", 185 lbs.

Was a manager on our team his freshman year; never gave up on his dream to be a Duke basketball player. Does anything asked of him; his maturity helps our guys. Unbelievably dependable. Tough. Sure.

Matt Christensen
Junior, 6' 10", 247 lbs.

Battles knee problems; on a physical roller coaster, but is there every day. Never able to give 100 percent physically; always there 100 percent mentally. Mild-mannered and gentle off the court. Dependable. Tough. Very team-oriented; very supportive of his teammates. Offers no excuses. Quiet; secure; mature.

Chris Duhon
Freshman, 6' 1", 186 lbs.

A reluctant superstar; has the "waiting-in-line" syndrome; Grant Hill and Shane Battier had it also; not a bad trait. On defense, he's like a bird flying free; reluctant, offensively. Amazingly talented. Will work like crazy. Shows great concern for his teammates; even though he could be a star, he wants their respect, love, and friendship. When he looks into your eyes, he's almost angelic.

Mike Dunleavy
Sophomore, 6' 9", 204 lbs.

Can do everything well. Wants to win and doesn't care who gets the credit for it. Is willing to step forward. Thinks of things in more depth than most. I want him to say more. Still growing physically; his body has changed and he's still learning how to deal with it; once his mind catches up to his body, he'll be one great player. Has a wit that challenges me and I like that.

Nick Horvath
Sophomore, 6' 10", 221 lbs.

A real believer. Solid player. Continually learning that he is good. Solid sixth or seventh man on our team. Great knowledge of the game; very intuitive; smart. Self-motivated; low-maintenance. Very well-liked by his teammates; able to help others improve. Big heart; unselfish.

Nate James
Senior, 6' 6", 200 lbs.

Quiet leader. At his best when he becomes a warrior. Confident. Great work ethic. Wants to be a part of something bigger than himself. 100 percent committed. At times, almost too team-oriented; a little bit too unselfish; that strength can also be a weakness. Sometimes he thinks too much and forgets his natural instincts; needs to think less in the heat of a game. A meat-and-potatoes player. Will defend until he dies. No one would do more for his teammates.

Reggie Love
Freshman, 6' 5", 220 lbs.

Wide receiver on the football team; very, very fast. Has great balance; has a lower, sturdy center of gravity. Doesn't complain; does whatever is good for the team. Very smart. Tough. Likeable. Fearless. Physical.

Dahntay Jones
Junior, 6' 5", 206 lbs.

Transfer from Rutgers where he was the marquee player; ineligible to play this year. Only the second transfer since I've been at Duke; a star; our best all-around athlete. Tough as nails; no excuses. Very intelligent. Dedicated. Aggressive. Patient. Wants to win. Outstanding defender. Loves to compete.

Casey Sanders
Sophomore, 6' 11", 218 lbs.

Didn't start playing basketball until he was 14. A great person. Accepts any role you put him in. Wants to get better; still learning; has the largest growth curve for the game; as he learns more, his eyes open up. Used to have excuses; not any more. Needs for us to tell him we need him. He's learned to like who he is and that he can be good being himself. Can really run the floor and block shots.

J.D. Simpson
Senior, 6' 4", 194 lbs.

Four-year walk-on; exceptional leadership ability. As well-liked and respected as anybody on the team. When he talks, people listen. Other members of the team want to be around him. Has charisma. Good shooter; intelligent player; understands our culture as well as anyone on the team.

Andre Sweet
Freshman, 6' 6", 203 lbs.

Team-oriented. Unselfish. Great attitude. Very homesick for his family and friends in New York; it impacts his studies. Never lets that be a distraction to the team. A good person.

Jason Williams
Sophomore, 6' 2", 196 lbs.

Incredible talent. Capable of tremendous belief; has a huge heart. If he hasn't done well in a game, he might come up to me and apologize for not playing well before I can say anything to him. At this stage in his life, he believes in me more than he believes in himself sometimes. Not completely sure of himself yet. Loves to play. Wants the ball in tough situations; has great courage. Unselfish. Incredible will to win.

The Assistant Coaches

Johnny Dawkins
Associate head coach, fourth year at Duke

Played for me from 1983–1986. Duke's all-time leading scorer. Consensus All-America and National Player of the Year (1986); retired jersey (Number 24) hangs in the rafters at Cameron Indoor Stadium. Nine-year veteran of the National Basketball Association. In charge of year-round player development program (skill development, individual lifting, conditioning). Mentor and friend to all the players and coaches. Quiet. Loves kids. Caring and kind. Passionate. Brings maturity and experience to the staff. Assessment of players is always right on the mark. If you want to have an assessment of a fine wine, you go to a wine connoisseur in France. If you want an assessment of a fine basketball athlete, you go to Coach Johnny Dawkins.

Steve Wojciechowski (Wojo)
Assistant coach, second year at Duke

Replaced Quin Snyder last year. Played for me from 1995–1998. Former captain of the Duke basketball team; NABC National Defensive Player of the Year. All-America Honorable Mention (1998). Former teammate of Shane Battier, Nate James, and J.D. Simpson. Former teammate of Coach Chris Collins. Works with the big men. Splits scouting and recruiting duties with Coach Collins. Chris Duhon was his first recruit. Great passion. Great heart. Amazing work ethic. Last name tougher to spell than Krzyzewski.

Chris Collins
Assistant coach, first year at Duke

Replaced David Henderson this year. Played for me from 1993–1996. Former co-captain of Duke basketball team. Former teammate of Wojo. Former assistant coach at Seton Hall University with Tommy Amaker. Former assistant coach with WNBA's Detroit Shock. Works with the guards and perimeter players. Splits scouting and recruiting duties with Wojo. Grew up around basketball. Father is a coach in the NBA. Great insights into all areas of basketball. Passionate. Gutsy. Great heart. A real winner.

Jeff La Mere
Director of basketball operations, sixth year at Duke

Former student manager at Duke from 1993–1995. Former assistant coach at the University of Delaware. Coordinator of all basketball-related activities, including scouting, videotaping, and assisting coaches in day-to-day operations. Very intelligent; reliable; has good insights about people and the game.

Mike Schrage
Administrative assistant, second year at Duke

Former student manager with Indiana Hoosiers basketball team. Former administrative assistant for the Mississippi basketball staff. In charge of academic coordination for all the players. Helps them with time management. Reminds them of papers due and exams coming up; stays on top of their progress. Provides me with a weekly written update. Thorough. Efficient. Dedicated.

Andre Buckner called me from Dallas one summer day and he didn't beat around the bush. "*Coach, I'm getting a tattoo,*" he said.

"Where are you going to get it, Andre—on your forehead or where?"

"*On my arm*," he responded with a laugh.

"Is it in good taste?"

"*Yeah, I think it is.*"

"Well, it's your right to do that. I'd advise you to think about it for a moment. Make sure it's something you want there forever—and that it's in good taste."

Twenty years ago, I wouldn't have handled Andre's call that way. I would have made it an issue. Back then, I was wired tight, and there was no way anybody on my team was going to get a tattoo. But with time, I've become more accepting, more understanding. And it's a good thing, too, because a number of the guys on our team have chosen to get tattoos.

Some people say that kids today have changed for the worse. But I bet adults were saying that when I was a kid. The group I hung out with were all good kids. We just did some things that were strange to adults. Well, the kids on my team are good kids, too. They just have a different culture. And as their coach and leader, I feel I need to get into their culture and figure out how to teach the principles of honesty, truthfulness, collective responsibility, and trust. It doesn't mean I have to dress like them, or get a tattoo, or have a body part pierced, or love hip-hop music. But it does mean I have to understand that they are allowed to do that. In general, I just don't let these things become obstacles to our having a high-quality relationship. They're good kids. If they want to wear earrings and have tattoos, that's all right—it's their culture.

*   *   *   *   *

In preparing for the upcoming season, I met frequently with my staff, and together we came up with some basic strategies.

First, conditioning was going to be a key for us. We had just moved into a new building—and our new weight, training, and locker rooms now lent themselves to year-round strength and conditioning. So we created a new program (called Individual Player Development) and put Johnny Dawkins in charge of it. I knew Johnny would be great at it, because he had to take great care of his body when he was a professional athlete in the NBA. He would now coordinate closely with William Stephens, our strength and conditioning coach, to see that all the players never got away from good conditioning.

Second, we decided to install a more up-tempo playing style and a system that would incorporate more depth. Last year, we weren't deep with players coming off the bench. This year we would be. We'd also be extremely fast. "I want this team to think fast," I told the staff. "So let's speed up practice this year. Let's create a fast tempo—even in how we go from drill to drill. Let's get the guys accustomed to never slowing down."

Third, we planned to take advantage of this team's shooting ability. Shots from beyond the three-point arc were going to be big for us this year. Our guys have the three key ingredients you need to be successful at it: confidence, intelligence, and unselfishness. So we decided to let our players trust their talent as much as we did. And we were going to hold to our maxim: Shooters do not stop shooting, at Duke.

> *"I don't think I ever heard 'Don't shoot' in my years here. What Coach K will get on you for is* not *shooting when you're open."*
>
> —Nate James

There were also some intangible things that we were determined to emphasize. We would show more video of past championship moments and great Duke teams. I wanted the kids to envision themselves hitting the big shot and celebrating a championship. I also wanted the team to have a primary focus on communication with each other. If you're a true team, you can go on the court and hear both the talk of the players and the squeaking of the shoes. If you hear just the squeaking of the shoes, something's wrong.

We vowed that we would learn from our mistakes and losses this season. Not too many negative things are going to happen to us twice. Paradoxically, we also plan to forget. We'll have to put things behind us quickly. Next Play is going to be a key phrase this year. THE FIST will also be big this year. We'll constantly reinforce the five points of THE FIST: communication, trust, collective responsibility, caring, and pride.

And we're going to talk to Jason Williams and Carlos Boozer about the NBA. I want them to know that it's okay to talk about going pro. We'll put together plans for them so we don't have them thinking things like, I have to score a certain amount so that I can make it to the NBA early. Besides, we should always have plans for our players and be involved in their decisions. We don't want to be providing input only at the eleventh hour. Talent alone does not require time. But the development of talent, the development of leadership, and the development of communication can only be developed through time and effort.

And finally, we're going to emphasize that basic fundamental of Duke basketball—defense. This year, we'll have more depth so we'll be able to keep a fresh unit on the court playing defense all the time. Half-court pressure, three-quarter-court pressure, full-court pressure, and forced turnovers result in fewer points for our opponents and more high-percentage shots for us. I've already got an appropriate quote picked out, and I'm going to put it on all the lockers before the first team meeting: "In all the research you do as a coach, studying other coaches in championship-type situations, you find that all those teams combine talent with great defense. You've got to stop other teams to win."

WE WILL PLAY GREAT DEFENSE. WE WILL STOP OTHER TEAMS.

*   *   *   *   *

The school year officially started on August 28, and our first team meeting was a week later, on September 5. Everybody was at that meeting—players, coaches, managers, staff—everybody. I wanted us all to be on the same page from the very beginning. "This is going to be a championship season," I said right off the bat. "So we'd best be champions before the season starts. Academics is key. Take care of your business *off* the court, so when the season starts we'll be able to take care of business *on* the court. Remember this, guys: There are not going to be any excuses for not doing well academically."

After my opening remarks, each coach and staff member spoke

about his various responsibilities and how he would be interacting with the players. And before the games began, we'd have similar meetings to reinforce attention to academics and appropriate behavior on campus. From time to time, we'd also bring in outside people to talk to the players about career planning. For instance, we brought an NBA official in to discuss some key points. He informed them that the average career in the NBA is only three and a half years and that 95 percent of NBA players work after their careers are over. It was another way of our preparing our players for life after college. Later, our staff typed up some bullet points and passed them out as reminders.

We also asked the deans of Student Affairs and Judicial Affairs to come in and speak about rules and regulations on campus. They talked about the No Cheating rule and just exactly what "cheating" meant. They talked about how a player at a neighboring university was recently arrested for drinking and driving, another for assault, and another for date rape. At the end of that session, I reiterated the only rule we have here: Don't do anything that's detrimental to yourself. Because if it's detrimental to you, it'll be detrimental to our program and to Duke University.

*   *   *   *   *

"Chris, shoot! Shoot, will you? Chris! Will you shoot the ball?!"

This isn't me encouraging Chris Duhon, it's the players on the court. We are working on connecting plays. It's a three-on-three drill and this is the idea: I dribble and pass to you, you shoot, we feel like it's our shot as well as yours. I penetrate to get your guy off you. Then I get the ball to you and you shoot. Well, the ball was thrown to Chris and he just wouldn't shoot. It was unbelievable. At first I thought he just didn't want to miss the shot or make a mistake. So I finally stopped the practice. "Look, Chris," I said, "if you're not going to shoot in practice, how do you expect to shoot in a ball game?"

"I don't know, Coach."

"Okay, then. Try it again."

But Chris continued to walk on eggshells—at least on offense. On defense, it was a different story. He was incredible—fast up and down the court, quick hands, smothering opponents. So I began to wonder why it was that the best high school shooter in the nation the previous year wasn't shooting. It was as if he had put himself in a cage and *couldn't* shoot. Then it hit me. On defense, he had the freedom to play aggressively and it didn't take away from anybody else. But, in his mind, if he took shots on offense, he was taking something away from Jason and Shane. So he was deferring to them. He was being unselfish.

This kid is the ultimate example of "team comes first," I thought to myself. But that great virtue can also become a great problem if it inhibits his performance. So, later, I stopped practice again. "Jason, what do you think about Chris as a player?" I asked Jason Williams.

"*Oh, he's terrific, Coach.*"

"Is it okay with you if he shoots the ball?"

"*Sure.*"

Then I turn to Battier.

"Shane, if you get two fewer shots in a game—and Duhon gets them instead, is that okay with you?"

"*Of course it is, Coach.*"

"You see, Chris," I said to Duhon. "It's okay for you to shoot the ball. So shoot the ball, will you?"

"*Yes, Coach.*"

This all happened during the first few days of practice in mid-October. And it was my way of trying to get all the guys—not only Chris—to shoot more. Early on, I wanted to establish a No Fear Zone where they were not afraid to shoot—where there would be no repercussions if they missed. I wanted them to develop the habit of stepping up and taking their shot when it was there. I wanted them to be confident shooters.

As practice progressed, I saw the guys begin to be bolder in their shooting. And, as a result, our three-point shot began to evolve. In the first practice, we took two three-pointers; in the second practice, only one. But in the third practice, we exploded with 24 three-point attempts. Now that was more like it. Throughout the season, the evolution of our success with the three-point shot was going to be the result of a lot of hard work. Going after it, day after day—as a team and as individuals.

One of my goals as a coach is to get every student in my program to realize the value of a hard-work ethic. "You bring yourself here every day at a certain high level," I ask of them. "Then I'll help you get better. I'm not going to help you get to where you can get by yourself. *You* need to do that."

Sometimes, people tend to get caught up in the process and lose sight of their destination. Basically, we want our guys to believe their destination is worthy of their effort. To be a championship team, then, what do you have to do to get there? The first thing you have to do is fall in love with the process. If you don't, you're never going to arrive at your destination. We want to create an environment where coming in for practice at 6:00 A.M. is not a punishment, where weight-lifting and sprinting are not drudgery, where intense workouts are just part of the program.

"When I first got here, working hard was just that—working hard! Now, working hard is just what you do. If you are around a certain level of performance all the time, and you stay around it, it just becomes how you're supposed to act. It's normal."

—Casey Sanders

"You learn the value of hard work and what it means. Work becomes something that's not negative. It's what you do."

—Shane Battier

*   *   *   *   *

Every day in practice we divided into two teams—Blue and White. The potential starters wore white jerseys—Battier, James, Williams, Boozer, Dunleavy, and Duhon. The rest of the guys made up the Blue team. However, they also wore white jerseys from time to time as we tried out different combinations. In game situations during the season, the Blue team, based on the scouting reports, always ran our upcoming opponent's offense or defense. In scrimmages, they went at the starters like it was a real game. That was their role.

Often, you can bust a second unit's spirit by having too good of a team. That's kind of what happened to our '99 team. The White team just dominated practices, often winning scrimmages by a lopsided score of something like 32–4. And at the beginning of this season, sure enough, the Blue team started out thinking that there was no way they could beat the starters. But they soon found an unusually effective weapon in their arsenal in the form of Dahntay Jones.

Dahntay had been a star player at Rutgers University the previous year—having averaged 16 points per game. When he contacted me in the spring and requested a transfer to Duke, I did not make it easy for him. I was immediately impressed that he was willing to put himself in a situation in which he wasn't the star. I told him that there would be no guarantees that he would start. I advised him to think about that and not to make his decision until he was 100 percent committed one way or the other. If he was going to leave his home and family in New Jersey, I didn't want him having any regrets. But because of NCAA rules, he could not play in games or travel with the team during his first year. However, he could practice with us. And he made all the difference in the world in preparing our team for each and every game we played. As soon as the guys on the Blue team saw what Dahntay could do on a basketball court, they immediately started to follow his lead. And that surprised him.

"People started following me early. That had never happened to me before. But once I saw they were looking to me for leadership, I gained more confidence in myself. From then on, I went into every practice trying to make everyone better. More than anything else, I tried to be a teammate to the players on the court. And sometimes, in my role, that meant getting in their faces."

—Dahntay Jones

That's exactly what I wanted Dahntay to do—get in the faces of the starters, force them to work hard, make them better. Before he came in, the starters were used to ruling the roost. Well, Dahntay rattled their cage. There were a couple of times when Shane really got out of character and threw a couple of elbows. But Dahntay came right back at him.

"Shane, you really surprised me," I said after one of the incidents.

"*He ticked me off!*"

"Well, you weren't that good then, were you? Don't you think somebody's going to do that to you in a game?"

Dahntay created a level of competition on a day-to-day basis that our starters would not otherwise have had. And in doing so, he lifted the entire Blue team up to a much higher level of performance and enthusiasm. They *knew* they could win with Dahntay. They *knew* they could make the starters play harder and better.

During the year, we practiced over 100 times. The Blue team approached every practice as if it were a game. If the White team didn't come in ready to play, they got embarrassed. That, in turn, created a situation in which the White team never turned off the competition mode. From the very first practice, every time they picked up a basketball, they were competing.

"When the Blue team went at it, they had no fear. 'We know you're the first unit,' they said. 'We know we're not going to start. But we're going to make you guys better because we're a team.' That meant so much to me. Dahntay could have been selfish. He's going to be one of the best players in America. He could have said, 'I'm not going to play, so why should I practice hard?' He came out and gave us his best every day—injured, not injured, tired, not tired. Every day, he comes out and gives you everything he has."

—*Chris Duhon*

*   *   *   *   *

We were preparing for our first exhibition game (the Blue-White Scrimmage at Cameron Indoor Stadium) when I noticed something unusual in practice. There seemed to be a little friction between Shane and Jason. It was a small thing, but I noticed it and I wanted to use it to make a point. As the White team was bringing the ball down the court against the Blue team, Jason had worked himself open on the perimeter. Shane, who had the ball, looked right at Jason, but rather than passing it, Shane turned toward the basket and forced a shot that he missed.

I immediately stopped practice and walked onto the court.

"Do you guys have a problem with each other?" I asked. "Shane, do you not like Jason?"

"*I like him, Coach.*"

"Do you not trust Jason?"

"*I trust him.*"

"Jason, do you like Shane?"

"*Yeah, I like him.*"

"Do you trust Shane?"

"*Yeah, I trust him.*"

"Then why won't you guys pass the ball to each other? What's your problem? You guys are the two best players on our team and you don't want to share the ball. I don't understand that. I think the two of you need to get together after practice and talk to each other about this."

What I really wanted to do here was put the two pillars of our team in a position to lean on one another. Shane was not being selfish when he took that shot instead of passing Jason the ball. He was just reverting back to the year before, when he was the leader. He was not yet in the habit of working with Jason as a leader also. Jason, however, viewed it as friction between the two of them. Well, friction can grow into jealousy. So I stopped it at the friction stage. Never letting little things like that go helped to create our No Jealousy Zone.

Sure enough, they did meet after practice. Jason reminded Shane that he had really boosted Jason's confidence when, in Hawaii, Shane told him he was the best player on the U. S. Select Team. And Shane told Jason that there would be enough awards to go around and that, if they just worked together, the team could win the national championship. After that, there was not a bit of trouble between the two of them the rest of the year—at least, not that I noticed.

Later in that same practice, I remember being really impressed with the way Mike Dunleavy was playing. Confident, sure of himself, making most of his shots, playing hard on defense, passing well, connecting—he was literally playing almost perfect basketball out there.

At one point, he made a great steal and was on a fast break to the basket when he saw Dahntay Jones quickly coming up to defend at the basket. At the last second, Mike hesitated and kind of threw the ball up high and missed the basket.

"Hold it! Hold it!" I said as I walked out on the court. "Mike, you can't do that. You're six-nine. Don't finesse it. Go right at the guy and make that basket. It could be the difference in winning or losing a ball game."

"As well as I had been playing, for Coach to come up and say something for this one little thing that I didn't do well showed me that he's a perfectionist and that nothing was going to get by him. And he was right about what I did."

—Mike Dunleavy

On October 28, 2000, our fans (nicknamed the Cameron Crazies) filled up Cameron Indoor Stadium to watch the Blue-White Scrimmage. Quite a few members of the local press also were on hand to sneak a peek at the team. We split up the guys to make the game a little more balanced—but it still turned into a blowout. The Battier-Dunleavy-Duhon group smashed the James-Williams-Jones group. It wasn't even close. The next day, when we reviewed tape of the game in front of the entire team, I really singled out only two people.

"You all played well," I said to the entire team. "But the guy who really played the best because of how well he's been practicing was Mike Dunleavy."

"Mike," I said, now looking straight at him, "you scored 23

points, grabbed 10 rebounds, and had 7 assists. Almost a triple double. Great game. Congratulations."

Then I turned my attention to Dahntay Jones. I knew this was the only game he could play with us all season. It was a great opportunity for me to make him feel like he was an integral part of this team. So, I made him the "star" of the moment. And even though everybody eventually goes through it, *nobody* wants to be the "star" of one of my review sessions.

I stopped the tape at a point where Dahntay held the ball out with one hand before making a drive to the basket. "What are you trying to show out there, son? What are you trying to prove when you palm the ball?"

"*Nothing.*"

"Then why do it? Hey, you may think you look good out there, but you really look like crap. And not only that, you're not *doing* anything."

I knew it was Dahntay's first game as a Duke Blue Devil. He was probably a little bit nervous and he was definitely showboating a little bit. So were all the other guys, for that matter. But by my stopping the tape and making him the "star," Dahntay was earning the respect of the rest of the team. Since this was the only time I'd be able to review him in a real game situation, I wanted to see how he'd take it. I also wanted him to know that he was part of *this* team and that he would be held accountable for his actions just like any player on *this* team.

In general, Dahntay's reaction was good. But at that moment, he really just listened—like they all do. It doesn't really make any difference what they *say*. It makes a difference what they *do* when they go out on the court the next time. In Dahntay's case, I really sensed he felt more a part of the team after that. It may have been at that moment that he said to himself, "*This group is worthy of everything I have to give.*"

On November 4, 2000, we hosted the EA Sports California All-Stars. Shane Battier was sidelined with a sprained left ankle, but Carlos Boozer was absolutely awesome. In filling in for Shane, he literally scored from all over the court. We won by a final score of 99–61. A week later, on November 11, 2000, we hosted the Grand Rapids

Hoops of the Continental Basketball Association. In that game, Jason Williams got into foul trouble, which forced Chris Duhon to play an extended amount of time. Chris played well, hit two big threes at key points in the game, and handed out quite a few assists. He looked good. Nick Horvath sprained his ankle in the second half. It didn't look like anything serious. Duke won the game, 107–74.

*   *   *   *   *

As we neared the start of the regular season, it was time to take stock of who we were as a group. We were still not a clenched fist, yet. We were not the best team we could be. We needed to talk more. We needed the sounds of a team on the court—talk *and* squeaking sneakers. The previous week I had to get on Shane for talking too much, if you can believe that. He was the only one doing any talking on the court. I actually had to tell him not to say anything at all so I could hear how vocal the rest of the team was. I think everybody got my message because they started talking. At this point, it was clear to me that the guys were searching for their roles on the team. That's really the reason they were quiet on the court. They were talking to *themselves*—thinking about what only *they* were supposed to be doing. But they needed not only to understand their roles, but everybody else's role on the team, as well.

The first step in identifying roles was for our staff to get together and make observations from practice. We did so, and here are some of the things we discussed: Shane can score in every way. He's our best three-point shooter; he's an outstanding foul-shooter; he can post; he can fill a lane; he has really improved in driving the basketball. He's always talking; he's alert; his mind functions in a continuous manner, and he can get other people to function that way. Three things—the blocking of a shot, the taking of a charge, and the steal—are all indicative of how well he moves when he's not covering the man with the ball. His position defensively is magnificent on almost every play. Shane's position is like a queen on a chessboard. He can do anything he wants. He's got to play at least 32 to 36 minutes a game. The timetable is set for Shane to be our leader. This is his team.

Jason dropped about ten pounds in the off-season and became a great outside shooter in addition to being an incredible driving inside scorer. The summer was more mental preparation than physical for him. He has much more confidence this year than he did last. The crowd excites him; injects him with emotion. Sometimes it gets him too wound up. Jason's a throw-back to the days when I grew up, when you just played ball because you liked to play and not for the fame and fortune it might bring. He starts—and he is our offensive floor leader.

Carlos first showed up at 286 pounds. His normal playing weight is 265–270. He's worked hard to get back in shape. Wojo's been putting in a lot of time with him. We need to motivate Carlos to do more. With his bulk, agility, and shooting skill, he's got the potential to be one of the best big men in the country. He's our most efficient scorer. He'll make 60–65 percent of his shots this year. He starts in the center position.

Nate needs to lather up, put on his war paint, and be ready mentally. He is in incredible physical shape—maybe the best of anybody on the team. He's an open jump shooter, and he plays defense and rebounds as well as anybody I've ever coached. This season he needs to live in the moment, not in the future. His teammates have great confidence in him. I see Nate making some really big plays this year. He's a fifth-year senior and our co-captain. We need his leadership. He starts.

Mike was 6' 8" last year. This year he's 6' 9" and still growing. He needs to grow mentally into his body. Once he figures out that he's not only a guard anymore, he'll be awesome. His versatility and his abilities will allow us to put him in almost any situation. He can play better defense, and we must work on that. He has the ability to step forward in any situation. But we'll have to prepare him ahead of time. Next year, he'll prepare himself. He starts.

Chris is coming along. This year, he's an understudy for Jason and Nate. When one of them comes out, he goes in. If Jason gets hurt or is in foul trouble, I think Chris is capable of being our floor leader. But let's remember, he's a freshman, so we'll have to get him prepared. Let's plan for more individual tape sessions with him. Show him his shots and remind him what a good shot is and what a bad shot is. And for God's sake, let's get everybody to encourage him to shoot. If he takes good shots and misses them, encourage him to take more. Chris is good enough to start, but right now, he comes off the bench—strong off the bench.

Nick worked really hard in the off-season. We need to boost his ego. He's not as confident as he should be. Nick is going to be really good. If he progresses this year, he has a chance to be a starter. We should plan for him to be an integral part of this team. He'll come off the bench in relief.

Casey is progressing well. We've been working on strengthening his shot-blocking. This year will be a tremendous growth period for him. Last year, he was personally disappointed that he didn't get to play much. This year, he'll have an expanded role. He'll come in to spell Carlos.

The Blue team is solid. They've been playing as one. Very impressive. Thanks to Dahntay's physical talent and J.D.'s charisma, they will keep the starters on their toes. Matt Christensen and Reggie Love (when he joins the team after football season) will provide much-needed enthusiasm off the bench. They both have the ability to give us a quick shot in the arm when needed. This may be one of the best Blue teams we've ever had.

Off the court, the guys have formed into small groups. That's natural. But I would like to see that change as the season progresses. We need to work on their interpersonal relationships. Let's strategically think about who rooms on the road together.

Finally, we need to bring Carlos to Shane and Jason's level. Potentially, we could have three guys who are the best in the country at their respective positions: Shane at wing, Jason at point guard, and Carlos at center. If we concentrate on developing those guys to be the best in the country at their positions, I see us winning the national championship.

*　　*　　*　　*　　*

Now it was time to meet with the players in the locker room and discuss their individual roles.

"We have a very unique situation here, fellas," I said to them. "As the season begins, our team has more than five guys who are good enough to start. We have two star players and several others who are going to become stars. How we talk about our roles, how we interact, is very important in preserving the No Jealousy Zone. Otherwise Duke can beat Duke. I'd just as soon talk about things straight out. Be very open. Anybody have a problem with this?"

Of course, there were no objections, so I turned and wrote the word *strengths* on the board.

"Strengths. What are our strengths, fellas?"

"*Shane,*" said one of the guys. So I wrote *Shane* on the board.

"*Jason,*" said another.

I wrote *Jason* on the board.

"*Carlos. Carlos is playing great in practice. Great.*"

Then I wrote *Carlos* on the board.

It was interesting to me that they had chosen as strengths the same three the coaching staff had chosen. Now I had more confidence to start discussing roles as I saw them for the upcoming season.

"I agree with you on our strengths," I said. "Shane is our leader on the floor. He will call all our defenses. He's our best player."

Now I'm concerned that Jason doesn't take that as an insult to him. "Jason, I want you to understand that that statement was not a knock on you. You are perhaps the most talented player in the country. You are becoming a great player, but don't let your incredible talent lull you into believing that you're the best you can be right now—because you can get better."

"*Coach, I know,*" said Jason. "*I know Shane's the best.*"

"Okay, then. Jason's our point guard. When he's in the game, he's running our offense. Jason, follow your instincts. You and Shane work together all the time."

"Nate, your role is to hit the open shot and defend. You are not a playmaker. You are a defender, a shooter, and a rebounder. Okay?"

"*Absolutely.*"

"Carlos, you are our most efficient scorer. You are our starting center. You need to touch the ball in the half-court offense. The entire team must understand that. Right?"

"*Right,*" said Carlos.

"Mike, you are a shooter, a passer, a rebounder. You're going to start. You have to realize that you are an incredibly unique player. In

1992, Grant Hill was a sophomore and he was also incredibly unique. You're going to be just like him. You're going to be a big part of what we do on both ends of the court this year."

Mike looked me in the eye and nodded.

"Chris, your main role this season is to be an understudy to Jason and Nate. You are in a learning mode, but you will see significant playing time. And when you're out there on the court, you're going to be aggressive and shoot the ball when you have an open shot. Is that clear?"

"*Yes, sir.*"

I addressed all the other players individually about their roles, and then I closed the meeting with a brief statement. "Fellas, remember, you need to be a fist," I told them. "Two is better than one if two act as one. Imagine what five guys playing as one can do. Be a fist."

*   *   *   *   *

During the last few practices of the preseason, Shane made sure that he and the other players encouraged Chris Duhon to shoot the ball. Shane was being a leader. He was setting up the No Jealousy Zone.

"*Look, Chris,*" Shane said to him, "*for us to be the team we can be, we need you to be Chris Duhon. And that's aggressive, exciting, and assertive—especially on the offensive end.*"

It's better for Chris to hear that from the players than from me. As a matter of fact, I had long since deferred to Shane in practices when he had something to say. After our second practice, for instance, I made an announcement to the staff.

"Tomorrow, I'm not going into the huddle at the start of the practice session," I said.

"Why not?" asked Johnny.

"Well, I've done it during the first two practices, and I've done it every day that I've been a coach. But in the first two practices, Shane spoke after me and he was better. So why not just let him speak? He's going to be speaking in the huddles out on the court when I can't be with them."

So I did not speak in a huddle at the beginning of practice for the next 99 practices. It demonstrated to everyone my confidence in Shane—and that Shane was an extension of me out on the court.

I've empowered my staff more this year, too. They're one of the youngest staffs in college basketball, they have tremendous energy and abilities, and I have great confidence in them. I'm going to let them handle the *X*'s and *O*'s much more this year so I can spend more of my time concentrating on the players. I'm also going to rely on Nate and Shane, our co-captains, as much as possible. They know how to win.

As we start the regular season, I have high expectations. This team can really shoot the ball. We are going to be a high-scoring team, and we will shoot many three-point shots. Our defense is really sound right now, so I think I'm going to back off on the up-tempo, breakneck-speed style we had been working on. Some of the guys were taking bad shots and getting too stretched out. They're just not ready to do it right now.

The ACC is a veteran conference, and because we've won the regular-season title four years in a row, the other teams will really come after us. I think it will harden us for NCAA play this year. We're going to have to keep the guys motivated to their highest level of performance. A key strategy for us this year is to make each other better by creating a unit where five play as one, where everybody is a family.

Speaking of family, my oldest daughter, Debbie, found out this summer that the due-date for her second baby was April 2, 2001—the day of the national championship game. "It's going to be a big week for us, Mom," she told Mickie. "I'm going to be having a baby, and we're going to win the championship trophy."

She might be right. We're ranked Number 1 or Number 2 in every preseason poll. Are we worthy of a national championship this year? Absolutely. Why? Because Shane Battier is here. I really believe this is his time. He deserves to win that championship ring. We're riding in his car this year, and his heart will lead us.

Preseason NIT

"Okay guys, listen up," I said as I handed each player a sheet of paper with a four-team bracket. "Tomorrow is our first game of the year and we're in the preseason NIT (National Invitational Tournament). It's a 16-team field, but this bracket is only for four teams. As you can see, we play Princeton in our first game here at home. When we win this one, three days later we'll play the winner of the Villanova-Fairfield game. The next round will be in Madison Square Garden the following week. But we won't worry about that now. We're going to treat each round of two games as if it is the Final Four and we are playing for the national championship. So let's get ready to play Princeton. It's the national semifinal game.

> *"It's my first game in college and Coach K is treating it like I'm playing in the Final Four. I tell you one thing, I wasn't looking ahead to the rest of the season. I was concentrating on* now; *focusing on the moment."*
>
> *—Chris Duhon*

"We are fortunate to play Princeton in our first game because they have a very deliberate, slow-down, ball-control team. Opponents usually do not score many points against them. This is a great opportunity for us to send a message to every other team that they're not going to beat Duke by playing the slow-down offense. We will set the pace of the game, not Princeton. We want them to adjust to us, not vice-versa.

"Our game plan will be simple. We're going to play really hard defense in the half-court. Put a lot of pressure on them all the time. We may get backdoored a few times. That's all right. Don't worry about that. I still want you guys out there pressing. Any questions?

"Okay, let's practice."

When the players hit the court, I had a surprise waiting for them. We brought in ACC referees to simulate game-like situations. I didn't want the players to develop bad habits by committing fouls that are not called in practice—then, all of a sudden, we're in a game and they're called against us. And that can take a team out of a game real fast.

At first, the refs gave the guys a bit of a clinic on how they're going to call 'em this year. Then they answered questions.

"*What if I put my knee into the other guy's leg?*" asked Carlos. "*Last year that wasn't a foul.*"

"Well, this year it's a point of emphasis. We'll call it a foul."

"*What if you touch a guy on the perimeter but don't change his direction?*" inquired Jason.

"This year, it'll be a foul. No rough play. No hand-checking, period."

After the mini-clinic, we ran two 10-minute scrimmages with the referees. Then, before we practiced several end-of-game situations, I recited one of my primary mottos: How you play in game-like situations during a practice session will eventually lead to how you play in a real game.

After that practice, we watched a couple of short video clips. We showed the team the last few minutes of the recent Kentucky–St. John's game in the Coaches vs. Cancer Classic. St. John's won because Kentucky ended up throwing the ball away. Either team could have won if the players had kept their heads. We also showed them the last minute of the 1999 Duke-UConn national championship game. The idea was to demonstrate how games can be won or lost in the last few seconds.

Now it was time to play our home opener. Naturally, there was a little bit of nervousness and anxiety in everybody, especially me. Cameron was filled to capacity, and when I walked onto the court, the crowd erupted in cheers. That has always made me a little bit uncomfortable. I wish I were a character on *Star Trek* and could be beamed from the locker room straight to the bench so I could just start coaching the game. That's what I'm really here to do.

Princeton at Duke

November 14, 2000—Senior Shane Battier established a new Duke single-game record with nine three-point field goals (two more treys than the entire Princeton team) on the way to a 29-point performance. Duke held a 22–20 lead with 10:09 remaining in the first half when the Blue Devils mounted a 27–5 run to end the half; Duke headed to the locker room with a 49–25 lead. The Blue Devils connected on their first five three-point field goals of the second half as they extended their lead to 64–30 with 16:11 remaining in the game. Sophomore Jason Williams scored 17 points and had seven assists while senior Nate James chipped in with 15 points and six rebounds. Sophomore Carlos Boozer had 11 points and four rebounds.

Final Score: Duke 87, Princeton 50
Overall Record: 1–0

After every game, the staff meets to review tape of the game and grade individual and team performances. Then, the next day, we meet with the players and provide feedback.

"Okay, fellas," I told the team, "We came out with passion against Princeton, we played hard, and we talked well. Our communication was very good. We also played without fouling, which is good for a slow-down game. Our defense and our shooting were good. Scoring 87 points against Princeton is like scoring 120 against another team. As a matter of fact, we scored more points against them than any team has in five years. We forced 20 turnovers—which was huge. We got accustomed to shooting the three and were 15-for-30. We set the pace of the game, not Princeton. That's the way it should always be with every team we play. Don't forget that. Don't ever forget that. Congratulations, it was a good win."

Next, we turned our attention to our upcoming opponent, Villanova, which had just beaten Fairfield. Chris Collins and Mike Schrage handled the scouting report for this game. They prepared a single-page report and a highlight tape, which they reviewed with me; then we had our session of "notebooks on the court" where we go over it with each of the players. Overall, scouting is the responsibility of my entire staff. Chris and Wojo take the lead in alternating games, with the help of Jeff La Mere and Schrage—all under the supervision of Johnny Dawkins.

My concern for this game was that it was going to be totally different from the game against Princeton. "Villanova is a good team," I said to the players. "We are going to have to play a really good game to beat them. They get solid guard play from Gary Buchanan and Jermaine Medley—and Michael Bradley, a Kentucky transfer, helps make them big and physical in the frontcourt."

After reviewing the report, we went back into the locker room and watched the scouting video that showed Villanova's offense and defense and how they work. Then we went back onto the court, and during the practice, we had a "walk-through" of Villanova's offense using the Blue team—and we showed the team how we wanted Villanova defended.

Villanova at Duke

November 17, 2000—Duke led most of the way in the first half, but tenacious Villanova would not go away until the final minutes of the game. Six Duke players scored in double figures. Carlos Boozer led the way with 22 points, 16 of which came in the first half. Shane Battier played all 40 minutes, had 18 points, and a team-high seven rebounds. With 1.8 seconds left in the first half, freshman Chris Duhon electrified the crowd with a three-point bank shot from 25 feet to give the Blue Devils a 51–40 halftime lead. Duhon scored 17 points that included 4-of-6 from three-point range. Sophomore Mike Dunleavy added 16 points on 6-of-8 shooting, while sophomore Jason Williams scored 13 points and dished out a team-high 10 assists. Michael Bradley led Villanova with a game-high 28 points.

Final Score: Duke 98, Villanova 85
Overall Record: 2–0

In the locker room after the game, I addressed the team like I always do, but something was different. Everybody seemed a little bit distracted. And some of the players were even grinning uncharacteristically. Then I remembered this game marked my five hundredth win at Duke. My brother, Bill, and many of my friends and former players had come into town to celebrate. I thought the team was just going to present me with the ball or something. But I knew it might be more than that when Duke's athletic director, Joe Alleva, pulled me aside and said, "Okay, Mike, we have something out on the court for you."

When we walked back into Cameron, the entire crowd was still there, and they erupted into thunderous applause and cheering. Mickie and our three daughters, Debbie, Lindy, and Jamie, were standing on the court—as was Nan Keohane, president of the university. Shane and Nate, on behalf of the team, presented me with the game ball. And then Coaches Dawkins, Wojciechowski, and Collins lifted a large black cloth off the floor and revealed the words: *Coach K Court*. I was told that, from this game forward, the basketball floor at Cameron Indoor Stadium would be named after me.

I was stunned. During the game, I had wondered why the guys were playing at such a frenetic pace. At the time, I didn't know why they were trying so hard. Now I knew why, and it moved me.

> *"Nate and I were told about Coach K Court a few days before the game. We approached Coach Wojciechowski and asked if we could tell the other players. He approved but said that absolutely no one else was to know. If there was ever a 'win one for the coach,' this was the game."*
>
> *—Shane Battier*

I was very emotional as I walked to the microphone. "I didn't know this was going to happen," I said. "I want you all to know that nobody could love Duke, this building, and the people in it more than I do. I'm so honored and humbled. I only wish my parents were still here to see this. My mother once cleaned floors at the Chicago Athletic Club to help me get here. So the K stands for Krzyzewski, and not just Mike. In naming the court in my honor, you also honor all of the players who played on Duke teams over the last 21 years. You could not honor me in a better way. Thank you. Thank you."

*   *   *   *   *

At the team meeting the day following the Villanova game, the first thing I did was to fill in the final slot on the four-team bracket with the name *DUKE*.

"Okay, fellas, we won that championship, now it's time to go to New York and win another one." Then I handed them the new brackets, which had us playing Texas in Madison Square Garden on November 22. In a way, this trip really *would* simulate a Final Four. We would be in a big city with a lot of media. It essentially *was* a four-team tournament. And, of course, we had to travel.

Since this was our first away game, we discussed what the players would wear on the road. In the old days, I'd have them dress in coat and tie, or coat and turtleneck. But, over the years, I found that some kids didn't have as much as others, and in a way, that created a problem for them. I also didn't want to say "Just wear something nice," because you never know what a kid's definition of "nice" might be. So we now have everybody wear their Duke travel warmups. The kids like them, they feel good wearing them, and they look great. So we decided to go with that again this year.

The first road game also meant we had to think about assigning roommates. Johnny Dawkins was the coach who really gave this issue a lot of thought, and I went along with his recommendations without hesitation. We put Jason Williams and Chris Duhon together because they were both guards and Chris was Jason's understudy. We wanted to build that relationship and have them get comfortable being together. Casey Sanders was paired-up with Mike Dunleavy because we believed Mike's experience and background in basketball would be great for Casey. And that's the way it turned out. Casey learned more about the details of the sport and Mike enjoyed talking about them. Johnny also thought it would be a good idea to have Carlos room with Shane. Shane is outgoing and Carlos is quiet and laid-back. We wanted Carlos to become more of a leader on the court. By sharing space with Shane, we figured some of Shane's leadership might rub off.

Some thought was given to having Battier room with Dunleavy. But we decided against it because they already shared an apartment in Durham. We didn't plan for them to do so, but when Shane and Mike told us that's what they were going to do, we immediately thought it would be good for the team. It would be good for Mike to be around a leader like Shane and, in turn, we were sure that some of Mike's wit and humor would help keep Shane loose.

When we arrived in New York and had our scheduled practice, I took the opportunity to speak about one of the elements of THE FIST—collective responsibility. Carlos had had a particularly great practice that day, so I decided to get the point across by talking to him in front of the other guys.

"Carlos, what caused you to play with such passion in practice?" I asked.

"*Just felt good, Coach.*"

"Well, remember that feeling in the game, will you?"

"*Okay.*"

"I like the fact that you're playing well, Carlos, especially on defense. Because when you're not playing well, Shane may have to come over and help out. Then he may pick up a foul. Well, that would have been your foul, but it's charged to him. So in reality, it's *our* foul, isn't it? And you know when you kick a pass back out to Jason or Shane or Nate or Mike and they take a shot and make it, that's *your* shot just as much as it is theirs. In fact, it's the whole team's shot. It's *our* shot."

Then I turned and addressed the whole group (who had been listening intently).

"*That* is collective responsibility, guys. It's a big thing for us."

Texas vs. Duke
Madison Square Garden, New York, New York

November 22, 2000—The Duke Blue Devils started the game with a 7–0 lead and never allowed Texas to get closer than five points. Nate James had six of those first seven points en route to a game-high 26 points. Duke outrebounded Texas, 47–38, with Carlos Boozer pulling down a game-high 11 rebounds. That repeatedly set the offense in motion. And with Duke playing fundamentally sound basketball at both ends of the court, it wore Texas down early. Despite scoring 20 points with seven assists, Jason Williams sat out much of the game with foul trouble. Chris Duhon stepped in, played 28 minutes, and ran the offense.

Final Score: Duke 95, Texas 69
Overall Record: 3–0

Two days later we were to play Temple in the final game of the pre-season NIT. It was a big-time match-up—and you don't get many opportunities to win a championship. During a scrimmage in practice the day before the game, there was a loose ball situation. Jason Williams tried to scoop it up by just bending at the waist. He missed it completely and the White team did not gain possession. So I stopped practice.

"Jason, you should dive for loose balls like that one. Why didn't you dive?"

"Didn't think about it, I guess."

"Well, *think* about it the next time, will you? It could be the difference between winning and losing a game. Okay?"

"Okay, Coach."

The last thing I did in the locker room before the team walked out onto the court for the start of the championship game was to fill in the bracket.

"I can tell you right now we're going to win this game," I said.

And then I wrote DUKE in the empty slot.

Temple vs. Duke
Madison Square Garden, New York, New York

November 24, 2000—Duke pulled out a thriller as Carlos Boozer netted a game-high 26 points, and Jason Williams took over the game in the last few minutes of play. The first half was low-scoring and close, with the Blue Devils holding a scant two-point lead at intermission. After Mike Dunleavy and Shane Battier hit three-point shots to start the second half, Williams and Boozer combined to score all of Duke's remaining points. With 3:38 left, Temple seized their biggest lead of the game on a three-pointer by Alex Wesby. That made the score 60–54. After Coach Mike Krzyzewski called a timeout, Duke played nearly flawless basketball—scoring on four of their final six possessions and not allowing Temple to score another point until there were only

1.6 seconds left in the game. Boozer scored six points in the final three minutes and Williams hit a key three-point shot that put Duke ahead, 61–60, with 2:05 left. After Wesby missed a three-pointer with 56 seconds to play, there was a hard fight for the rebound. Shane Battier slapped the ball out of a Temple player's hands. And Jason Williams dove for the ball, extending the full length of his body to bat the ball away from a Temple player who, in turn, pushed it toward Wesby, who was breaking toward the basket. Williams then dove hard at the ball again, slamming himself against the floor. This time, he gained control of it and called timeout with 46 seconds left. Williams then dished a pass to Boozer, who scored a lay-up to make the score 63–60 with 17 seconds remaining. After a foul, Temple made a free throw and the game ended.

Final Score: Duke 63, Temple 61
Overall Record: 4–0

After the game, John Chaney, Temple's coach, was asked how he felt about having to play us again the next week. "I like to schedule good teams," he said. "But playing Duke twice is like scheduling two *L*'s."

I was asked about the key to the game. "From that timeout [with 3:38 left] on, we just played great basketball," I responded. "We made play after play, and Jason Williams just played great. He put us on his back."

> *"In practice before the game, I didn't dive for a ball and Coach got on me for it. It's so weird that the same situation happened again. The only thing I could think about was that I wanted to win the basketball game. Coach sure was right. In this case, it* did *mean the difference between winning and losing a game."*
>
> —*Jason Williams*

Carlos Boozer was named the MVP (Most Valuable Player) of the preseason NIT—the first big-time event of the year for Duke.

You would have thought that Shane, with all his preseason publicity as probable national player of the year, would have won that trophy. But he really didn't play all that well in the NIT. After a standout game against Princeton, he faded a bit—with 18 points against Villanova, 16 points against Texas, and only eight against Temple.

He could have been a little resentful. I mean, how would most people feel if they had the lead in a Broadway musical, and all of a sudden, a supporting actor nails a song and gets all the fanfare? I think they might react with a little jealousy. But I was watching Shane as Carlos received his well-deserved trophy. Shane went up to Carlos and hugged him.

"I'm proud of you," he said, "It's about time you played like that. We need Carlos Boozer to play like that. Great going, Carlos. Keep it up."

I know that really meant a lot to Carlos. Many times, a superstar will create a ceiling on performance for everyone else. He doesn't want his teammates to get past a point where they take away from him. It happens all the time. Well, Shane Battier wanted all the guys to be stars. After a game, in the locker room, when he's slapping everybody on the back, they know it's not phony. Shane's security is in who he is—and that sets the tone for everyone else giving each other their hearts. It keeps them from putting a ceiling on their performances.

Now I'm feeling terrific. We really *do* have a No Jealousy Zone. This is going to be one heck of a year.

Early Regular Season

Less than 24 hours after winning the Preseason NIT in Madison Square Garden, we were back at Cameron Indoor Stadium for a game against my alma mater, Army. I had purposely scheduled these two games back-to-back, and by planning to play Illinois on November 28, it meant we'd have three games in five days. At this point in the season, our plan was not to do my team any favors. We're trying to put them in situations that would get them ready for March Madness.

> *"Coach put it to us this way. He asked us, 'What would you rather be doing? Practicing or playing a game?' We all knew the answer to that one."*
>
> —Nate James

Our annual game against Army is always interesting for me. I'd not only graduated from West Point, I had been head basketball coach there for five years before coming to Duke. Twenty-one years later, I still had many connections. Army's head coach, Pat Harris, played for me while I coached there, as did Assistant Coach

Marty Coyne. Robert Brickey, also an assistant there, started on my Final Four teams in 1988, 1989, and 1990. And my daughter Jaime's boyfriend, Chris Spatola, was a starting guard for the Cadets.

Army at Duke

November 25, 2000—Carlos Boozer scored all of his 22 points in the first half as Duke shot 71.1 percent from the field and forced 13 Army turnovers. At halftime, the Blue Devils led the cadets 67–26. Casey Sanders logged two minutes before suffering a pulled hamstring, but Nick Horvath scored ten points after missing several games with a sprained ankle. Shane Battier played only 19 minutes and scored nine points. Jason Williams added 10, Mike Dunleavy, eight, and Chris Duhon, seven. In the second half, Coach Mike Krzyzewski let the rest of his bench play for much of the game. Freshman Andre Sweet logged 18 minutes and scored eight points, while Matt Christensen tallied five points in 19 minutes.

Final Score: Duke 91, Army 48
Overall Record: 5–0

Our next game was a big one. We faced the University of Illinois (ranked Number 8 in the nation) in the marquee game of the ACC/Big Ten Challenge in Greensboro, N.C. Illinois was projected to be a Top Five team and contend for the Big Ten Conference championship. And in my mind, if they did that, they'd contend for the national championship.

Illinois vs. Duke
Greensboro Coliseum, Greensboro, North Carolina

November 28, 2000—The Duke Blue Devils, now ranked Number 1 in the nation, won a nail–biter with the help of 23 points from Jason Williams and 21 from Mike Dunleavy (both matched career scoring highs). Duke was lackluster in the first half as they allowed Illinois to score 10 of its 35 first-half points on second and third chances on the offensive boards. Coach Mike Krzyzewski spent halftime chastising his team for poor rebounding and lack of intensity. After a seesaw battle for most of the second half, Duke took a 77–70 lead with 2:02 left in the game. But Illinois made a three-point shot, and Duke seemed to come unraveled as they fouled and committed an uncharacteristic turnover to allow Illinois to make it a one-possession game in the last minute. With 13 seconds left, however, Chris Duhon anticipated an inbound pass and forced a turnover by deflecting the ball off an Illinois player. The win improved Duke to 125–18 alltime as the nation's top-ranked team. But this one didn't come easy against a physical Illinois team that out-dueled the Blue Devils on the boards, 42–27.

Final Score: Duke 78, Illinois 77
Overall Record: 6–0

After every game, our first practice is a feedback session with the entire team present. In other words, before moving on to the next game, we take care of ourselves first. I'm particularly interested in not allowing any negatives, whether physical or psychological, to fester and build upon themselves. We discuss the things we did well and the things we didn't do well. Essentially, I'm trying to develop pride in our performance. Pride—one of the five points of THE FIST.

After the Illinois game, we had one hell of a feedback session. I mean, I just hammered the team.

"As good as we were against Temple," I said starting my soliloquy, "that's how bad we were against Illinois at the end of the game. We were ahead 77–70 with 1:30 left in the game—and we won 78–77. That is unacceptable! We missed free throws; we fouled; we even fouled a three-point shooter, for God's sake. Our end-of-game management was horrible. Don't you think we should take pride in all 40 minutes of a basketball game and not just the first 38 1/2 minutes? We had that game won, but then they scored seven points and we only scored one point— ONE! It was like you guys were afraid to lose instead of playing to win. Well, in November and December, you can't be afraid to lose. This is the time you can learn how to win the close ones you'll encounter in the heart of the ACC season and in the NCAA tournament.

"Another thing is that we got obliterated on the boards, 42–27. 42–27! Did you guys forget all you know about rebounding? You need to *think* out there on the court. Didn't you remember the scouting report about how good they are going to the boards? I tell you one thing, we were lucky to win that game—LUCKY! Jason saved us with his 23 points. You created a lot of shots for us. But late in the game you fouled a three-point shooter, Jason. A THREE-POINT SHOOTER! You can't do that again. It could have cost us the game. Defensively, we were very good. We forced 26 turnovers. Overall, our defense is winning games for us, but we haven't found our identity on offense yet. But the worst thing—THE WORST THING—is that we didn't make each other better out there. We were doing individual stuff. It wasn't *our* shot. It was *my* shot. *My* play. We need to make each other better. We're doing it defensively, but we're not doing it offensively. We're not connecting. We're not *communicating* as well as we need to on the offensive end of the court. We need to keep our spacing and keep *talking* to one another. 'Hey, I'm open over here!' 'Jason, I got you.'

"We're going to work on all of that *before* we ever look at a scouting report on Temple. Let's start playing like we can play, not like we've been playing. Okay, let's go."

I was furious with the guys and I blasted them. But it needed to be done because they were falling into one of those "valleys" the season always seems to produce. I had to snap them out of it and get them headed back toward a "peak."

In practice that day, we put in the exact same game situation we had against Illinois: 1:30 to go; Duke 77, Visitors 70. "Figure out different ways to win, guys," I said out on the court. "This is winning time—winning time with your head, winning time with your heart, winning time with your mouth. Talk! You gotta talk!"

Then we had them focus on communication. "Carlos, you see Jason open, you pass it to him, and you say, 'Shoot it, J.' When you say that, you're showing *trust* in him—and then he feels more trust in himself. In turn, that gives him more confidence in his shot. He's less afraid to shoot. You're helping us create the No Fear Zone. It also shows that you *care* about Jason. *Trust* and *caring*, guys. Don't forget. Trust and caring—two points of THE FIST."

During this drill, I found a quality of Boozer's that I hadn't really noticed before. He really likes to pass. If you hit him (and he's a big target), he'll get you the ball back. Not many big guys do that. But I could tell Carlos liked it because I could see his eyes light up. So I stopped practice for a moment.

"That's damn good, Carlos! You like doing that, don't you?"

"*Yeah, Coach. I do.*"

"How do you other guys like it when Carlos does that?"

"*Yeah, that's cool,*" they all agreed enthusiastically."

"Okay, Carlos, keep doing it. This is what we call a 'relocation three-pointer from the post.' It makes the defense move in a different way. It makes them go in and out like an accordion."

We also used "penetration and kick" drills to foster this type of communication. Jason "penetrates" into the lane, the defense converges on him, and he "kicks" the ball out to an open man on the perimeter. It tends to foster more three-point shots—and that is exactly what I'm after this week. I want to build up our offense and I want them to shoot more treys.

The three-point shot has to be taken with *courage*, it has to be taken with *unselfishness*, and it has to be taken with *intelligence*.

Courage comes about from the confidence derived in our No Fear Zone culture. The players know it's okay to shoot. They don't worry about missing a good shot. It gives them confidence—and with confidence comes courage.

Unselfishness is part of our No Jealousy Zone. We're always looking for the open man. We're playing as one. Our fist is closed. It's not your shot, it's *our* shot. Don't worry about missing *our* shot.

Intelligence is reinforced through practice. We have to think about keeping spacing among the players. When my teammate moves here, I have to go there. Court-spacing on offense is critical to the three-point shot. And it takes brains to make it work.

By teaching the proper way to take a three-point shot, we promote these three qualities. But ideas have to be followed up with action. You can't just talk about courage and unselfishness and intelligence. There's something you have to do to show courage. There's something you have to do to show unselfishness. There's something you have to do to show intelligence. In a university, we live in a world of theories. And that's good. But those theories need vehicles. What is your vehicle for courage or unselfishness? How do you *show* it? The three-point shot is a vehicle to show a player's courage, his unselfishness, and his intelligence. That's the way I teach it.

It is also incredibly important to our basketball team. People fear Duke's three-point shot. It keeps us in a game. We have the potential to blow a game wide open. Our opponents can lose leads faster—and our lead can widen faster. Moreover, it can really impact the opposing team's thinking. A coach thinks his team has been playing really well. But all of a sudden, he looks up at the scoreboard and sees that instead of being up by 10 points, he's only up by three. Holy mackerel! he thinks, I don't know if we can play any better than this. I believe the three-point shot is worth more than three points because of the psychological impact it can have on opponents.

Winning basketball has more to do with psychology than it does with the X's and O's. And that's really what I spend a large percentage of my time on as a coach—getting inside a player's head, understanding where he's coming from, helping him get to where we all need to be as a team. A perfect example is the attention I paid to our superstar, Shane Battier, at this point in the season.

You might naturally think that the preseason pick to be National Player of the Year wouldn't really need much coaching. But Shane was in a major slump. After his 29-point performance against Princeton, other teams started to double-team him and chase him off the three-point shot. We had gone five games now, and he just hadn't come around to playing up to his potential. So I asked Johnny Dawkins to spend more time with Shane because the two of them had a lot in common. Johnny had been a National Player of the Year and a high lottery pick in the draft. His influence on Shane was noticeable as they worked out together, ate together, and had many one-on-one conversations. Johnny knew that Shane was simply putting too much pressure on himself to perform up to everybody's expectations. He had been thinking too much about things other than his own performance. And he was being too much of a mother hen to the other guys on the team. So Johnny advised him to stop pressing, to focus on what he could do well. He could still be the leader of the team and not worry about every little detail. With Johnny Dawkins' help, I figured it would just be a matter of time before Shane was back to his old self.

*   *   *   *   *

We flew to Philadelphia the day before the Temple game and had a great practice at the Philadelphia 76ers' practice facility. Billy King, the 76ers' general manager, who was the captain of my 1988 team and the National Defensive Player of the Year that season, was on hand to give us support. Everybody was talking, and our penetration and kick was working well. In preparing for this game, we had concentrated on communication and the three-point shot as a strategy to defeat their zone defense. The night before the game, we showed the team videotape of our earlier game with Temple and pointed out how poorly we had played against their match-up zone. Then we showed the guys a composite tape of their past three-point shooting successes—and contrasted the two.

We had just played John Chaney's team a week ago and won with what would be our lowest scoring effort of the year—63 points. This time, I wanted Duke's offense to come alive. I didn't want it to be close. I wanted to destroy their zone.

Duke at Temple
First Union Center, Philadelphia, Pennsylvania

December 2, 2000—Top-ranked Duke thrashed Temple with 17 three-point shots before the largest crowd to witness a college basketball game in the state of Pennsylvania. The Blue Devils' first eight baskets of the game were all three pointers done by penetration and kick-out, and making the extra pass. Jason Williams scored a career-high 30 points and was 8-for-10 from beyond the three-point arc. Chris Duhon had 12 assists (also a career-high) and Shane Battier rebounded out of a minor slump with 18 points and nine rebounds, while also leading Duke's smothering pressure defense. At the end of the ball game, a Temple player almost handed the ball to Jason Williams in a sign of total frustration and exasperation. During the postgame press conference, Temple coach John Chaney paid Duke a high compliment. "I've never seen a team as good as this team," said Chaney. "I felt like Butch Cassidy and the Sundance Kid. Every time I looked up, someone was shooting. . . . I just don't want to see Duke anymore."

Final Score: Duke 93, Temple 68
Overall Record: 7–0

In the locker room after the game, I praised the team. "Fellas, that was beautiful basketball. We dribbled, penetrated, then passed. We had 26 assists tonight—and Chris Duhon had 12 of them. That's an incredible statistic. Let me give you another incredible statistic. We were 17-for-30 from three-point range. Let me put that in perspective for you. On two-point shots, 17-

for-30 is 34 points. On three-point shots, it's 51 points. So, 17-for-30 is 57 percent shooting. To score 51 points with 30 two-point shots, you'd have to hit 87 percent from the field. If Temple went 17-for-30 with twos at the same time we were going 17-for-30 with threes, they would still be losing by 17 points. *That* is the power of the three-point shot, fellas. Our performance was a little bit scary for somebody looking to scout Duke. It was powerful . . . powerful.

"Also, tonight, you demonstrated your courage, your unselfishness, and your intelligence. Tonight, you were a clenched fist. You talked to each other all night. Great *communication*. You *trusted* one another with each other's shot. You were *collectively responsible*. Tonight it really was 'our' shot. You *cared* about your teammates enough to pass them the ball. You all made the extra pass tonight. The connections that were made on some of the plays were as beautiful as you could ever hope to see in the game of basketball. And fellas, it was obvious you took *pride* in your performance this evening. We hit on all five points of THE FIST tonight. Don't you feel proud? I do. And I'm very proud of all of you."

> *"Tonight was like the beginning of the season. We felt we had something to prove, and we did."*
>
> —*Jason Williams*

*   *   *   *   *

After the Temple game, we went on a roll. Over the next three games, we would score an average of 101 points on offense, and on defense, we'd hold our opponents to an average of only 62 points. Before each of these games, we showed videotape of the Temple game and just said, "This is great. Keep doing this."

Davidson at Duke

December 5, 2000—Jason Williams scored 25 points and Nate James added 20 as the Duke Blue Devils hit the century mark for the first time this season. Davidson stayed close for most of the first half until Duke went on a 22–10 run to take a 16-point lead into the locker room. In the second half, Williams hit three straight treys in a span of 2:11 to put the game out of reach. Duke's defense forced 33 turnovers on the way to their eighth consecutive win.

Final Score: Duke 102, Davidson 60
Overall Record: 8–0

*   *   *   *   *

Michigan at Duke

December 9, 2000—Duke handed Michigan its fourth-worst loss in school history, as they jumped out to an early 34–2 lead and never looked back. The scoring outburst was fueled by Duke's reaction to Michigan's pregame tactics that had their players forming a football-type huddle at center court and stomping on the Duke *D*. Duke senior co-captain Nate James commented after the game that when they saw that, "we decided to go out there and play our rears off and shut these guys down." The Blue Devils led by 41 points at the half, 59–18. Shane Battier led the way with 21 points as six players scored in double figures. Jason Williams scored at least 20 points for the fourth consecutive game. Afterwards, Coach Mike Krzyzewski praised his team's defense: "Our defense played at a different level in the first half than it has at any time so far this season. It seemed to hurt [our players] when Michigan scored. That's how I want us to play." Michigan coach Brian Ellerbe commented, "Our young kids were intimidated. . . . We couldn't function in this environment."

Final Score: Duke 104, Michigan 61
Overall Record: 9–0

After the Michigan game, we had a 10-day hiatus due to final exams. Exam week was a difficult time for the players, some of whom had as many as four exams and papers due. At this stage, Mike Schrage, our academic coordinator, really earned his wages as he constantly worked with the team to help them balance their study time with their practice time. And this week, as always, we made certain the guys understood that academics would not slide. They must do well, and we will support them any way we can.

Each student was on a different schedule, so in lieu of our normal practice regimen, we mixed things up a little bit to try to help them. Our goal was to keep everybody in shape, so we did more running and lifting. We tried to practice as often as we could with as many of the players as we could. Usually, we tried to have at least three limited sessions with the whole team. Some of the kids could miss as many as three straight days, so we also scheduled individual sessions, which allowed them to come in at their convenience.

This week I could see how committed the guys were. We scheduled a number of optional practices and pretty much everybody showed up. They were all feeling good about the team—really good—and so was I.

*   *   *   *   *

Nick Horvath had injured his foot in a practice just before the Michigan game. It was a freak injury. He was running sprints, turned his foot at one point, and felt a sharp pain. The doctors said it was a bone bruise and that he would have to wear a boot for a couple of weeks. We had to watch this situation and see how it developed. Not having Nick might hurt us, especially if anybody else got injured.

*   *   *   *   *

I went over to Duke Children's Hospital this week to visit a friend of mine. Jonathan Patton is waiting for a new heart. Now 25 years old, he's had eight open-heart surgeries, has had three valve replacements, and has been in and out of Children's Hospital since he was three days old. He always wears a hat that has the words *Always Positive* embroidered on the front. He always has a smile on his face and he helps me remember to be positive. And he tells me that I help him when I come around. Maybe that's what friendship is all about. I invited Jonathan to come into the locker room after the next home game against North Carolina A&T. He already had met most of our players earlier in the preseason. Even though Jonathan is a transplant candidate, he still has more heart than most people I know.

*   *   *   *   *

I prepared brackets again for another NCAA tournament simulation. This time we made a West Coast trip where we'd first play the University of Portland in a big arena before a huge crowd. That would simulate the national semifinal. When we won that game, we'd fly down to Stanford to take on the Number 3-ranked Cardinal basketball team. That would be the championship game—and a big test for us, especially with only one day to prepare. At that point, we'd say to the kids, "Hey, I know you're going to be tired, but we've got a championship game on Saturday. We've got to get ready." After the Stanford game, we'd all fly home for the holidays. It was just like what happens in the Final Four—everybody goes his own way after the last game. There really is a kind of finality to it.

*   *   *   *   *

We scheduled the Portland game, in part, for Mike Dunleavy. This was where he went to high school. His dad was coach of the NBA's Portland Trailblazers, and we would play in their arena. The game attracted the largest crowd to witness a college basketball game in Oregon history, and when we were in the locker room, I ribbed Dunleavy a little bit, "Hey, Mike. I didn't know you had this many girlfriends in Portland." The other guys laughed and kidded him. He just grinned.

Duke vs. Portland
The Rose Garden, Portland, Oregon

December 19, 2000—Portland was playing Duke basket for basket in the early going of this contest. But with six minutes left in the first half, Jason Williams took an elbow just above his left eye that knocked him to the floor and left him bleeding. Game officials did not see the blood and motioned for Williams to get up, as though he'd tried to draw a foul. Incensed, Duke players ran off a 26–3 run to end the first half with a score of 52–28. After the game, Carlos Boozer explained the inspired play. "I got in the huddle and was fired up," said Boozer. "I told everybody, 'It's time to go. We can't let this stuff happen to us.' " Boozer made all 11 shots he attempted and led Duke with 22 points and six rebounds. Williams, who scored 17 points despite the injury, took five stitches at halftime to close the cut. He returned to the game with about 15 minutes left in the second half. Mike Dunleavy added 18 points in his homecoming.

Final Score: Duke 97, Portland 64
Overall Record: 10–0

The upcoming game against Stanford was part of the annual Pete Newell Challenge. One of the reasons we made this trip to the West Coast was out of my respect for Coach Newell. He coached at Cal and is a legend. He's also one of my mentors. I met him through Coach Bob Knight when I was an assistant coach at Indiana. One of the best pieces of advice he ever gave me was "Always be yourself in coaching. Always teach the fundamentals. Be a teacher. And take care of your family."

Coach Newell had invited Duke to participate several times in the past, but we couldn't take part because it usually conflicted with exam week. This time, Coach Newell made some special arrangements for us to be able to play. Our only other previous meeting with Stanford was in last year's opening game in the Coaches vs. Cancer Classic at Madison Square Garden. We lost that game by one point, 80–79, after having a five-point lead with 32 seconds left in the game. I didn't want that to happen again.

Duke vs. Stanford
The Arena, Oakland, California

December 21, 2000—The largest crowd to view a college basketball game in the state of California showed up to see the Stanford Cardinal host the Duke Blue Devils in the annual Pete Newell Challenge. Duke outplayed and outran Stanford in the first half and enjoyed a 13-point lead at intermission, 43–30. The lead grew to 15 points in the second half, but things went downhill from there for the Blue Devils. With 4:45 to go, and Duke leading 73–62, Carlos Boozer fouled out. That allowed Stanford's two big men, twins Jason and Jarron Collins, to take control of the game and score 11 of the Cardinal's final

22 points. In response, Duke went to a smaller, faster lineup with Shane Battier at the center position. At the four-minute mark, Stanford went on an 11–1 run and tied Duke at 79 with 1:09 remaining. After Mike Dunleavy made a two-point bank shot, Shane Battier picked up his fifth foul with 35 seconds remaining and had to sit on the bench. Stanford called a timeout with 16.9 seconds left after scoring a lay-up. Duke was leading at that point, 83–82. . . .

During that timeout, I knew we were going to be fouled, so I was diagramming a play with Mike Dunleavy throwing the inbound pass to Chris Duhon, who had just made two free throws. Shane usually inbounds the ball under the basket, but he had fouled out. I was thinking that Mike was tall, he's aware of time, and he'll make a good pass. But Dunleavy interrupted me in the huddle.

"*Why don't you let somebody else take the ball out so I can be on the court and take the free throws,*" he said.

I stopped diagramming and looked at him. I could have said, "No, I'll call the play. Just shut up." But I thought, It's December and I have a sophomore who wants the ball; I like that. At that moment, I was thinking about bigger things than winning the Stanford game. I wanted to let Mike Dunleavy know that I had confidence in him. After all, how many times do you have a chance to show someone that you love them, or trust them, or have confidence in them. I wasn't going to let that opportunity slip by. So I changed the play.

"Okay, we'll go with it," I said. Then I diagrammed the play so that Chris Duhon inbounded the ball to Mike.

> "*In the huddle, everyone else was looking a little puzzled. I felt they were looking for somebody to step forward, so I did. Going down the stretch, I had made some shots and I felt strong and confident. I was on a roll. And I wanted to win. So I asked for the ball. I was sure I could make those free throws.*"
>
> —*Mike Dunleavy*

. . . When Duke inbounded the ball, Stanford fouled sophomore Mike Dunleavy, sending him to the line for two free throws. A 75-percent free throw shooter, Dunleavy hadn't been to the line in the game to that point. He missed both shots. . . .

"As I walked to the foul line, I saw Coach and Shane and Carlos over there, and I got nervous. Then I started thinking about trying to win the game for them because they were on the bench. I just missed the shots. No excuses. I just missed them."

—Mike Dunleavy

. . . On the next possession, Casey Jacobsen drove to the left side and banked a two-point shot off the glass to give Stanford the lead 84–83. Then, with 3.6 seconds remaining on the clock, Jason Williams rushed back down the entire length of the court and put up a lay-up that was touched by Jarron Collins just enough to keep the ball from going in the basket. Nate James's follow-up went through the hoop a split second after the buzzer sounded. Jason Williams and Shane Battier each scored a game-high 26 points. Although Duke led for more than 38 minutes in the ball game, they shot just 29 percent in the second half. Stanford scored on its last 11 possessions and held the Blue Devils to only one basket in the final eight minutes.

Final Score: Stanford 84, Duke 83
Overall Record: 10–1

It was not a pretty sight in the locker room after that game. Everybody was upset, especially me. We should have won. Shane made two stupid fouls and fouled out. Carlos hardly played the last 10 minutes of the game after getting his fourth foul. Then he fouled out right after we put him back in. Mike Dunleavy was sitting in the middle of the locker room with a look of bewilderment on his face—like he couldn't understand what had happened.

"I walked off the court in shock. It wasn't the end of the world, I knew that. But I was confused about what happened. I was shocked that I missed those free throws."

—Mike Dunleavy

He was up there at the free throw line alone and he got hugged by the bear. Why did he miss those free throws? As Johnny Dawkins so aptly phrased it, he let the game become bigger than himself by taking on too much pressure. Mike wanted to take the entire team's burden on himself. He was alone on the line, but we never want one of our players to feel he is in that position. When he goes to the line, the entire team is with him. That's collective responsibility, one of the five points of THE FIST. And it serves to give a player in that situation sustenance and confidence.

The first thing I said when I addressed the team was directed at Mike. "It would be selfish of you to think that you lost this game for us," I said. "Shane should have been in the ball game. Carlos, you should have been in the ball game. We lost this game together. Mike, it's the same as if somebody hits the winning shot. He can't go away from here saying, 'I won the game.' And Mike, you can't go away from here saying, 'I lost the game.' When we walk out of this locker room, we all say together: '*We* lost the game. So now we move on to the next game.' Let's get out of here."

As I headed to the postgame press conference, I passed Stanford coach Mike Montgomery. As we shook hands, he said to me, "There *is* a Santa Claus!"

Well, that made me really mad. Not at Mike Montgomery—he's a friend and a good guy. I was mad because he was dead right. We handed Stanford a gift. Duke never does that. We get beat. But we never give it away—never.

*   *   *   *   *

It was a long plane ride back to Durham—five and a half hours long. Mike Dunleavy and J.D. Simpson stayed behind and went to be with their families for Christmas in Oregon and California. Mickie and I took two seats on the plane behind the team.

I just sat there and stared straight ahead. I was hot, angry, emotional. And the longer I sat there, the worse it got. We were up by 15 and lost it! We should have won this game. We were kicking their butts. We lost to them last year, too, by letting them come from behind, and it made me mad that we let it happen again. Shane made two dumb fouls, and he's out of the ball game. He can't foul out. He has to play all 40 minutes. Carlos is out. He can't foul out, either. We need him in the low post. He's critical to the team. We can't win against big teams without Carlos. The small, up-tempo offense we went to didn't work, either. Damn! What a game!

After thinking about all this for a while, I decided to pull out the video machine and watch tape of game. That is one of the ways I usually get past all the emotion. But the machine was broken. I couldn't get it to work for anything. Now I couldn't analyze the game! I felt like throwing the damn thing against the wall. All I could do was just sit there and rack my brain trying to figure out how we let that game get away from us. How could we let that happen? That never happens! It must have been two hours before I said anything at all. I just sat there and boiled.

> *"Coach and Mrs. K were sitting behind me on the plane. And every so often, I would look back to see Coach's facial expression. There were times when I saw him beating his head on the back of the seat — thinking of things he could have said, things he could have done differently. I could see the pain on his face because we lost a game we should have won. From then on, I totally believed in Coach — seeing that he wants the best for us. Also that he wants to win — and wants us to win the Duke way."*
>
> *—Chris Duhon*

I was snapped out of my trance by some of the guys laughing and joking around. Do you guys care that we just lost this game? I wondered to myself. It was obvious that they did not have my level of commitment. I looked over at Johnny and he seemed to be disturbed as well.

Up to that point, Mickie had just been sitting there quietly waiting, I think, for me to say the first words. I guess she knew me well enough that I would speak when I was ready. Finally, I leaned over to her and said: "These guys don't care. They just don't care."

"That's not true," she responded. "Look at Chris. Look at Nate."

I looked over at Nate James, who was still quite somber. He was supposed to have guarded Casey Jacobsen, who scored the winning basket. It was his first huge test against an All-America player, and he felt bad that he hadn't stopped the shot. Chris Duhon was very quiet also.

"Yeah, you're right," I responded.

"Shane gave permission, you know," said Mickie.

"What?"

Mickie's comment caught me off guard. She looked at me and said, "Shane was the first one to laugh, the first one to be lighthearted. That let the guys know it was okay to move on."

After I thought about it, I realized Shane was probably more right than I was. The kids were just getting on to the next thing. And the next thing for them was their Christmas vacations. They were just following one of my key maxims—Next Play.

We arrived back at the Raleigh-Durham airport at 3:30 in the morning. Most of us got on the team bus for the ride back to campus. Some got on a van that would take them to other gates for their flights home. Before we took off, I climbed into the van and gave the players and managers a hug and wished them a Merry Christmas. After the bus arrived home, I did the same for the others. Everybody was going their separate ways. It was like the end of the season—just like we had lost in the Final Four.

When Mickie and I got home, she went to bed and I put the game tape in the VCR. I never slept that night. Later that day, I called Mike Dunleavy to make sure he was doing okay.

*   *   *   *   *

When the guys returned from the Christmas holidays, they were still feeling pretty bad about the Stanford loss. Being scattered across the country for a week wasn't good for a couple of reasons: First, they didn't have each other to help them get over it. And second, they couldn't get back on the practice court so they could move on. The loss lingered in their minds. They dwelled on the negatives and they were all worried about what I was going to do.

At the first practice, I spoke to them in a quiet tone of voice.

"I watched tape of the game over Christmas," I told them. "And I can tell you that I've not yet rebounded from feeling that loss. And you know what? It's a feeling I want to keep with me for the rest of the season—so I'm motivated to see that it doesn't happen again. It makes me think about all the little things that we usually do, but we didn't do in that game. A couple of people couldn't make shots. We missed a couple of free throws at the end. It really makes you hurt. But I think it's good to bring that hurt to practice every day, because it makes you play harder."

That's really about all I said to the team before sending them out on the court. We had done enough dwelling on the loss. Now it was time to reacquaint them with the process. It was time to get them ready for our next game against North Carolina A&T.

After practice, I took time to meet with three players individually. First, I spoke with Dunleavy and asked him how he was doing.

"*Okay,*" he said. "*But yesterday, I got it in the grocery store.*"

"What happened?"

"*Oh, some guys yelled out, 'You choker!' They were probably Carolina fans.*"

"Well, get used to it, son. You're probably going to hear that in every visiting gym we go to. They'll try to harass you. 'Dunleavy, huh? Choke artist Dunleavy.' The only way you can stop that stuff is to play great. So what are you going to do?"

"*I'm going to play great.*"

"Okay, get out of here."

Then I had to meet with Andre Sweet. I'd received Andre's grades and they just weren't up to par. So for academic reasons, he had to be suspended from the team for an indefinite period of time. When he walked into my office, he knew it was coming and he already felt really bad. So did I. I told him that he wasn't going to be able to play or travel with the team, but he could still practice—and I expected him to practice. I didn't want to prolong his pain, so it was a short meeting. But it had to be done.

Finally, I met with Shane Battier. In the Stanford game, he had made two really stupid fouls. He jumped into somebody and he committed a foul 90 feet from the basket. I couldn't let that go without addressing it.

"Shane, you cannot commit fouls like that," I told him. "When we're playing a championship game, I'll need you to play with two, three, four fouls. And so, I'm going to put you in positions where you have to play with multiple fouls—and you have to learn to do that."

"*I will, Coach.*"

"You're too valuable. You cannot foul out of a game. You need to have more discipline. We would *not* have lost to Stanford if you were on the court. There's no way. Do you understand?"

"*Yes, Coach. It won't happen again.*"

North Carolina A&T at Duke

December 30, 2000—Third-ranked Duke rebounded from its first loss of the season in a big way. During a 25–3 run in the first half, Shane Battier went on a three-point barrage as he made three long-range shots in a span of 57 seconds and added another with under one minute left to give the Blue Devils a 63–32 lead at the half. Battier scored 27 of his season-high 31 points in the first half, while Nate James added 25 points (with three treys) and Jason Williams had 23, including 7-for-11 in three-point shooting. Overall, Duke set a school record and tied the ACC record with 18 three-pointers in 38 attempts. North Carolina A&T's J.J. Miller scored a career-high 34 points and received an ovation from the Cameron Indoor Stadium crowd when he left the game with under a minute to play.

Final Score: Duke 108, North Carolina A&T 73
Overall Record: 11–1

In the locker room after the ball game, Chris Duhon was crying. We had won by 35 points and he was crying! I thought he must have gotten into a fight or something. Before I could say anything, Johnny Dawkins motioned to me to go easy. He had already talked to Chris and to the team before I walked in.

"What's wrong, Chris?" I asked.

But he couldn't answer.

"Coach, it's because of the amount of points Miller scored," said Johnny.

I looked at Chris, who had guarded Miller in the game, and asked, "Is it about Miller?"

He nodded that it was.

"Well, that's good. I'm glad you're crying. I'm glad it means that much to you. In order for us to be a really good team, we need to care about our performances. The fact that you, as a freshman, can feel that bad is terrific. It's great that you have enough pride in your performance to care that much. I'm proud of you, Chris."

*   *   *   *   *

The next day, I began to think about the situation with our big men. Carlos Boozer had not played against North Carolina A&T because of a virus he had picked up over Christmas. So we played Casey Sanders and Matt Christensen in his place. I thought Carlos might be more motivated if he perceived that these two guys were vying for his position. But they did not play well. Casey was nervous and tentative. And Matt's knee problem limited his performance. So I began to get frustrated, especially since Nick Horvath was out with an injury and I didn't know when he would be able to play.

As I started to think about Carlos, I realized that he was playing very inconsistently. He had played great against Portland but had done very poorly against Stanford—having scored only four points with four rebounds. To top it off, he got into foul trouble and fouled out with over five minutes left in the game. Carlos was our only proven inside player and we just could not afford to have him foul out of any more games. I thought part of the reason for his inconsistent play was that he had not completely unpacked his bags here at Duke. I knew it was his dream to play in the NBA and that he was considering leaving after this year to go into the draft. But I knew he was simply not ready. He had a lot of growing to do as a player, and I really wanted him to learn more so that he could be better than just an average pro. I wanted Carlos Boozer to be a great pro—because that was the potential he had. So I felt it was time for me to have a heart-to-heart conversation with my big man. The purpose of the meeting was for him and me to become closer and for us to have the same game plan for his future.

On New Year's Eve, Carlos came over to my house and we sat in my living room to talk. It was just the two of us. As Carlos sat down, I could tell he thought I was going to hammer him. He's only 19, but at 6' 10" and 270 pounds, he looks much older. And there is a tendency to think he should have the wisdom of an older person. But that's not the case and I have to keep reminding myself of that fact.

"Look, this is a man-to-man talk," I began. "I'm going to tell you the truth and I want you to tell me the truth. There's nobody here. Whatever's said will stay between you and me. But we're going to be here until we get a good understanding of each other. Okay."

"*Okay,*" Carlos agreed.

"I feel like you've come to Duke with a plan of staying either one or two years and then going pro. Is that right?"

"*Yeah, that's right, Coach. I want to be a pro.*"

"Well, there's nothing wrong with that. But, as a result of that thinking, you're only a good basketball player. You're not great. You're not living this moment, Carlos. You haven't completely unpacked your bags and you are definitely not making the most of me, your teammates, or Duke University."

"*Well, what do you want me to do?*" he asked.

"First of all, you have to unpack your bags. There's a part of you that's always in the future. We need that part of you to be here—so you can be as good as you can be right now. The future will happen. Second, I want you to believe in me. I'm going to tell you some things that are not meant to hurt, but they're a true assessment of where you're at. Is that okay?"

"*Sure.*"

"Carlos, you're not really that good right now. Whoever is talking to you about going pro and being a really high draft pick is wrong. That is not going to happen at the end of this year. In the upcoming NBA draft, there will be a lot of big guys being selected."

"*Yeah, I know.*"

"Based on the way you're playing now, you'd be a late first-round pick. You didn't come to Duke to be a late first-round pick; you came here to develop into a great, great basketball player, didn't you?"

"*Yes, I did.*"

"Well, you are not even one of the top three players on this team at the moment. Can you be good enough to be a high pick? Absolutely. But wouldn't it be smart for us to be on the same page in regards to your plans for the future? While I'm coaching you , I'm not thinking about the next kid I'm going to recruit to take your place. I'm coaching *you* right now. I'm on your side, Carlos. Let me be on your side completely. What do you say?"

"*Okay, Coach. I'm with you,*" Carlos responded. "*That's what I want to do.*"

So Carlos Boozer and I outlined a plan together. We agreed that the main goal was not about his becoming a professional basketball player—it was about his becoming an excellent basketball player who will eventually go pro. There was a difference. Carlos pledged to work harder for the next seven weeks. He also agreed to stay for his junior year and take enough classes in order to be close to graduation. I committed to do my best and get him ready to be a Top 10 pick in the NBA by then. I also promised to always be honest with him and tell him the truth. When he was ready, I'd let him know. If he wasn't working hard enough toward his goal, I'd let him know that, too.

When Carlos walked out of my house, I really felt we were closer than we had ever been before. It was a big step in our relationship. And it felt good.

> "*I was relieved when Coach K didn't hammer me. But I was also really excited that we were talking in such a personal manner. It really wasn't like a coach-player kind of conversation. It was more like teacher-student or father-son. I always appreciated Coach K before that night. Now, I was completely committed to him.*"
>
> —*Carlos Boozer*

*   *   *   *   *

As we marked the end of the year 2000, it was easy to note we had been through a lot. We'd been to New York and played in Madison Square Garden. We'd been to Philadelphia and played at First

Union Center in front of the largest college crowd in the history of Pennsylvania. We had been to Oregon and played at the home of the Portland Trailblazers and followed that with a big game at The Arena in Oakland. Those two games had also been played in front of the largest crowds in the history of Oregon and California. All big arenas, all big events, all big crowds.

We were 11–1, and the only game we lost, we felt we should have won. We were improving as a team, and I had reached a new level in my relationship with Carlos. I had every reason to be optimistic about 2001.

ACC Regular
Season

The new year started out on a sad note. Lute Olson, Arizona's head basketball coach and a good friend of mine, lost his wife, Bobbi, to cancer. I was concerned about Lute, so I called him and we spoke for about 20 minutes. Sometimes all a friend can do in a situation like that is listen, which I did. I also let him know that Mickie and I were thinking about him. Lute stepped down from his coaching position for a little while. But he has a strong family and they rallied around him. I felt sure he'd be okay and back at the helm of the Arizona Wildcats in due time.

The new year also meant that we would begin conference play—and what a year it was going to be. The ACC had five teams in the top 20. Maryland was Number 17, North Carolina Number 13, Virginia Number 8, Wake Forest Number 4, and we were Number 3. All these teams had great starters, quality depth, and experience. The other teams in our conference, North Carolina State, Clemson, Georgia Tech, and Florida State, also had good teams. And when you play an away game in the ACC, anything—and I do mean anything—can happen.

At our last team meeting before the regular ACC season started, I wrote on the board, *0–0*—meaning Duke, like every other team was 0–0 in conference play. We had a new lease on life. Everyone was fresh.

And we all had high expectations. Each season, I get a little anxious starting out the league. But I really look forward to it because this is when our kids become men. This is where we become a basketball team.

*　　*　　*　　*　　*

In our first week of play, we took on Florida State, Clemson, and North Carolina State. We pretty much steamrolled Florida State and Clemson, but North Carolina State, an older team that really demands respect, played us very tough.

Before the Florida State game, we showed the team a one-hour tape of the *Charlie Rose* show in which he hosted a discussion with legendary UCLA basketball coach John Wooden and hall-of-fame players Bill Russell and Bill Walton. I wanted our guys to have a sense of the history of our sport, to see some of the true geniuses of basketball, and to hear them talk about their passion for the game and the hard work it takes to be great.

Duke at Florida State
Leon County Civic Center, Tallahassee, Florida

January 4, 2001—In Duke's first ACC game of the year, Shane Battier, Jason Williams, and Nate James combined for 70 points (only two points shy of Florida State's total for the game). Williams scored 26 points, hitting 6-for-10 from behind the three-point line, while Battier and James each scored 22. Together they connected on 13 of Duke's 15 three-point shots. Center Matt Christensen sparked the Blue Devils with two blocked shots, a dunk, and a drawn charge. Duke's lead never dropped below double digits as they out-rebounded the Seminoles, 43–29. Carlos Boozer, playing his first game after getting over a stomach virus, scored six points with nine rebounds. Only 4,337 fans showed up for the game. Florida State fans may have been in mourning over their football team's loss last night to Oklahoma in the national championship game. After the game, team co-captain Shane Battier quipped, "I could hear myself think."

Final Score: Duke 99, Florida State 72
Overall Record: 12–1 **ACC:** 1–0

*　　*　　*　　*　　*

Clemson at Duke
January 7, 2001—Third-ranked Duke scored more than 100 points for the

fourth time in a row at Cameron Indoor Stadium. Carlos Boozer led the way with 25 points. Shane Battier and Nate James contributed 21 points each. Boozer had a perfect shooting performance. He was 8-for-8 from the field and 9-for-9 from the foul line. During the first half, the Blue Devils scored 18 unanswered points during a stunning 37–5 run against the Tigers. Nate James contributed a sterling defensive performance against ACC leading scorer Will Solomon. As the Cameron Crazies (Duke student fans) chanted "Nate Dogg! Nate Dogg!" James held Solomon to 5-for-12 shooting. "Coach told me that my role is to shut down the other team's top gun, and that's what I tried to do tonight," said James.

Final Score: Duke 115, Clemson 74
Overall Record: 13–1 **ACC:** 2–0

*   *   *   *   *

Duke at North Carolina State
Entertainment and Sports Arena, Raleigh, North Carolina

January 10, 2001—Number 2–ranked Duke got 22 points each from Shane Battier and sophomore Jason Williams. But Williams was scoreless in the first half, possibly due to his turning an ankle after a collision with an NC State player. Shane Battier, however, stepped forward and scored most of his points on hot three-point shooting to give the Blue Devils a 10-point lead, 41–31, at the intermission. Commenting on Battier's performance, Wolfpack Coach Herb Sendek stated, "It doesn't take a lot for the lead to go from 18 to 30 by the time you take another sip of Coke." . . .

> *"At the half, I had a talk with Jason. I told him I'd love to hit 20 threes, but that we were not going to win this game unless everybody played their role and that, instead of sulking about his ankle, he needed to go out and play like I knew he could. Then he got that look in his eye."*
>
> *—Shane Battier*

. . . With less than five minutes to play in the game, NC State completed a 14–4 scoring run that reduced Duke's lead to only six points, 67–61. Jason Williams then came to the rescue by continually driving to the basket and getting fouled. In the final 48.6 seconds, he made eight free throws to preserve the Duke victory. Overall, Williams was 15-for-18 from the free throw line, with all of his 22 points coming in the second half. Near the end of the game, the official clock was stuck for over half a minute, and when asked about it after the game, Coach Mike Krzyzewski quipped, "Even being Polish, I could figure out the clock should be running."

Final Score: Duke 84, North Carolina State 78
Overall Record: 14–1 **ACC:** 3–0

To win our first three ACC games felt good, but we didn't have time to savor the victories. It was Next Play. We had to prepare for a Top 10 team—and one of the best in our conference. Virginia had several strengths we had to be very careful about—and our strategy revolved mostly around defense.

We knew that they made a lot of lay-ups, so we drilled our big guys on stopping them from getting close to the boards, and we directed our perimeter players to stay in front of the ball handler at all times. In addition, I wanted to remind our team that a lot of forced turnovers could really make the difference in a game with a high-caliber opponent like Virginia.

So I drew a comparison to a pinball game in which bonus points are rapidly added to the score. "Duke always forces a lot of turnovers," I said to the guys. "Just look at what we did in our last three games. Against Florida State we forced 15, against Clemson 22, and against NC State 19. But unlike a lot of teams, we have a very high percentage in scoring off turnovers. So they're like bonus points on a pinball machine—they really add up."

At first, because Virginia was an extremely fast team and penetrated well, my strategy was to slough off a little bit when they brought the ball up the court. In other words, don't attack them, wait for them to come to us, and then play our standard half-court defense. At our afternoon practice the day before the game, we worked on that strategy. But the kids showed no pizzazz at all. They just kind of went through the motions. So I got mad at them and kicked them all out of practice. "Okay, okay, stop the practice," I said. "You guys aren't playing worth a damn! And I have no patience for this kind of attitude. Get the hell out of here!"

> *"We didn't come out with the intensity we should have. Coach wants us to play every game like it's the national championship game. 'If you guys will match my intensity, we'll have no problems,' he often says."*
>
> —*Chris Duhon*

But when I got back home and started to wonder what went wrong, I had more and more doubts about my slough-off strategy. Maybe the players took me too literally and that was the reason they showed no life. I didn't really have a concrete reason. I just sensed the team didn't have an edge. You can call it intuition if you want, but I decided to reverse the game plan a full 180 degrees. I called Wojo right away and asked him to get everybody back to the gym at 10:00 that night. "Have them go right to the court," I told him. "Oh, and there's something else. I want to see a couple of hundred sheets of paper with the word ATTACK up on the locker room walls."

"We'll take care of it," responded Wojo, who immediately got on the phone with Jeff La Mere (director of basketball operations) and told him about my special request. Jeff, who was still at the office, immediately ran off two hundred 8½ by 11 copies with the word ATTACK on them and called a couple of the team managers over to help him tape them up in the locker room.

But because it is a big locker room, when they finished, Jeff felt the sheets looked spotty and wouldn't convey the message I wanted to get across. "Obviously, we need more signs," he said to the managers. So he ran off another 2,000 copies and they proceeded to wallpaper the entire locker room. All the walls were covered, all the lockers were covered, all the chairs, and even the floor so the guys would be walking on the word ATTACK. They even put them up in the bathroom—on the mirrors, in the showers, in the stalls, on the toilet seats, and in the urinals. I mean, it was absolutely unbelievable!

That night, the entire team gathered out on the court and I immediately apologized to them for giving them the wrong game strategy. "Look, guys," I said, "I screwed up. I gave you the wrong plan. I was compensating. I was thinking, We're not going to be able to do this; or We'll pick them up at the top of the key; or We're not going to be able to do this, so don't contest, don't deny. Well, I was over-coaching and I was wrong. When I kicked you out of practice, I basically kicked myself out. I was wrong and I'm sorry.

"But I've got it right this time and here's what we're going to do: We're going to attack them from the get-go. No let up. We're going to attack them on offense, but we're especially going to attack them on defense. We will pick them up higher on the court—three-quarter court, full-court pressure. We want them to react to us—not the other way around. If we get into that mode, it will have a real positive impact on our offense. We're going to force turnovers and we're going to score off those turnovers. This strategy will put us in a very positive frame of mind. Now let's go watch tape."

Carlos was the first one into the locker room and his eyes almost popped out of his head. If you can imagine a room where you're used to seeing wood all over the place and then walking into that same room and it's now totally white, you can start to get the idea of the visual impact it had on the players.

The expressions on their faces were priceless. They were surrounded by the word *ATTACK*. They were walking on the word *ATTACK*. They were sitting on the word *ATTACK*. Heck, they were even going to the bathroom on the word *ATTACK*.

> *"We all pretty much got the point."*
>
> —*Mike Dunleavy*

"Okay guys, I'm going to assume that you've all got my message," I said. "We're not going to slough off, we're going to do what?

"*ATTACK*," they all said in unison.

"Okay, then, let's watch some videotape."

As the screen rolled down from the ceiling, there was one sheet of paper in the middle of it that Wojo had placed there. So when we watched the tape, the word *ATTACK* was always in the background. Now it was also a subliminal message.

It might seem to some that we overdid it with this little motivational tactic. And, to tell you the truth, even I was shocked when I walked into the locker room and saw thousands of sheets of paper instead of hundreds. But I had to make sure the guys heard me say "Attack." I had to get them to turn around 180 degrees and I wasn't going to take a chance that anybody misunderstood me. I wanted them to embrace the new strategy without having any residue from the old strategy.

Now I felt we were ready to play Virginia.

Virginia at Duke

January 13, 2001—Second-ranked Duke used a 23–0 run in the first half to top the 10th-ranked Virginia Cavaliers, which helped them attain a school record for the biggest margin of victory over a Top 10 opponent in school history—42 points. The lead mushroomed to 39–9 with six minutes left in the first half as the Blue Devils outplayed Virginia in all aspects of the game. With his team ahead 53–20 at intermission, Coach Mike Krzyzewski urged them not to let up on either offense or defense. . . .

In the locker room, I told the guys that they were now in a position where many teams would let up. "There's another 20 minutes left in this ball game," I said. "And Virginia's good. Don't forget they're ranked Number 10 in the nation. I know they're going to come back. There's a lot of time left in the game. There's going to be a run or two in them. Now, let's come out strong and really hold them."

At that moment, it wasn't about running up the score on an opponent. It was teaching the players not to let down. I knew Virginia could come back. They were that good.

> *"We wanted to keep increasing the lead. When we were up by 30, we wanted to increase it to 40. When we were up by 40, we wanted to increase it to 50. This will prepare us for games later on. We can't afford to slough off."*
>
> —*Jason Williams*

"In every game, there are what we call 'breaking points.' When we push the margin into the high teens, we try to bear down even harder to make the other team make a decision. They can either quit or fight back."

—Shane Battier

. . . Duke led by 40 points, less than two minutes into the second half. With 19 points, senior Nate James led five Blue Devils in double-figure scoring. Battier had 18 points, Williams 17, Boozer 16, and Dunleavy 12. James also held Virginia's leading scorer, Roger Mason, to five points. The entire team forced 21 Virginia turnovers for the game. Cavalier head coach Pete Gillen said after the game, "We just got unnerved and then it becomes a tidal wave and that's it. This is the toughest place to play in America." Virginia stand-out Donald Hand, a senior playing his final game at Cameron Indoor Stadium, remarked, "I'm glad I don't have to come back here anymore. [Our team] needs to play with the kind of passion Duke showed today—and that ain't happening."

Final Score: Duke 103, Virginia 61
Overall Record: 15–1 **ACC:** 4–0

During our staff meetings—which were held at regular times *and* whenever I felt the need to get together—most of the time we talked about people, not the *X*'s and *O*'s. It wasn't: "How's Jason's jump shot?" It was: "Schrage, what's going on with Jason academically? What do you guys think? Is all this talk about the pros getting to him? And what about Duhon, Coach Collins? When you're shooting with him, what do you see? Is there something bugging him?" We spent most of our time talking about things like that— about people and how they connect. We were constantly looking for ways to connect more.

In mid-January, we decided to focus on our four big men because we sensed there was some weakness and, quite possibly, some distance between them. After all, Carlos was getting all the playing time. Casey Sanders had started in the North Carolina A&T game when Boozer was sick, and he had not played well. Nick Horvath was still out with a foot injury, which, for some reason, just didn't want to heal. And Matt Christensen was hobbling around on bad knees almost all the time, so he wasn't getting much playing time. So we met with all of them—individually and as a group.

First we spoke with Carlos, who really worked hard after our New Year's Eve conversation. But even Carlos would admit that he needs somebody to rev him up. So Wojo decided to increase the number of workout sessions they did together. On many days, you could see Carlos and Wojo both on the treadmills or the stationary bikes having a contest to see how many calories they could burn over a half-hour stretch. It was really gratifying to see Wojo's fire and intensity motivate Carlos.

We also spoke with Matt in some detail about his role on the team and how we expected him to play when we brought him into games.

"Coach K emphasized a few things he absolutely expected me to do— rebound aggressively, protect the basket on defense, and play hard with a lot of energy and enthusiasm. I was glad to hear that, because those are all things I do well."

—Matt Christensen

In Casey's situation, I really didn't think he was ready to compete against Carlos. In other words, he wasn't about to try and get the starting center position. But that's what I wanted. I thought it would motivate both players. So we decided to have Casey increase his personal workout schedule from two per week to four per week. And much to my delight, it really got him going. It was our way of showing that, even though he wasn't getting the playing time, we still believed in him. His positive reaction was very important to me. I didn't want to lose him for the rest of the season just because he didn't play much.

Nick Horvath went into the same training schedule with Casey—four workouts a week, only limited to lifting in his case. Because of Nick's ambiguous status from week to week, I could not spend as much time with him as I did with the starters. But Dawkins,

Collins, and Wojo spent a lot of time with him. So, too, I found out later, did Shane Battier. Shane had Nick over to his apartment quite a few times and talked to him a lot about how he was feeling and how he was doing. As one of our captains, that was a great thing for Shane to do—and exactly what I would expect from one of the leaders of our team.

Speaking of leadership, it was right about this time that we decided to name J.D. Simpson a captain, joining Nate and Shane as one of three tri-captains. J.D. was a senior and was well-liked by all members of the team. He was already one of the leaders of the Blue team and was as dedicated a player as I had ever coached. I first spoke with Shane and Nate about the move, and they endorsed it wholeheartedly and enthusiastically. There was no trace of jealousy or selfishness in their reactions. When I told J.D. about his new title, he reacted by saying: "*Wow, thanks. I can't believe you're giving that to me.*"

"Now, wait a minute," I said. "I'm not giving you anything. You earned it."

"*I know that, Coach. I know that. You wouldn't give me anything unless I earned it.*"

"Well, congratulations, J.D. Because of your role on the team, we are a *better* team. We're going to get even better because of you being a captain. I'm sure of it."

*   *   *   *   *

Our next game was a step out of conference against a very good Boston College team that eventually would go on to win the Big East Conference. Playing a game like this during the regular ACC season created a tough situation for our team—one that I wanted them to experience. This year, we did it twice—in January with Boston College and in February with St. John's. The ACC schedule allows a team to have two byes during the nine-week season. But instead of taking time off, we set up these games to get our team more tournament-tested. In essence, we were preparing them for March Madness.

Boston College had a record of 12–1 and had started the season 10–0. "The most important thing I know about this team," I told our guys, "is that they win. They're having a hell of a year."

Boston College at Duke

January 16, 2001—Jason Williams scored a career-high 34 points and had nine assists as Duke won its sixth straight game. Boston College pulled within two points, 44–42, at the beginning of the second half, but led by Williams, the Blue Devils clicked off 11 straight points in less than two minutes. That streak was part of a 34–17 run that kept BC at bay for the rest of the game. Shane Battier and Carlos Boozer each added 22 points to the victory. With 2:41 left to play and Duke ahead by 19 points, Shane Battier elicited wild cheers from the home crowd when he dove head-first onto the floor with both arms extended and swatted a loose ball over to Jason Williams. While running out the clock with 20 seconds remaining in the game, Jason Williams smiled and faked the ball several times at BC's Kenny Walls, who retaliated by shoving Williams into the scorer's table. A technical foul was called and Walls was ejected from the game. As the game ended, both teams walked off in opposite directions at the request of game officials who wanted to avoid a potential confrontation. After the game, Coach Mike Krzyzewski was asked why Shane Battier dove for that ball when Duke was ahead by 19. "Does a great singer sing a bad song at the end of a performance? Does a great actor screw up the last line of a play? Basically, he's a perfectionist. It's what makes Shane one of the best players. He plays all the time and doesn't want to get out of character."

Final Score: Duke 97, Boston College 75
Overall Record: 16–1 **ACC:** 4–0

At our very next practice, Jason came up to me and apologized for the incident at the end of the game. I spoke with him privately and asked him what happened.

"This kid had been trash-talking me the whole game and there we were in the last few seconds and he was still doing it. I just lost it. Coach, I'm sorry."

"Well, you're going to get criticized and you deserve it," I said in response. "That kind of behavior is not acceptable. Because of your talent, you're always going to be a target. Opponents are going to trash-talk you to try and throw you off. And you never want to be at the point where you come down to their level. That's part of the game, you have to get used to it. You have to be more composed. What if that happens in the NCAA tournament and it's you who gets thrown out of the game or suspended? You don't want to lose the national championship because you got in a fight, do you? Are you kidding me?

"Jason, if you're going to be a champion, you have to do uncommon things. Uncommon things have to be common. Now, don't let it happen again. Let's get on to the next play. All right?"

"Yes, Coach."

*　　*　　*　　*　　*

For our next game, we traveled to Atlanta to meet Georgia Tech, a team with a good mix of older and younger players. They were pretty hot at the moment, having just beaten Virginia and Wake Forest, two Top 10 teams. Our game was slated for 12:00 noon, which was a bit earlier than normal for us. So I asked the managers to play some music at breakfast to wake up the players. They surprised me by bringing in a boom box and playing some really old rap music. That got the guys laughing and it really did wake them up. It woke me up, too, but for a different reason.

Hip-hop isn't my favorite type of music, but I'm getting more used to it. And besides, it's part of the players' culture. Once, I asked my daughter Jamie (a freshman at Duke this year), "What's cool right now, music-wise?" She informed me, and the next day during workouts, I walked through the weight room (where the music is always blaring) and shouted: "Okay, shut this music off!" The music was shut off immediately and everybody just stared at me. "All right," I said, "if any of you ever take one of my CDs again, I'm going to kick the crap out of you!" Then they all started laughing. But when I said, "Now if you really want to hear somebody good, you'll play Jay-Z or Lil' Wayne," they all turned and looked at each other like, Hey, Coach knows hip-hop!

Duke at Georgia Tech
Alexander Memorial Coliseum (The Thriller Dome), Atlanta, Georgia

January 20, 2001—Second-ranked Duke built a commanding lead in the first half on the shooting of Jason Williams and Carlos Boozer, who combined for 34 points before the intermission. Early in the game, Mike Dunleavy took an elbow to the jaw and started bleeding from the mouth. Shortly thereafter, Dunleavy air-balled a three-point shot, and the Georgia Tech crowd chanted "Air ball!" every time he touched the ball after that. Carlos Boozer was then called for throwing a flagrant elbow against the individual who had popped Dunleavy. In the second half, Georgia Tech center Alvin Jones picked up his fourth foul and was relegated to the bench for the next few minutes. . . .

> *"Right after Jones picked up his fourth foul, I called everybody together in a huddle and said: 'This is the time we have to jump on them.'"*
>
> —*Shane Battier*

. . . Co-captain Shane Battier then put on a dazzling offensive display in which he scored 20 straight points for the Blue Devils. The first 14 of those points was scored in 95 seconds. During that stretch, Coach Mike Krzyzewski kept calling plays from the bench specifically for Battier, because he was hot. For the game, Battier hit four three-pointers and scored a season-high 34 points. . . .

> *"I was in the zone. I felt detached, like I was on the outside looking in on a basketball game. It was an out-of-body experience. It all happened because I played a poor first half and I didn't want to let down my teammates in the second half."*
>
> —*Shane Battier*

Near the end of the game, when Duke had an insurmountable lead, the home crowd began chanting, "We want air ball! We want air ball!" When Mike Dunleavy finally did check back in, he committed two turnovers on back-to-back possessions—and the crowd really let him have it.

. . . For the game, Mike Dunleavy connected on only 2-for-9 attempts from the field on his way to a season-low four points. With this win, Duke extended its road game winning streak in the ACC to 22 games.

Final Score: Duke 98, Georgia Tech 77
Overall Record: 17–1 **ACC:** 5–0

In the locker room after the game, I talked about Battier's performance. "How'd you guys feel with Shane scoring all those points?" I asked.

"*Good. Man, that was great! Terrific!*"

"Well, remember, those weren't Shane's baskets, those were *our* baskets. It is collective responsibility. We take pride in his performance. There's no jealousy on this team. We're proud of him. He's our teammate."

I also addressed the intentional-elbow call against Carlos Boozer. "Carlos, I know you were upset about what happened to Mike and were just playing more aggressively. But you cannot be called for intentionally elbowing an opponent again. I just won't have it. It makes us look bad as a team, and it is just not the way we play. If you want to get back at them, get back at them by stopping them on defense and by putting the ball in the hoop. That's the way we take revenge on the basketball court. Got it?"

"*Yes, Coach.*"

Later, I called the ACC offices and told them that I had addressed the matter and that this type of thing wouldn't happen again. I was told that Georgia Tech head coach Paul Hewitt had done the same. I think every coach in the league should admonish their players to "Play tough, play clean, and don't let your emotions get the best of you."

*   *   *   *   *

After we flew back to Durham, our staff met from 8:00 P.M. to 12:00 midnight to watch tape and review the game. Overall, I was not pleased with the team. They had not reacted well to the physical play of Georgia Tech, and besides, THE FIST was beginning to loosen up—the guys just weren't coming together like they had in the second Temple game, when they had played some of the most beautiful basketball I'd ever seen.

"In this game," I said to my assistants, "Georgia Tech was coming after us. They wanted to muscle Shane and Jason. And the rap on Mike was clearly, 'If you get in a good lick, he'll get timid and weak and not play well.' And guess what, they were right. It worked."

Something needed to be done to light a spark. We had been winning, but we just weren't playing as well as we should have been.
The kids needed a good talking-to, and I felt the assistant coaches
could do that effectively. And besides, it would be good for the team
to hear a different voice.

So at 3:00 the next afternoon, Coaches Dawkins, Wojciechowski,
and Collins met with the team for two hours. I stayed out of the
room. They told the kids that, as former Duke players, they understood the dynamics of what happened in the Georgia Tech game—
and if something wasn't done to address it now, we would forever
have to be a victim of rough, physical play.

"A lot of people don't like all the things that Duke has accom-
plished," said Chris Collins. "They think Duke is soft. They don't
like our whole clean-cut image. So they are going to challenge us
physically; and if we are weak and timid and allow that to happen,
we play into their strategy."

Johnny then ran the tape session and showed the physical nature
of the play. The kids saw how Dunleavy had been cracked in the
jaw. They saw how Jason had been taken out on a breakaway lay-
up when an opponent knocked him into the support and was
called for an intentional foul. And they saw that when Shane went
for a loose ball, a guy came down with both knees right in his
back. The players were shocked at the physical nature of the game.
They were so immersed in their own play that they didn't realize
the full extent of what was happening.

"This is what people are saying," said Johnny. "That you guys are
weak, that you guys are soft. Are we going to fight back or not? Are
we going to let people continue to be physical with us? Or are we
going to stand our ground and not take it anymore?" The assistant
coaches really got on the kids—and they seemed to respond. I could
see more of a fire and intensity in their eyes as they took the court
after that meeting.

The Georgia Tech game was also the low point of the season for
Mike Dunleavy. Mike is a very proud, confident player. But in this
game, he was weak, timid, and just not playing naturally. He did not
react well to the rough physical play. He had four fouls in the first

half. He took poor shots the whole game. As a matter of fact, he didn't score at all after he took that elbow to the mouth.

"When Mike returned to our apartment after the game, he just sat there on the couch in the living room staring into space. 'Everybody's pretty worried about you,' I said. 'They're wondering if you're sick or if you're getting enough sleep.' At that point, Mike hit the couch with his fist. 'That makes me so mad,' he said. 'I hate it when Coach worries about me.' Then I tried to cheer him up. 'Don't worry about it. You're human,' I told him. But Mike would have none of it. I tried to get him to go out to a movie with some friends, but he just stayed home and moped."

—Shane Battier

It was time to have a one-on-one with Dunleavy. Only this time, I thought it should be with Chris Collins rather than me. So the next day, Chris sat down with Mike and reviewed videotape of his performance in the Georgia Tech game. When the video concluded, Chris just looked at Mike and said, "Well, what do you think?"

"It's my fault. I can't play like that. I owe my team and you guys more than that. It will never happen again."

Mike Dunleavy did not offer one excuse for his poor performance. He just accepted responsibility for it and vowed to change. Chris Collins told me he believed Mike was going to turn the corner and make a big jump. I thought so, too.

"We lost to Stanford and Coach was okay with me after I missed those two key foul shots. But after the Georgia Tech game, which we won by 20 points, he wasn't too pleased with me, to say the least. The truth is, he was right. I was absolutely awful, and I pledged to never play like that again. It was nobody's fault but my own."

—Mike Dunleavy

*   *   *   *   *

We had a big week coming up in ACC play. Over the next eight days, we would play Number 9 Wake Forest, Number 8 Maryland, and Number 4 North Carolina. It would be a big test for us.

Wake Forest at Duke

January 24, 2001—Mike Dunleavy matched his career-high of 21 points as he teamed with Jason Williams (27 points) and Shane Battier (22 points) to lead Duke to their sixth straight ACC conference victory. Dunleavy had three three-pointers out of four attempts and seemed to show up all over the court in what some observers called his best game of the season. The sophomore also had two steals, two blocks, and seven rebounds. The first 14 minute-span of the game was evenly matched until Williams scored three straight Duke baskets. Inspired by their point guard's play, other Duke players slapped the floor in excitement. "When we slap the floor," said co-captain Nate James, "that means we are together, on the same page, that we want to shut 'em down on defense." A 21–3 run by the Blue Devils in the first half pretty much slammed the door on the Demon Deacons' hopes for an upset of Number 2–ranked Duke. In the second half, the Duke bench erupted in cheers when sophomore Casey Sanders, backing up Carlos Boozer at the center position, hit the floor with a thunderous thud after stepping in front of a screen and taking a charge.

Final Score: Duke 85, Wake Forest 62
Overall Record: 18–1 **ACC:** 6–0

*   *   *   *   *

"Hold it! Hold it! Holy mackerel! I can't believe it!" I yelled during the middle of a practice scrimmage. All the guys stopped and looked at me. They didn't know what was coming.

"Casey! This is the spot! This is it!" I said, holding my hands down, pointing to the floor, and moving my foot around in a circle.

Casey looks up at me and all the guys are looking and wondering, What spot?

"This is the spot where you were born. This is the spot where you became a player. This is the spot where you took the charge yesterday. Forget about Coach K Court! This is *the spot!*"

Now all the guys are laughing and Casey has a big broad grin on his face. I wanted everybody to know, especially Casey, that he had made a huge leap as a player in the Wake Forest game. And this was a way of doing it without holding a meeting and declaring it in a solemn, serious tone. And the guys picked up on it right away—and then they kidded Casey as the scrimmage continued. "*Oops, I just walked across Casey's spot!*" "*Geez, Dahntay. Don't walk across Casey's spot! It's sacred!*"

We had been working hard to get Casey to be more aggressive and passionate. And with his four-a-week workouts, he was beginning to feel stronger and more confident. As a matter of fact, just before the game, Wojo, who had been working with him almost daily, reminded Casey to "play hard, run the court, and try and take a charge." Something was different about Casey Sanders in this game. I don't know exactly what caused it, but I was certainly gratified to see him come on like he did.

> "*I admitted to myself that I didn't know anything. I started paying more attention in practice. Before, whenever my teammates would say something to me, I would think, Well, that may work for them, but it doesn't work for me. But I stopped saying that to myself and really started listening to them. And I basically just tried to do everything the coaches said. It started in the Wake Forest game. I didn't play that long, just a few minutes. But you would have thought I was the hero of the game the way the coaches and players carried on. It just made me feel great.*"
>
> —*Casey Sanders*

In that same practice, we had a great 12-minute scrimmage between the Blue and White squads. At one point Jason fell on a player and twisted his ankle pretty hard. He kept playing, but there was a noticeable limp. The Blue team actually beat the White team in that scrimmage. And the starters were upset about it. "*How did they beat us?*" screamed Shane in frustration. Jason came up to me and wanted to play again, but I refused.

"No, Jason. You lost and that's it. This isn't like 'Mommy, I want to do it again.' You're not going to be able to do that against Maryland when we're at Cole Field House on Saturday. You'll have to beat them before the buzzer goes off." Then I turned to J.D. Simpson, Dahntay Jones, and the rest of the Blue team. "Way to go, guys. You just played great. Maybe we should start you against Maryland."

There are two things that are very bad for players—to think they've been forgotten, and never to be yelled at. After the Blue team beat the starters, I praised the Blue team and chastised Jason and the starters. It had to be done.

*   *   *   *   *

This week started on a sad note. Al McGuire, the former Marquette basketball coach and one of our more colorful television broadcasters, died at the age of 72. Al had a street-wise intelligence and a brilliant understanding of people that I appreciated very much. He had been ill with a form of leukemia, and he had needed frequent blood transfusions. A few weeks earlier, I had called him to see how he was doing, and he had made it easy on me by being upbeat and taking over the conversation. He started talking about how good our team was this year and how he had been impressed with us after seeing several games on TV. When I asked him how he was, he said, "I'm at peace, Mike. You know me. I got everything out of life—great friends, great family, always did what I wanted to do. When I get the blood transfusions, I feel better. I'm getting tired of them, though."

Al liked to go to flea markets and buy odd items that interested him. Well, not long after our phone call, I received a package of six miniature West Point soldiers. The note said: "Saw these and thought of you. Al." He died before I could write him a thank-you note. I keep those toy soldiers in my office in a prominent place so everyone who walks in will see them. I'm going to miss Al McGuire.

*   *   *   *   *

When we arrived at Cole Field House, I knew it was going to be a war. Maryland had some great ballplayers in Juan Dixon, Lonny Baxter, Steve Blake, Byron Mouton, and Terence Morris. I mean, they just had a terrific team—a genuine contender for both the ACC title and the national title.

This would be the toughest game we had played to date. Not only that, but we were entering enemy territory—literally. Cole Field House is the most hostile environment for us in the ACC. Mickie does not attend games there because of it. The Maryland fans were waiting for us, too. Most of the students, and numerous adults, wore shirts with F*CK DUKE emblazoned on the front. As our players were being introduced, they shook open newspapers in front of their faces like they were not paying attention. And after the introductions, they crumpled up the newspapers and threw them at the Duke bench. And throughout the game, sometimes they'd throw stuff at the bench—ice, aluminum foil from hot dog wrappers, stuff like that. It's a tough place to play.

Before our team went out on the floor after preliminary warm-ups, I grabbed all their attention for one last statement. "We're not going to lose this game," I said. "At any point, if you think we're going to lose this game, look over to me on the bench. You'll gain confidence that we're going to win."

Duke at Maryland
Cole Field House, College Park, Maryland

January 27, 2001—After being outplayed for nearly the entire game, Duke overcame a 10-point deficit in the final minute of regulation and won the game in overtime. It was one of the greatest comebacks in NCAA basketball history. The Blue Devils led for almost all of the first 11 minutes, until Maryland went on a 20–4 scoring run to take a 44–29 lead with just 2:39 remaining in the half. Jason Williams committed 10 turnovers in the game's first 25 minutes. With 1.4 seconds remaining in the half, Maryland's Tahj Holden missed a shot and the half appeared to expire. But game officials ruled that the shot had missed the rim, which was a shot-clock violation. So 1.4 seconds were put back on the clock and Duke was awarded the ball. Coach Mike Krzyzewski then called the same play that beat Kentucky in the 1992 NCAA East Regional final when Grant Hill passed it to Christian Laettner, who shot the game-winner as time expired. This time Mike Dunleavy threw the ball the length of the court to Shane Battier. Dunleavy overthrew Battier but Jason Williams grabbed it and banked home a shot as the buzzer sounded. That cut Maryland's lead to nine points at intermission and gave the Blue Devils some much-needed momentum. . . .

In the locker room at halftime, I didn't say much to the kids. Actually, I felt we were lucky to be down by only nine points, as poorly as we had played. So I turned and wrote up on the chalkboard in big letters, *WE WILL WIN!*

"Look guys," I said, "we're playing poorly. They are playing as well as they can play. And we're only down by nine." Then I reiterated what I said before the game began. "At any point, if you think we're going to lose this game, look over to me on the bench. I'll give you the confidence you need to win."

. . . In the second half, Duke drove the ball to the basket, which served to get Maryland into foul trouble and slow down the game. The Blue Devils converted numerous free throws in the second half. But that strategy just appeared to be postponing an inevitable Maryland victory. With 1:51 remaining in the game, Maryland's best ball handler, Steve Blake, fouled out—and 10 seconds later, Shane Battier picked up his fourth foul. At the 1:05 mark, with Maryland leading 89–77, Nate James hit a three-pointer to cut the lead to nine. Duke then called a timeout, at which point ESPN conceded a Maryland victory and announced Steve Blake (11 points, nine assists) as the Player of the Game. . . .

> *"After I made that three-pointer with about a minute left, we went to the bench and I told Mike Dunleavy, 'Hey, this is going to be on Classic Sports every night. We're going to come back and we're going to win. Everybody's going to be talking about this game forever.'"*
>
> —*Nate James*

. . . After Maryland made one of two free throws to take a 10-point lead with 1:00 left on the clock, the fans in Cole Field House began chanting, "Overrated! Overrated! Overrated!" . . .

Althea Williams (Jason's mom): "As soon as I heard that cheer, I thought to myself, 'Uh, oh. Jason really hates that cheer. Maryland's in trouble now.'"

Mike Schrage: "I was sitting at the end of the bench next to three security guards, one of whom was talking into his walkie-talkie. 'All right, they want us over at the football stadium,' one said to the others. 'They're scared the fans are going to tear down the goal posts when we win, just like they did when we beat Duke last year.' Then all three of them took off running to go to the football stadium."

... Then, with no timeouts remaining, Duke pulled off the "Miracle Minute."

53.5   Jason Williams drives the length of the court and lays in a basket.

         Score: Maryland 90, Duke 82

48.7   Jason Williams steals the ball after an inbounds pass and immediately shoots and hits a three-pointer.

         Score: Maryland 90, Duke 85

48.7   Andre Buckner fouls before the clock starts. Maryland misses both free throws.

         Score: Maryland 90, Duke 85

40.4   Jason Williams hits a three-point shot.

         Score: Maryland 90, Duke 88

21.9   After a Maryland timeout and an inbound pass, Nate James steals the ball for a Duke possession. Mike Dunleavy misses a three-point shot and Nate James is fouled on the attempted tip-in. James sinks both free throws in front of 14,500 screaming Maryland fans.

         Score: Maryland 90, Duke 90

00.0   Maryland holds the ball for the final shot; misses a three-point attempt at the buzzer.

         Score: Maryland 90, Duke 90

         End of Regulation.

Mike Schrage: "I looked over to my right, and those three security guards were sitting next to me again."

In overtime, the Blue Devils seemed to be fresh and revitalized, while the Terrapins appeared tired and demoralized. With 3:52 left in overtime, Shane Battier hit a three-point shot that gave Duke the lead, 95–92, which they never lost. Battier scored all six of Duke's final points and then blocked Juan Dixon's last gasp shot to end the game.

Final Score: Duke 98, Maryland 96, OT
Overall Record: 19–1 **ACC:** 7–0

When the final buzzer sounded, I just stood up and said, "We won!"

After shaking hands with Maryland's coaches and players, who were understandably dispirited, we began to walk off the court. Chris Collins suddenly ran up to Johnny Dawkins, put his arm around him, and yelled: "Incoming! Incoming!" As Chris tried to hustle him off the floor, Johnny looked back toward the stands and saw all kinds of debris being thrown out of the crowd, into the Duke fan section, and onto the floor.

I wouldn't have thought much about it, except many of our players' parents were pelted with some of that junk. Pat James and Nate Sr. were hit. Two water-filled plastic bottles struck Althea Williams and Vivian Harper, Chris Duhon's mom. Carlos Boozer's mom, Renee, was hit on the head by a glass object of some kind and suffered a concussion. And just about all of them were verbally abused by some of the Maryland fans. An internal investigation into the incident revealed that "more than 100 items were thrown at the Duke families in the 50 most intense seconds of the barrage." The University of Maryland's president later sincerely apologized for the conduct, and that was good enough for me. I just hope it never happens again.

In the locker room after the game, all the guys were hooting and hollering in a wild celebration. Colonel Tom Rogers, my long-time friend and part-time assistant, went up to the chalkboard, erased the WE WILL WIN! that I had written at halftime and scrawled in big letters: WE WON!

"Congratulations, fellas," I said to the team, "it was an amazing victory. Simply amazing." Everybody cheered and hollered again.

"Let me tell you what we learned in this game. In that last minute, we learned how to play like a clenched fist, again. Before that, two of our fingers, Shane and Jason, weren't performing to the level they usually do. In fact, both of them were playing so badly, they could easily have said to themselves, 'I want to get out of here. Where is the *bus*!' But the other three, Nate, Mike, Carlos—and Chris when he was in—were holding us together and kept us in a position to win the game.

"Then, all of a sudden, Jason, who was playing terrible basketball up to that point—I think you had around 10 turnovers, Jason—suddenly scored eight points in 14 seconds. Eight points in 14 seconds! That has to be the ultimate example of Next Play, Jason. And Shane, you carried us in overtime. You were incredible. That block at the end of the game, after playing more than 40 minutes, will go down as one of your greatest moments. What a play!"

The guys patted Shane on the back and pushed him around. His grin showed everybody how big his heart was at that moment.

After a pause, I turned to Jason.

"Jason," I asked, "what the hell got into you, son?"

"*Coach*," he responded, "*I hate that cheer!*"

*   *   *   *   *

Following each game, we usually tied everything up in a nice tight package, provided feedback to the team, and then moved on to the next game. This time, however, that was exceedingly difficult to do.

After reviewing the game, it was clear to me that we really did lose to Maryland. They outplayed us for 39 minutes. And if it had not been for that incredible last-minute finish, I probably would have killed them in practice. A lot of times, I'm tougher on a team after a win where we don't play well than after a loss where we gave a really good effort. But I couldn't do it after this game.

The truth is they had done an extraordinary thing. I couldn't get on them that much, because it was one of the greatest comebacks in basketball history. It was being shown over and over again on ESPN and touted as an instant classic. The buzz about that game just didn't go away, and the kids just weren't coming back down to earth.

So we had a double shot of distraction—which is unusual with a North Carolina game coming up. When you're preparing for them, you have to be in a mood to win and compete. In some respects, *losing* to Maryland would have been better preparation—not that we want to lose, but our team clearly did not have a true sense of reality about who we were. So now we were living on a false sense of pride. We were in the awkward position of being undefeated in ACC play, but the truth was that we really weren't playing very well.

And now we had to get ready to play our archrival in a very important game. Both teams were 7–0 in ACC play. We were 19–1 overall, and UNC was 17–2 and had won 14 games in a row. Whoever won this game was going to take over sole possession of first place and have a major psychological edge as we headed down the stretch of the season. We were playing at home, and people just figured we were supposed to win this game.

Every year, our home game against UNC is an event. There's a tremendous amount of media hype. It's kind of like the Super Bowl of the college basketball regular season. Our collective sixth man, the students who call themselves the Cameron Crazies, camp out for a month in the tent city they named Krzyzewskiville in order to get into the game. There are a lot of parties going on all the time, and the night before the game, I come out and talk to everybody.

This year there must have been 2,000 people in the Cameron courtyard—sitting on the stairs, sitting on the walls, standing. It's really not a pep rally, it's a team meeting. And these kids know it. There's no press allowed. They'll kick the press out if they show up. Mickie was with me, along with Jason Williams and Chris Duhon. Because I was concerned about our players not being as ready as they should be, I wanted to bring our sixth man more into the game. So I talked about THE FIST.

"We are all one of these five fingers," I told the students as I held my open hand up high. "When we take the court, we have to be together—like a fist." Then I closed my hand and made a fist.

"If one of us is weak, the rest of us will make us strong. We won't succumb to one person's weakness. We will go in the direction of THE FIST. When you're having a bad day, you must allow the others to step up for you, or to pat you on the back and say, 'C'mon, get with it!' or to get in your face and try to snap you out of it. And you, in turn, will not say, 'Leave me alone, I want to be miserable today.' That is unacceptable on our team. Our team is not allowed to have a bad day. How do we *not* have a bad day? We do not have a bad day because we observe the five points of THE FIST:

"Point One: Communication
I'm going to tell you the truth if you're doing something bad, if you're doing something mediocre, or if you're doing something great.

"Point Two: Trust
When we tell each other the truth and talk to each other face-to-face, trust is going to develop. It's amazing. How many of you really trust someone? Some of you may not trust anybody. But if you're part of something that's bigger than you, something that you identify with, something you throw yourself into, then you will be more apt to be able to trust the people in that room. And that's what we're trying to build. A team where we trust one another; where we have confidence in one another.

"Point Three: Collective Responsibility
We win and we lose together. It's not Jason Williams's shot or Chris Duhon's shot, it's *our* shot. This is *our* game. This is *our* court. A fist embraces plural pronouns.

"Point Four: Caring
We care for one another. If something happens, we're there for each other, all the time. All the time.

"Point Five: Pride
If we do all these things over and over, we develop the pride of being in that fist—whether it's a team fist, a church fist, a family fist, or a business fist. We're proud to say, 'I belong to the Duke basketball program.'

"With these five points, all of a sudden you're part of something bigger than yourself. That's what being a fist is all about. You throw yourself completely into the group—by communicating, by trusting, by being collectively responsible, by caring, and by having pride. If you continue to do that through the years, you will develop a tradition of excellence. And that is what we have here at Duke—a tradition of excellence.

"Do you all notice what the players and I do at the beginning of a game? We put our fists together in the huddle and we say '*One, two, three—Win!*' Five guys as one. Well, tomorrow, so that you'll be part of what we're doing, when we get into that huddle, I want you all to reach out from the stands and put your fists in, too. If you do that, I believe we're going to win. I believe in us and I want you to believe in us, too.

"For the rest of this year, I don't want you to get caught up in bashing any individual player. Get caught up in being part of THE FIST. Don't throw anything on the floor. You all know what happened at Maryland. That can never happen at Duke. Never. When we need help, don't downgrade the other team. Uplift your team. Uplift us. Be innovative in what you do. Be creative."

Then I took my Duke warm-up jacket off to reveal I was wearing the same shirt that all the Cameron Crazies wear—the one that says: *Sixth Man.* Everybody cheered when they saw it. And when they quieted down, I ended my talk by saying, "I'll be wearing this under my shirt during the game to keep you guys close to my heart."

*   *   *   *   *

Normally when the opposing team is being introduced, the Cameron Crazies will say, "Hi, Joe" (whatever the name of the player is who's being introduced). But during introductions for UNC the next night, the place went dead silent and all the kids held out their fists. Many of them had even painted their fists Duke blue. When our players were introduced, the place erupted in cheers and the kids held their fists up high. And when we were in the huddle, all the Cameron Crazies reached out with their fists and participated in our cheer, "*One, two, three—Win!*" It made the players feel great. It made us all feel like they were really behind us.

North Carolina at Duke

February 1, 2001—North Carolina relentlessly attacked Duke on the inside by feeding star center Brendan Haywood. At the same time, Duke's stellar defense seemed to wane, as the Blue Devils did not pressure the ball well. After trailing 41–34 at halftime, Duke made an 11–2 run on the shooting of Shane Battier—finally taking the lead 50–49 on a Jason Williams jump shot. The lead seesawed for the rest of the game. Duke stayed in the game down the stretch on the play of Mike Dunleavy, who made a crowd-pleasing dunk and then a clutch three-point shot to tie the score at 83–83 with 9.2 seconds left in the game. With 1.2 seconds left, however, Shane Battier fouled out of the game after committing an uncharacteristic foul against Brendan Haywood. Haywood, who is only a 48.6 percent shooter from the line, nailed both free throws to give North Carolina the victory. . . .

> *"We employed a trap and someone threw a deep pass to Haywood. I was in the backcourt. When I saw the pass, I thought: Okay, I'm going to intercept it, take one step, take a half-court shot, and maybe win the game. The only problem was, when I went to break on the ball, I came out of my shoe. It made me stumble and I ran right into Haywood. As soon as the foul was called, I wanted to crawl into a hole. I'm so used to being on the right side of plays, I just felt awful. The worst feeling was that I let my team down. I felt personally responsible for losing that game."*
>
> —Shane Battier

. . . UNC guard Joseph Forte led the Tar Heels with 24 points and 16 rebounds. Jason Williams led the Blue Devils with 32 points. Carlos Boozer scored only four points and was confined to the bench for seven minutes with foul trouble. Duke shot a season-low 13-for-27 from the free throw line and missed 44 shots total. With the loss, Duke fell out of first place in the ACC for the first time since 1997. With the win, North Carolina gained the inside track on the East region top seed in the NCAA tournament in March.

Final Score: North Carolina 85, Duke 83
Overall Record: 19–2 **ACC:** 7–1

As usual after the game, I did a press conference, and predictably, the reporters wanted my perspective on our second loss of the year. "Sometimes you want it too much," I responded. "I sensed it from the beginning—they were too ready, too emotional, and, really, I spent most of the game trying to settle them down. . . . We just did not shoot the ball well, especially from the free throw line. We've been an 80 percent free throw-shooting team. Tonight, we shot less than 50 percent. Our offense also affected our defense. We didn't see the ball go in on some open shots. You've got to be mentally tough to go on to the next play. I don't want to take anything away from North Carolina. They played a great game. We'll work harder now than we did before this game. This will just make us more determined."

After the press conference concluded, Mickie came up to me. "There are still students out there," she said. "They've been waiting for you."

"What? The game ended an hour ago. Why didn't somebody tell me?"

I hustled back out to the court and there were about 100 students standing at center court with their fists raised in the air. They told me that the Carolina team and fans had lingered on the court celebrating, but our students had stayed in the stands holding out their firsts and surrounding the court in silent unity.

I felt like crying. Are you kidding me? What these kids have done tonight is better than any lesson they could get in a classroom. They were telling me, "*You are not alone. We win and lose together.*"

"I'm sorry we lost the game tonight," I said to the students. "You could not make me feel better than you do right now. For you to be out here like this is really wonderful. That's winning. We're going to be okay. We're going to be fine."

Then I brought them all together. "We're going to do the same thing I do with the players. Okay, everybody get in here. Put your fists together on top of mine."

So 100 students crowded together, reached out their fists toward me, and we did the cheer: "*One, two, three—Win!*"

*   *   *   *   *

"My mom was in town, so I went to dinner with her after the game. When I got back to the apartment, it was Shane who was slumped down on the couch this time. He didn't look good. He was channel surfing and couldn't find

anything he wanted to watch. I smiled, but he didn't respond. Then I jumped on him and started wrestling with him. 'C'mon, cheer up,' I said. 'It isn't like you just blew the game against North Carolina or anything.' Then Shane smiled and started to loosen up a little bit. 'Okay, that's better,' I said. 'Now, quit changing channels. Put on ESPN and let's watch the highlights of our game.'"

—Mike Dunleavy

*   *   *   *   *

Players listen better after they lose. The sophomores and freshmen had never experienced a loss to North Carolina and had never experienced being out of first place in the ACC. So they took the North Carolina loss very hard. When I gave them feedback, you could have heard a pin drop. I mean, their attention was undivided.

We were thoroughly outplayed inside, I told them. We had wanted to neutralize or get over their inside players, but we were not able to do that. Carlos was ineffective. He had only four points in 29 minutes and was in foul trouble most of the game. We intended to defend well against Joseph Forte, UNC's outstanding wing, but we were not able to do so. Forte had a great game against us. Shane's foul at the end of the game differed from the dumb fouls he committed against Stanford. This play was going to be a steal, but he just came out of his shoe. He made a mistake doing a positive act. I'll never have a problem with that. The final thing I told the team was that we had not handled the aftermath of the Maryland game well, at all. We had not put the excitement of the win behind us in order to prepare for the next big game. Next Play is not just about putting losses behind you, it's about putting wins behind you, too. I told the team that if they wanted to do well in the NCAA tournament this year, they had better learn to do that effectively.

"The good news is that feeling the sting of defeat on February First is a lot better than feeling it on April First."

*   *   *   *   *

Jason Williams had scored 32 points against North Carolina and was now being touted as a Player-of-the-Year candidate. Shane was pleased Jason was playing so well and also seemed relieved to have some of the burden off his shoulders.

"*Jason, you're going to be National Player of the Year,*" he joked.

"*No, Shane,* you're *going to be National Player of the Year,*" Jason shot back.

The fact that there was no jealousy between these two superstars allowed Shane to relax and get back to his peak performance. He kind of sneaked in the back door while everybody was praising Jason and quietly put up better numbers. But with the national praise, Jason was also put under tremendous pressure to turn pro after the year ended.

Concerned for their son, Jason's parents traveled down from New Jersey to have a meeting with me. It was just the three of us. Jason met with his parents later. I wanted to have their view on the entire situation and they were really prepared to discuss the subject. His mom had a decision flow-chart that we talked about in great detail. Then I recommended they go talk to Paul Haagen, the associate dean of our law school, so they would be completely informed legally on everything related to a player jumping to the NBA early. It was a good meeting because we both wanted what was best for their son.

The day before the Florida State game, I met with Jason alone in my office. He and his parents had decided that he should come back for his junior year and be close to graduation before he went into the NBA draft. Graduating was very important to him and his parents. I agreed with his goal, and together, we laid out a detailed plan to make it happen.

"I talked to Coach right before the game and we discussed what my parents and I had talked about. I liked the fact that he did not try to make my decision for me, but rather, along the way, helped me come to my own conclusion. At the end of our talk, Coach told me he thought I was an uncommon kid. I love Coach K. I'd go through a brick wall for him."

—*Jason Williams*

Florida State at Duke

February 4, 2001—Duke rebounded from its second loss of the year on the offensive play of Carlos Boozer, who had 23 points, and Shane Battier, who had 21. In the last 11 minutes of the first half, Duke ran off a 29–8 run that provided a 41–24 lead at the half. The Seminoles then fell victim to Duke's pressure defense in the second half as the Blue Devils had two runs of 15–4 and 21–0 to put the game out of reach. While Jason Williams finished with only eight points, his defensive presence on the court was sterling. He finished with six steals, committed only two turnovers, and had 10 assists. In the locker room after the game, Williams announced to the press that he was passing up the opportunity to be one of the top choices in this spring's NBA draft and would stay in school through the 2002 season. "I'm not going to the NBA this year," said Williams. "I plan to get my degree at Duke. Don't ask me about it anymore. This is a final decision. I'm coming back to Duke next year. This is where I want to be."

Final Score: Duke 100, Florida State 58
Overall Record: 20–2 **ACC:** 8–1

*   *   *   *   *

Duke at Clemson
Littlejohn Coliseum, Clemson, South Carolina

February 7, 2001—Duke overpowered Clemson to win its 24th consecutive road game in the ACC—a conference record. Fifth-year senior Nate James hit 10 of 14 shots from the field, including 3-for-5 from three-point range on his way to a career-high 27 points. James scored Duke's first eight points then steadily stung Clemson with his shooting. He also held Will Solomon, the ACC's top scorer to only 11 points on the night. Shane Battier added 15 points, and Mike Dunleavy finished with his first career double-double (17 points and 17 rebounds). After the game, Coach Mike Krzyzewski commented, "I'm pleased with the development of Dunleavy and James. And pleased that somebody different stepped forward. Everybody says Nate James is an unsung guy. But now, he's sung."

Final Score: Duke 85, Clemson 64
Overall Record: 21–2 **ACC:** 9–1

I had been looking forward to Reunion Weekend all year, and it was finally here. This was to be the 10th anniversary of Duke's first national championship, and nearly all the members of our 1991 team were back on campus for a celebration.

We had a private dinner the night before the NC State game in the Duke Sports Hall of Fame for all the players, managers, and their families. It was a very emotional evening, with lots of laughter and tears, as a number of people spoke and we watched the 10-year-old team videos. At 10:30 that night, this year's team began assembling downstairs in the locker room for a final pregame get-together. The banquet was winding down when I got up to address the crowd.

"If the families don't mind," I said, "I'd like all the guys from the '91 team to come down to the locker room with me. We're having a team meeting in preparation for tomorrow's NC State game." Then I looked around and said, "Okay, guys, let's get our butts moving." And they all got up and came with me. It was just like the old days. Bobby Hurley, Christian Laettner, Marty Clark, Greg Koubek, Clay Buckley, Kenny Blakeney, and Bill McCaffrey followed me into the locker room, shook hands with our young players, and everybody sat down.

"Welcome back, '91," I said. "I want you younger guys to be around successful people—and there's nobody more successful than these men. Not only did they win a national championship, they were the most improved team I have ever coached. We had an incredibly tough schedule that year, and they just kept improving. They were a resilient group and believed in themselves thoroughly. They had great heart—just like this year's team. And there are some other common factors between these two teams: a great point guard from New Jersey—Hurley and Williams; uncommon leadership from one of the players—Laettner and Battier; and a young versatile star—Hill and Dunleavy. But more than anything else, the most common thing between these two teams is their hearts—their *hearts*. Let's watch the team video from the 1991 championship team and you'll see what I mean."

After the video was over, I asked the younger guys what they saw in the '91 team that made them successful.

"*They were real close*," came one reply.

"*There was communication*," came another.

"Right," I said, "and that's what we have to do against State tomorrow."

After I talked a little bit about game strategy, I concluded the meeting by saying, "Okay, everybody, let's get together."

As I put my fist in the center and all the kids started to gather around, Shane Battier looked over to the older guys and said: "*Hey, '91, you guys get in here, too*." So we all put our fists in the center and it was a unified: "*One, two, three—Win!*" After that, the two teams had a chance to talk and share stories.

Part of my thinking for getting these two teams together was that I wanted the younger guys to get a sense of history. I also wanted them to see how happy the '91 team was and how they could reflect on their accomplishment 10 years later. This team had their moment back in 1991. They still had that moment—and would always have it. I wanted our team to understand that.

North Carolina State at Duke

February 11, 2001—All five starters for Number 3–ranked Duke scored in double figures as the Blue Devils shot 53 percent from the field and forced 24 turnovers. The Wolfpack led 9–7 after the first three minutes, but Duke then went on a 17–0 run. At one point, Duke's defense held NC State without a basket on 13 consecutive possessions. At the start of the second half, the Blue Devils continued their hot shooting by hitting their first eight shots and 11 of their first 12. By the 11-minute mark, the lead had ballooned to 30 points. Jason Williams led all scorers with 23, while Carlos Boozer added 17 on 7-for-10 shooting from the floor. Nate James contributed 19, Shane Battier 18, and Mike Dunleavy 13. Duke's 1991 national championship team was honored at halftime ceremonies. A co-captain of the '91 team, Greg Koubek, stated to the crowd that "the best way to honor our team is to win another national championship."

Final Score: Duke 101, North Carolina State 75
Overall Record: 22–2 **ACC:** 10–1

*   *   *   *   *

"Chris Duhon! When are you going to start shooting the ball?" This time it wasn't the players asking Chris to take more shots, it was me. Chris just looked down at the floor.

"Jason, is it all right for Chris to shoot the ball?"

"*Sure it is, Coach.*"

"Do you see, Chris? It's okay with Jason if you shoot the ball. Shane, is it all right if Chris shoots the ball?"

"*Yes.*"

"You see. Shane says it okay, too. Are you listening to me, Chris?"

"*Yes, Coach,*" he replied, as he looked up from the floor.

"Okay. Tomorrow, we're playing a very tough Virginia team. I am turning you loose for that game. I want you to stop worrying about everyone else and just play your game. Do you understand?"

"*Yes, Coach.*"

"Good, then you will be shooting the ball tomorrow, won't you?"

"*Yes, Coach.*"

"Okay. Now everybody listen up. Chris Duhon is now our sixth starter. He's going to play against Virginia as our sixth starter and he is going to shoot the ball. I'm turning him loose. Does everybody understand that?"

"*Yeah.*" "*Yes.*" "*Sure, we got it.*"

"And is that okay with everybody—if Chris is now our sixth starter?"

"*Uh-huh.*" "*Yup.*" "*Yeah.*"

"Good, now let's get back to practicing."

It was time we did something more with Chris—partly because I was worried about Jason. Against Florida State and Clemson, Jason had scored only eight points in each game. After he had decided not to go pro, I think he just started dishing the ball off to the other guys instead of being himself. I spoke to him about it, and he did pick it up for the NC State game with 23 points. But also, I believe Bobby Hurley's presence in the locker room the night before clearly inspired Jason's performance in that game.

So I was ready to create a little competition for Jason. I didn't tell Chris and Jason, but that is, in part, what I had in mind. The other part is that I didn't want Chris to feel like an understudy or a supporting actor for the entire season. Essentially, I was telling him that he was not an understudy anymore.

Another thing that motivated my action was my concern about Virginia. This was a very good team we were about to play. They had fluctuated between sixth and 12th in the national rankings since the last time we played them, and they were hungry to play us again. Virginia fans had been camping out for two days waiting to get tickets. I knew University Hall in Charlottesville would be rocking on Wednesday night.

Wojo took extra time to get the big men ready. He led a lot more physical workouts, for example. At one point, he taped a picture of Virginia's big man, Travis Watson, on the big blue body pad. Then he got behind the pad and used it to muscle Carlos, Casey, Matt, and Reggie. The big blue pad is a body-length cushion that protects the users from getting hurt as they put pressure on the players during drills that simulate the physical nature of a real game. Sometimes the managers use the pad. Sometimes Wojo uses it. Chris Collins calls it "Wojo's Girlfriend" because Wojo hugs it so tight during the drills. At any rate, we needed the big men to be ready for this game. Virginia was a tough, physical team.

In the visitors' locker room in Charlottesville, I wrote a statement up on the chalkboard: *We will give our best effort and we will play Duke basketball.* Then I had every player come up and sign his name on the board. It was the last thing they did before they went out on the court.

Duke at Virginia
University Hall, Charlottesville, Virginia

February 14, 2001—Twelfth-ranked Virginia ended third-ranked Duke's 24-game ACC road streak despite the heroics of freshman Chris Duhon, who had a career-high 20 points, including 5-for-5 from three-point range in the second half. . . .

> *"My teammates had been giving me a lot of confidence in practice telling me to shoot the ball. When Mike Dunleavy got into foul trouble and had to come out, I knew someone had to step forward."*
>
> *— Chris Duhon*

. . . With 14.3 seconds remaining in the game, Shane Battier sank two clutch free throws to tie the game 89–89. Nate James then blocked Cavalier Roger Mason's shot under the basket. But Adam Hall picked up the loose ball and put in the winner with less than a second left on the clock. It was a sub-par night for Jason Williams, who went 5-for-21 and scored 14 points. Mike Dunleavy and Carlos Boozer were in foul trouble for much of the game. Boozer had only six points, Dunleavy five. Casey Sanders filled in ably for Boozer in the low post with a strong defensive effort. Duhon played 35 minutes in place of Dunleavy. After the Valentine's Day game, Duke coach Mike Krzyzewski observed, "Virginia had the most heart today. The team that should have won did win."

Final Score: Virginia 91, Duke 89
Overall Record: 22–3 **ACC:** 10–2

In the locker room after the game, I didn't say much to the team. But I was extremely upset, especially with the poor play of Jason Williams. So I calmly said to him, "Jason, you disappoint me. I don't know if you were worried about your ankle injury. But whatever it was, you let your team down tonight. You didn't really *care* tonight. You didn't care about your performance. You didn't *care* about your team. You just didn't care."

> *"After we lost that game, I was in the locker room and I was starting to cry. And Shane came up to me and looked at me, and he didn't have to say anything. I knew what he was thinking. He was thinking, Don't you dare cry. You have nothing to cry about. You didn't play your heart out tonight. I thought about it for the entire bus ride back. And I realized Shane was right."*
>
> *— Jason Williams*

At the beginning of the four-hour bus ride back to Durham, I talked to the coaching staff and singled out Chris Duhon and Casey Sanders. "We may have lost tonight and not everyone played well—but two good things may have come out of it. Tonight we may have found two real players—Casey and Chris. Casey had a major impact inside. It was a turnaround game for him. And Chris finally started to shoot and show what he can do. This was a breakout game for Chris Duhon."

For the rest of the four-hour bus ride back to Durham, I watched videotape of the game. And the more I watched, the more frustrated I became. And by the time we arrived at Cameron, at four o'clock in the morning, I was really steamed. "Okay, everybody into the locker room," I said before anybody could get off the bus. "We're having our feedback session right now."

Once everybody was seated, I tore into them. I questioned their level of commitment going down the stretch run of the ACC regular season. We had lost to UNC, then we won three games, and now we played like this. We were back to being inconsistent and I hammered them for it.

Then I made Jason Williams the "star" of the session. "Jason, this was your worst game of the year, your low-point of the season," I said. "I don't know where you were tonight. You didn't have your head in the game. You seemed to be in a daze. You didn't lead us. You took bad shots. You made turnovers. In shooting, you were 5-for-21! Five-for-21! Are you kidding me? That's not the Jason Williams we all know."

Then I turned my attention to Mike Dunleavy.

"Mike, you've got to be careful not to foul so much—especially in the early stages when I have to keep jerking you in and out of the game. You cannot commit stupid fouls, do you understand? You cannot be on the bench instead of on the floor. We can't have Mike Dunleavy not play in a game. Do you understand?"

Then I let Carlos have it. "Carlos, you had six points and four fouls. You almost committed more fouls than you scored points! You weren't on the court long enough to make a difference in this game. Don't you see that we have trouble winning when you're in foul trouble? You fouled out in the Stanford game—and we lost. You fouled out in the North Carolina game and we lost. You got into foul trouble in this game—and we lost. Our only three losses have come when you took yourself out of the game. Come on, man! We need you."

By then, I was so exasperated, I even got on Duhon. "Chris Duhon, you had a terrific game. I'm sorry we didn't support you better. We had a hot guy, and we didn't get him the ball enough. Jason, why weren't you throwing Chris the ball? Part of that is your fault, Chris. You weren't calling for the ball enough. When you're hot, you have to *call for the ball!* Chris, maybe we didn't pass you the ball enough because we're not accustomed to you shooting. You can't go four games or four practices with only taking two shots and then all of a sudden hit 20. That's unfair to the rest of the team. You have to be more consistent."

After I vented, I sent them all home and told them I'd see them at 3:00 P.M.—about ten hours from then.

*　*　*　*　*

That afternoon, Jason came right up to me and apologized.

"*Coach, I'm sorry I wasn't good last night,*" he said.

"Don't worry about it, Jason. Next Play," I responded. "Is there anything wrong?"

"*No, I'm all right.*"

Later in that practice, Shane went up to Jason and had a conversation.

"*I may be telling you something you already know,*" said Shane, "*but we know you're a better player than you showed at Virginia. How do you feel about the game?*"

"*I turned it over too much,*" said Jason. "*I forced shots. I didn't play smart.*"

"*Well, there you go. I can't tell you anything you don't already know about the situation. The important thing now is how you respond. How you respond to the bad games and the adversity will determine how great a player you are.*"

I thought it was interesting that Shane did not berate or encourage Jason. In his own way, he challenged him.

The next day, Chris Collins watched tape with Jason and evaluated his performance. Chris pointed out how Jason was just walking around. He'd see a Duke fast break with four Duke guys and five Virginia guys—and Jason just trotting behind everybody. He didn't have any steals. He wasn't talking. He wasn't playing defense. He was a body on the court and nothing else. Then Chris pointed out to Jason that his facial expressions gave him away.

"It looks like you're waiting for someone to take your hand," said Chris, "and ask, 'Jason, are you all right? Are you okay?' "

"After that session, I learned that when things don't go exactly right, you have to have that look on your face that says, 'Okay, it doesn't bother me. Next play.' After that session, I wore a look of confidence on my face. Even if I missed a shot, I showed a look of confidence."

—Jason Williams

Duke at St. John's
Madison Square Garden, New York, New York

February 18, 2001—Duke rebounded back into the win column on the floor leadership of Jason Williams, who scored a game-high 26 points. Williams had seven rebounds, six assists, and three three-pointers, and he was 7-for-9 from the free throw line. Five Blue Devils scored in double figures on the night: In addition to Williams, Battier had 18, Duhon 15, Dunleavy 14, and Boozer 10. Duke's defense smothered Red Storm guards Cook and Shaw, holding them to a combined six points for the game. It was St. John's worst defeat in four years. Duke continued its poor free throw shooting in the first half by going only 2-for-10 from the line. They ended up 17-for-29 for the game—still way below par for the Blue Devils.

Final Score: Duke 91, St. John's 59
Overall Record: 23–3 **ACC:** 10–2

The morning of the St. John's game, the media was writing Duke off as ACC regular-season champs. We had no chance, no chance, they said, to get the Number 1 seed in the East region of the NCAA tournament, which was to be played in Greensboro—about 45 minutes away from our home. If North Carolina won their game at Clemson later that afternoon, it would be over for Duke. But when we returned to Durham, somebody at the airport told us that Clemson had defeated UNC. Now we were only one game behind North Carolina instead of two.

> *"It's a whole new ball game. They were two up on us and now they've lost one, so I guess you could say it's kind of given us a new life. We've got hope, but we've got to play better and get after it because now we're back in the race."*
>
> —Nate James

* * * * *

Shortly before our upcoming game with Georgia Tech, Mickie and I sat down with Shane for a private moment.

"Shane, we have something important to tell you," I said.

"*Yes?*" he said, looking slightly perplexed.

"Before the next game, there will be a small ceremony. The university has decided to retire your jersey. You are the 10th Duke player to be so honored. Number 31 is going to be hoisted to the rafters with all the others. Congratulations."

Shane's eyes widened and his smile grew long, as he began to comprehend what he had just heard. I think he must have been thinking about all the resolutions he had on his walls at home, all the dreams he had had as a kid. This was one of those dreams come true. But the guy who is never at a loss for words could manage just one.

"*Wow,*" he said softly. He didn't need to say any more.

* * * * *

Fifteen minutes before the Georgia Tech game, on February 21, 2001, Duke University president Nan Keohane and Duke athletic director Joe Alleva formally retired Shane Battier's jersey. It was an emotional moment for our star player. His brother and sister was there, his parents had flown in from Birmingham, Michigan, and all his teammates stood with him. As Shane held up his framed Number 31, the Cameron Crazies went wild. They held up posters with all his career statistics, and they chanted Shane's special cheer, "Who's your daddy? Battier!"

"I'm truly honored," said Shane to the audience, *"and I'm humbled by the ceremony today—to think that my name will be added to the pantheon of greats who have played here. I'm still pinching myself. It is truly special to be able to share in this with my family, with my friends who are in attendance, and, most of all, with the guys I play with."*

As Shane stood out there on the court, my mind drifted back to the early 1990s, when I was in Michigan on a recruiting trip. We were trying to convince Chris Webber to come to Duke, but he eventually chose Michigan instead. While I was there, Kurt Keener, the basketball coach at Detroit Country Day School, told me that his was a school that would produce Duke-caliber players. "As a matter of fact," said Keener, "I have a real young kid who's coming up and he's going to be really good. He'll be like Webber—but in a different sort of way. His name is Shane Battier."

Now, here was that same kid having his jersey hoisted to the rafters at Cameron Indoor Stadium. It gave me chills.

When we all went back into the locker room for the final time before the game introductions, I asked Johnny Dawkins to think of some reason to get Shane out of the locker room for a few minutes. Then I addressed the rest of the team. "Look here, fellas, Shane has done everything in the world for you guys. Everything. He's not jealous of any one of you. He's demonstrated great leadership. It's time we do something really, really special for him. We should win this one for Shane. We should play a game befitting the guy whose jersey has been retired."

I knew they all wanted to win this one for their captain. There really wasn't much I needed to say.

Georgia Tech at Duke

February 21, 2001—After retiring Shane Battier's jersey before the game, fourth-ranked Duke handed Georgia Tech its most lopsided loss in 29 years. Duke's defense forced a stunning 29 turnovers and scored 35 points in the first half off turnovers alone. Battier had a steal that led to a dunk and a three-point play. That was followed by a long three-pointer that capped a 14–0 run to put Duke up 29–15, with 10:01 remaining in the half. Casey Sanders played a season-high 18 minutes and was very effective in neutralizing Tech's center, Alvin Jones. Sanders also scored five points and hauled in four rebounds. Jason Williams led all scorers with 25 points. Mike Dunleavy added 18, Nate James 13, Chris Duhon 10, and Carlos Boozer nine. The win marked Coach Mike Krzyzewski's 200th in ACC regular-season play, making him only the second coach to gain that many victories. "I thought we played a game befitting the kid who had his jersey retired," said Krzyzewski after the game.

Final Score: Duke 98, Georgia Tech 54
Overall Record: 24–3 **ACC:** 11–2

We had rebounded well from our loss to Virginia and now had two games in which we had scored more than 90 points and, at the same time, held our opponents to under 60. You'd think I might be happy thinking about all that, but I was really very worried, because Carlos Boozer had just played three poor games in a row. He had gotten into foul trouble against Virginia and scored only six points. Against St. John's, he'd had four fouls and garnered 10 points. And he had scored only nine against Georgia Tech. He just wasn't performing like I knew he could. In the seven weeks or so since our talk on New Year's Eve, Carlos had played pretty well. But I thought he was still having problems against some of our opponents' older big guys. He still wasn't over the hump yet. And with his performance in these last three games, I began to think he was regressing. Maybe our previous meeting just didn't take hold, I thought. Maybe he didn't believe in me. Maybe he still had his own plan, his own speed. It was gnawing at me.

Then I heard through the grapevine that Carlos was concerned that his teammates weren't getting him the ball enough, and that was the reason he hadn't been playing very well lately. Whenever there is a minor thing that might turn into something major, I always jump on it immediately. Well, this was one of those things. So after practice the day before the Wake Forest game, I called my wife, who was at home preparing for some dinner guests.

"Mickie, I just have to meet with Carlos. I'm going to be late."

"Go ahead," she replied. "You're at your best when you have those individual meetings with the players. That's when they get the most out of you. Besides, something productive always follows."

So Carlos and I met in my office along with Johnny and Wojo. I got right to the point. "Carlos, do you think you're not playing well because you're not getting the ball?"

"*Yeah,*" he replied.

Carlos was honest with me, I had to give him that. At that point, I laid into him. "It isn't your teammates, Carlos, it's you," I said matter-of-factly. "You're not in great shape. You don't demand the ball. You're not willing to pull your weight in making other people better. You're a room-service guy, Carlos. You want your stuff delivered on a tray. You're not helping Shane get better. You're not rebounding. You're not a presence down low, defensively.

"The reason for all this is that ultimately, you don't believe in what we're saying. And until you believe in what we're saying, you're never going to reach your full potential. Do you know what your full potential is, Carlos? Well, let me tell you. If you learn the value of hard work, and *really* believe it, you will be another Karl Malone. I kid you not. Karl Malone!

"But I don't think you really believe in us. I don't know if you have the ability to believe and care. Because if you did believe, you would be the player you want to be and the player we need you to be."

"*You know I believe in you, Coach,*" said Carlos.

"No I don't. If you really believed, then the things we work on every day, the things we talked about on New Year's Eve, would translate into what we do in a game. And that is just not happening."

"*Coach, I do believe. I want you to believe that I believe.*"

"Well, you need to show it, Carlos. You need to show it to us in some way other than just telling us. You need to do it in games— and do it consistently."

Then something unusual happened. Carlos Boozer—all 6' 9", 270 pounds of him—started to cry. He started to cry and he couldn't stop. Tears quietly streamed down his face and the sadness in his eyes just touched me to the core. I looked over at Wojo and his eyes were moist, too.

After a long pause, I finally broke the emotion of the moment. "You know what, Carlos? By crying, you are showing me you have a heart. You're showing me that I'm in your heart. We're going to be okay, Carlos. That's the best thing you could have done for me."

"*It's always been hard for me to show that kind of passion and heart,*" said Carlos at last.

"I know, son," I replied. "And I know that you do care, that you do believe. You're going to have a great game tomorrow, Carlos."

*   *   *   *   *

On the bus ride over to Winston-Salem the next day, I started thinking about our next three games—at Wake Forest, home against Maryland, and at North Carolina. All three games were the last home games for each team. That meant we were going to play three Senior Day games in a row—games in which all the seniors are honored for their time at the school. Parents fly in from all over the country, awards are given out, and other special things are done. Teams are highly motivated on Senior Day. It's an extra incentive. *Nobody* wants to lose on Senior Day.

When Chris Duhon got on the bus to go to Winston-Salem, he had a basketball under his arm. "How are you feeling, Chris," I asked. "*Good, Coach,*" he responded. "*I slept with my basketball last night.*"

Duke at Wake Forest
Lawrence Joel Coliseum, Winston-Salem, North Carolina

February 24, 2001—Carlos Boozer scored Duke's first two buckets of the game. And Chris Duhon scored the last on an off-balance shot at the buzzer. In the first half, Duhon fell to the floor after being accidentally hit in the face by a defensive player. No foul was called, but an official timeout had to be called while Trainer Dave Engelhardt and Coach Mike Krzyzewski tended to Duhon and helped him off the floor. Later, with 5:54 remaining in the half, Krzyzewski was charged with his first technical of the year, after Mike Dunleavy was knocked to the floor and no foul was called. Both teams had stretches of red-hot shooting in the first half, with Duke holding a one-point, 41–40 lead at intermission. With 5:24 left in the game, Duke trailed by nine points, 75–66. . . .

"Some teams fold when they're down, but we are a very confident team with veteran players. When we were down by nine, we were pretty calm in the huddle. We said we would win the game."

—*Shane Battier*

. . . Duke quickly went on a 14–2 run. With two minutes to go, Carlos Boozer made a great dunk, was fouled, and converted the free throw to tie the game 77–77. Duke's bench, led by Boozer's backup, Casey Sanders, erupted in cheers. At the 1:23 mark, Chris Duhon missed an off-balance floater, and Coach Mike Krzyzewski soon called Duke's last timeout. . . .

Duhon's shot is called a "giant killer." Instead of going all the way to the basket, he kind of floats it over the big men before they have a chance to jump and block it. We worked on it in practice. I called that timeout because I didn't want Chris to lose confidence in himself because of that missed shot. He was a freshman and he still thought that missing a shot was a mistake. But a missed shot is not a mistake. A bad shot is a mistake. Well, that last shot was not a bad shot. When he came off the floor, I went straight to him.

"Chris, you weren't sure of that shot, were you."

"*No,*" he said.

"Well, that was a great shot. That's your shot. It's going to be a signature move for you. You have the ability to take it. I want you to shoot that shot. So when you have the opportunity, I want you to take it again."

. . . Duke scored the next three points on a Mike Dunleavy free throw and a Jason Williams bucket. But then Wake's senior guard, Robert O'Kelley, playing in his final home game, hit a deep three-point shot with 7.5 seconds left, to tie the score at 80–80. With no timeouts left, Duke's Jason Williams drove the length of the floor but couldn't get an open shot, so he passed it off to Chris Duhon at the top right of the key. Duhon then took three steps around his man and launched a 15-foot "giant killer" at the basket. The ball went through the hoop as time expired, giving Duke a thrilling victory. . . .

"I didn't think about the shot, I just played off my instincts. I knew when it left my hand that it was good, but it seemed like the ball stayed in the air for three hours. It's something Chris Collins showed us in practice in order to get shots from the lane up over the hands of athletic big men."

— Chris Duhon

. . . Carlos Boozer was dominant in the paint and finished with 20 points and a season-high 13 rebounds.

Final Score: Duke 82, Wake Forest 80
Overall Record: 25–3 **ACC:** 12–2

After it was all over and I was getting ready to go down the tunnel to the dressing room, I walked past Mickie and my daughter Debbie, who were in the stands. My grandson, Joey, was leaning over the rail and he reached for me, so I just picked him up and took him into the locker room. All the guys were, of course, extremely happy with the win. They all came up and said, *"C'mon, Joey, give me a high five."* And Joey obliged.

Then, on the bus ride home, I noticed Shane get up and go over to sit down next to Chris Duhon. *"Way to go, buddy,"* he said. *"Do that more. You can hit big shots. We have the utmost confidence in you to take those shots."*

Life was good that day.

*   *   *   *   *

At our team feedback session the following afternoon, we began the tape review session with Duhon's last shot, and Chris Collins and Wojo pointed something out that I had not noticed at the time.

Right after Chris made his shot, I jumped up and threw both my hands high into the air. Seeing that, Johnny tried to give me a double high five. But I did not see him and dropped my hands at the last second, and Johnny almost fell over when he missed me on his follow-through. Everybody started laughing when they saw that on the screen. Of course, they all realized that I went back to being calm and stoic because I had to shake hands with Wake Forest's coach, Dave Odom, whom I have a lot of respect for. I didn't want to be jumping around and celebrating. It would not have been appropriate. "Okay, okay, Johnny," I said. "I owe you a double high five. But I'm not going to give it to you until we win the national championship."

The rest of that feedback session was upbeat for two reasons—Chris Duhon and Carlos Boozer.

"Chris, do you think Jason had time to think about passing you the ball at the end of the game?" I asked. "Do you believe he was thinking: I better throw the ball to Chris right now? No! He instinctively threw it to you because he believes in you—just like all these other guys. They all believe in you." Chris, we thought, was finally over the hump. Now he would shoot without being asked.

And everybody patted Carlos on the back for his sterling performance. The grin on his face was a mile wide.

"Carlos, you were terrific," I said. "You dominated the game. You were physical. You demanded the ball. You were passionate the whole game. You were alert. And you let your body react instinctively. That was one of your greatest performances. Congratulations."

All the guys knew we had found something special in Carlos.

"Carlos provides us such an extra boost. We're still deadly from the outside, and now for us to have an inside presence like him, it's what we're going to need to win the whole thing. There are some guys who are bigger than Carlos, but he not only has the body of a man—he has the heart of a man."

—Jason Williams

*   *   *   *   *

As we entered our final home game, I didn't think our team's level of confidence could go any higher. But we had to be careful in preparing for this game.

First of all, it was Senior Day—the final game at Cameron for Shane Battier, Nate James, J.D. Simpson, and Ryan Caldbeck. All their families would be in the stands. There would be special introductions before the game, and afterwards, they would come back out to address the crowd. We also had two senior managers and all the seniors in the stands who were part of the Cameron Crazies, our sixth man. It was their final home game, too.

All in all, Senior Day is a tricky time for a coach. There are a lot of emotions, so we don't give the players too much in the way of mental preparation—largely because the emotion causes them not to remember everything we tell them. So we keep it real simple.

But one thing was for sure—we were not going to win this game just because it was Senior Day. Our opponent was Maryland—the team with perhaps the greatest depth in the ACC. After we beat them at Cole Field House with the "Miracle Minute" comeback, they really became demoralized. They lost five of their next six games. But that was last month. Maryland had long since regrouped, were on a winning streak, and now were playing their best basketball of the season. The truth is that they were the hottest team in the country. They also had real motivation for this game—revenge. They wanted to make up for that previous loss. They had also beaten us in Cameron last year and had confidence they could win here. They were going to come out strong. I knew it was going to be a tough game.

Maryland at Duke

February 27, 2001—After falling behind 5–0, Maryland took control of most of the first half, until Duke scored 15 points in five possessions to take a 50–43 lead into the locker room. Carlos Boozer was having a great game, scoring 16 points and pulling down seven rebounds in 23 minutes of play, until he had to leave the game with an injury. . . .

With about 15 minutes to go in the second half, Carlos was going for a rebound when he landed in a crowd and heard something pop in his right foot. Limping badly, he came out of the game and had Duke trainer Dave Engelhardt wrap his foot. At that point in the game, we were leading 60–55, and I sent Casey Sanders in to replace Carlos.

. . . The Blue Devils maintained the lead until Boozer returned with a little over 11 minutes remaining in the game. He stayed only a short time, though, then left the court with a noticeable limp. . . .

Dave Engelhardt then took Carlos back into the training room for a quick fluoroscope, and word was sent back to me that it was a break. *Carlos had broken his foot!*

When I heard that word "break" instead of "sprain," it was like, See you later, Charlie. That's it! He's gone and we're not going to win the national championship. Of course, I didn't want to let my players know that's what I was feeling, so I was careful not to give it away in my facial expressions or body language. I did, however, tell them that Carlos had broken his foot and may be out for the season. That is not something I could keep from them. It was just too important.

. . . Krzyzewski then used a number of different lineups with Casey Sanders or Matt Christensen in the backcourt with Chris Duhon or Jason Williams. He also moved Shane Battier down into the low post to try and offset the play of Maryland standout, Lonny Baxter. Nothing seemed to work, however, as the Blue Devils went cold offensively. They made only one of their next 13 shots and, at one stretch, went more than eight minutes without a field goal. Maryland then seized the opportunity and finally took the lead for good on a Juan Dixon floater with six minutes remaining. . . .

Sometimes when a team looses a key player, it will go to a higher level —and sometimes it will drop. When Carlos went out, we dropped.

After analyzing it, I think our team went into shock. Their eyes were staring into space. Some of them looked like they had just had a lobotomy. Others just looked like they were somewhere else. I was yelling at them—trying to snap them out of it, trying to get them to run different plays. But they just didn't respond. Even the crowd wasn't in the game because, I found out later, word had spread among them, too, that Carlos had broken his foot. It was the only time this year when it looked like our guys didn't believe that they were going to win the game.

We had gotten into a dependency during that game of getting Carlos the ball. And then, all of a sudden, he was gone. The guys also were fast-forwarding their thinking. It was the end of the year. We were in the ACC race. We were gearing up for March. And now, all of a sudden, Carlos goes down with a broken foot. Damn, it may be over.

The players were working hard, but they were working as individuals, not as a team. In essence, THE FIST was gone. So it was a loss punctuated—no Carlos and no fist.

We started throwing up a lot of threes that missed. Shane tried to win the game all by himself. For the first time this season, no one else stepped up. By the end of the game, our guys didn't even *want* the ball. To top it all off, Maryland was really playing well. This was not a mediocre team. This was an excellent team and they took advantage of our disorganization.

. . . Juan Dixon led the Terrapins with 28 points in a dazzling offensive display. Shane Battier garnered 31 points and Jason Williams 13 in the losing effort.

Final Score: Maryland 91, Duke 80
Overall Record: 25–4 **ACC:** 12–3

For the people in the stands, the game ended in shock. Parents were in shock. Fans were in shock. But a small group of students rushed out onto center court and immediately stood around the Duke *D* with their arms interlocked. As the Maryland team was celebrating, Lonny Baxter unintentionally backed into the circle and a short blonde coed gave him a big shove in the back to push him away. Surprised, Baxter turned and looked down about a foot and a half, saw the fire and passion in the young woman's eyes, and just walked away. There were also some Maryland fans out on the floor—but they didn't get near that *D.*

Meanwhile, the locker room was like a morgue. Guys were crying, they were angry, and they were confused.

"I really felt bad for the seniors. Just to see the faces on Shane and Nate made me cry. We were winning that game. I mean we had it. And then, all of a sudden, Carlos was out, I was in—and we lost it. It got me down and I really felt bad."

—Casey Sanders

"This was not the way I envisioned playing my last night in this building. I just can't believe it. It was like a nightmare. Shane played his heart out, but I did not play my best, and that makes it hurt all the more. This is going to stick with me for the rest of my life. I'm never going to forget this game."

—Nate James

I took only a few minutes to address the team. I was upset and I was angry. "We were winning," I said. "We were playing great and we had the momentum. Then Carlos went out and we gave up. We should have fought harder without Carlos, but we didn't. We should have won that game, but we didn't because we gave up.

"Coach was right. We did give up and I was ashamed."

—Jason Williams

"I've never been around a team that gave up just because of a little adversity. I'm disappointed in you guys. Now our center's gone and I just don't know what to expect from you guys. Be at practice at 6:00 A.M. Thursday morning."

"As Coach walked out of the locker room, I took the call for a 6:00 A.M. practice as a punch. I thought of it as punishment for giving up."

—Chris Duhon

The seniors then had to go back out into Cameron and address the crowd. Usually, this is an upbeat time—a time when the players thank the crowd for all the years of support. And, of course, Shane, Nate, J.D., and Ryan did speak and thank everybody. But, as one preacher in the audience noted, "It was like being in the middle of a funeral wake for the loss of a dear friend. There was no passion in their voices at all. It was like the world had just come to an end. It was like their season was finished and they had no chance of winning the national championship."

All the sportswriters seemed to agree. "Boozer will be out for the season," they said. "Williams is hobbling on bad ankles." "James is in a horrible shooting slump." "The entire team is not shooting well from the free throw line." Dick Vitale of ESPN noted, "The loss of Carlos Boozer is unbelievable this late in the season. The one guy the Blue Devils couldn't afford to lose was Boozer on the interior."

Nearly all the experts believed that we might not win another game all year and that we were definitely out of the championship race. In essence, Duke was left for dead.

And the truth is that we were about as dispirited as a team could be. We had one game left at North Carolina, and because of this loss, we didn't think we had a chance to play for the regular-season championship. With Carlos out, things didn't look good for the ACC tournament or the NCAA tournament. We were in a real black hole.

Chris Collins summed it up best when, as he walked off the court after the loss, he asked, "What now?"

Final Regular-Season Game

From the locker room, I went straight to my office and closed the door. I wanted to be alone for a little while. I had to be alone. I didn't want my assistants to see me in doubt and I needed time to recover. My daughter Debbie, who had hurried to see me, was sitting in the far corner of the room. At that time, she was eight months pregnant and on her way to having a very large baby. I didn't even notice her. I was feeling sorry for myself and was too much into my own thoughts. She told me later that my face revealed a crestfallen, devastated man.

I went over to my desk and just held my head in my hands for a little while. When Mickie walked in a few minutes later, I was slumped way down in my chair with my arms folded. She sat down next to me but didn't say a word. After about five or six minutes of total silence, I finally looked up. "I'm going to be here all night," I said. "Don't worry. I'll be all right. Why don't you just go on home and I'll talk to you later."

Sitting alone in my office, the first thoughts that raced through my mind were: Okay, Carlos is out and it's not going to happen this year. We're not going to win the national championship. We were fortunate to get this far, but it's over. It's over.

But then I thought about Shane. In my 26 years of coaching, I had never felt anyone deserved to win a national championship more than he did. He had worked so hard over the past four years; I just felt that it was his time

And then I thought about the rest of the players, This team really deserves to win. They're great kids—unselfish, caring, lots of pride. Thinking of the players made me feel better. They gave me confidence.

I also thought about my work with the Children's Hospital. I thought about all the kids over there who have much bigger problems than I did at that moment. I thought about Jonathan Patton and his Always Positive hat. "Are you kidding me?" I said to myself, "You're lucky just to be able to feel bad."

After about an hour, I had gotten over feeling sorry for myself and was mentally ready to meet my assistants. But first, I went into the bathroom, splashed water on my face, and looked in the mirror. I couldn't show any pessimism. Rather, I had to display determination because I knew they were going to be down.

Sure enough, when I walked into our meeting room, Dawkins, Collins, Wojo, La Mere, and Schrage showed a combination of fear and worry in their eyes. They were concerned not only about the future of the team, but also about me personally. Normally, I would come right in after a game to review tape. But an hour's delay was inordinate.

"How are the kids?" I asked. "How are they doing?"

"They're down," said Johnny. "They're wondering what's going to happen to our team now. And they're concerned about Carlos."

Then I mentioned that Frank Bassett, who is part of our medical team, informed me that Carlos apparently had suffered the same injury as Bobby Hurley back in 1992. "We'll get a hard x-ray tomorrow," I said. "But that's something to be grateful for, because Hurley made it back in three weeks.

"Right now, we're going to watch the tape of the game and find out what the hell happened to us tonight."

Instead of getting into a long, drawn-out conversation, I felt the best thing to do was to review the game. That would get us all focused on something and force us to start talking to each other—which we did. But even after analyzing the *X*'s and *O*'s, we didn't have an answer as to what our new strategy would be. But we knew we will had good players. We had Shane, Jason, Mike, Nate—and Duhon was emerging. Our meeting finally broke up at four o'clock in the morning so the guys could get some rest. The players had a mandatory day off, but we coaches were going to put in a full day.

Once at home, I got in bed and lay there for about 10 minutes but I couldn't sleep. All I could think about was that we had to make a major adjustment—not just for our upcoming game against North Carolina, but also for the entire postseason because Boozer might not be back at all. A strong sense of urgency overwhelmed me, so I got up and went downstairs to watch video of North Carolina. As I stared at the television, I began to formulate a course of action. We have to protect the low post, I thought. We have to improve rebounding. We have to transform to a more up-tempo style—like we were going to do at the beginning of the year. It didn't work then. But we weren't ready then. Now, the kids were more seasoned. They were ready for it now. It could work. It's got to work. Duhon. Duhon is the key. He's fast. He's a great defender. He can shoot. He'll free up Jason to do more.

The more I thought about it, the more fired-up I became. So I showered, changed, and went into the office. I was there only a few minutes when my daughter Jamie walked in. Mickie had called her the night before and said, "Your dad's feeling really down. It would be great if you could stop by the office tomorrow and give him a hug. Tell him you love him. He really needs that right now." So Jamie came over and gave me a big hug and asked how I was doing.

"Do you think Reggie Love can guard Brendan Haywood?" I asked her.

Jamie quickly picked up the phone to call Mickie. And all she said was, "Mom, he's okay."

Jamie was right. I was okay. I had moved on, and it was Next Play for me.

*   *   *   *   *

Our staff meeting began at 9:00 and lasted all day. "We're not leaving this room," I said right off the bat, "until all of us are on the same page about how we're going to play, what we're going to do to get the most out of this team, and how we're going to be a championship team with what we have." Then I set about trying to convince my staff that we could do it—that, despite the loss of Carlos, we could still win the national championship.

I may not have completely believed it myself at that point, but the more I said it, the more I believed it. A leader has to purge himself of all doubts—and the only real way to do that is to keep taking shots. So I took my shots with the staff.

"We need to change the personality of our team," I said. "We need to start Duhon. We'll get more speed that way—and better defense on the perimeter. No one else can put pressure on the ball handler like Chris can. It will also free up Jason to take more shots because he won't have to defend the ball as much. It will keep him fresher."

"Who do we start at center, then?" asked Wojo.

"Casey," I said. "But we'll rotate with Matt and Reggie."

"But that means Nate won't start," cautioned Johnny.

"That's right. Nate is going to be the key to making this strategy work. He's got to accept his new role without reservations. Having him come off the bench will give us a big punch. It's going to work."

"But Nate is a fifth-year senior, Coach," said Chris Collins. "Not starting has got to impact him. We'll have to handle this carefully."

"I think Nate will be okay. It might even make him better. If he comes off the bench, making a grand entrance. As our sixth man, he could have a huge impact."

"Nate hasn't been playing great," said Johnny, who clearly had the most reservations. "We don't want to completely shatter his confidence. We don't want him to think that we don't need him anymore."

"You're absolutely right, Johnny," I said. "It would be a disaster if we lost Nate. But he'll be okay. I remember when I first saw him in high school. He was the team leader and totally committed to his teammates. When I met with him, I can remember looking into his eyes and saying to him, 'I want to coach you because you have the ultimate ability to believe. You're going to be my captain one day.' I have the utmost confidence in Nate's ability to handle this situation. We have to do what is best for the team."

Next, we started evaluating our core strengths—and we soon came to the conclusion that speed and the three-point shot were what we did best. If we could just recapture the magic of the second Temple game, we'd be awesome. But was it possible for us to consistently win games without a major presence inside—with three-point shooting as our focal point? That's where speed became so crucial. We had the two quickest, fastest guards in the country—so we determined to utilize those strengths. In the Maryland game film, I had noticed that when Jason brought the ball up the court, he was standing upright. "I want him leaning forward when he brings the ball up the court," I said. "That means he'll be going faster and the opponents that run with him will have to run that much harder."

An up-tempo style would mean that we would be taking the ball right at our opponents. We would be pushing them, keeping them on their heels. If we sprinted up and down the floor every time, our opponents would have to do the same—otherwise we'd get lay-ups all the time. Then, if they're thinking that they have to get back quick, they won't be crashing the offensive boards with as many players as they normally did. That, in turn, would open up more defensive rebounds for us. I thought we'd be able to tire out our opponents. This is where our early-season focus on conditioning would really pay off.

We also had to take a close look at our big men, but we did not think our problem would be solved by just plugging someone else into the center position. We thought that Casey, Matt, and Reggie would not give us the low-post presence we needed. So we had to devise a strategy that would allow us to get Shane into that position. Then it hit us: We would simply let the big men do what they did best. Casey could run up and down the court fast—that was one of his strengths. He had been lifting four times a week since the first of January, so he'd surely be stronger.

The fact that at this point in his career, Casey wasn't a big scorer inside was not a negative. All he had to do was run, play defense, set screens, and rebound. Matt Christensen's knees were going to limit his playing time. But with his bulk, and with his passion, he would be able to spell Casey at key points in the game.

Reggie Love would be another key ingredient in this whole strategy. He had been working out with the football team in their spring session. So we knew he was in unbelievably good shape. He also had a low center of gravity, had good balance, could jump, and was unafraid of physical contact. But the key point about Reggie was that he was fast. He ran a 4.5 40 for the football team. All of a sudden, we were salivating. Reggie was like the one vegetable that made this meal right. I mean, it was perfect!

By the end of the day, I was sure of the approach we had to take. We were forced into making some changes—and we had to make those changes fast. Our new plan could be really great or really disastrous. It wasn't going to be middle-of-the-road. I believed it was a strategy that would not only beat UNC and take us through the tournaments but would also get the players out of shock. It was so radical that it had the potential to completely change their focus and capture their imaginations.

But what I saw and what the kids would believe were two separate things. Now it was my job to make them believe.

*   *   *   *   *

"The day after the game, I was filled with a lot of doubt. We just needed some time to get away, to think about what was going on, to do a lot of soul-searching. Everybody just went in their own directions."

—*Chris Duhon*

"After the game, every one of the players came into the training room to see me. They all asked if I was all right, told me not to worry about anything, to take care. It let me know how close we were as a team. But I felt like I had let them down by getting hurt. I felt like I had let myself down, too. I had finally found my groove and then I was out of the line-up—just like that!"

—*Carlos Boozer*

"Back at the apartment, I apologized to Shane for losing on Senior Day. But neither of us wanted to talk that evening. We were confused. Our big guy was out and we didn't know where this was going to take us. But the next day, we just hung around the apartment and talked about it. 'What is it going to be like with Carlos out?' 'What's going to happen?' 'Guys will sure have to step up if we're going to go all the way.' We had our doubts."

—*Mike Dunleavy*

*   *   *   *   *

At 6:00 the next morning, everybody assembled in the locker room. The players were apprehensive. They were not sure of what was going to happen. After they were dressed, I came in with an upbeat attitude and asked for their attention. They expected to be blown out, but I was calm as I spoke to them.

"Look, if you believe in what I say, if you do everything I ask you to do, *we will win the national championship.* Do you understand that? If you do everything I say, we are going to win the national championship. I promise you. I promise you." I looked into their eyes for reactions. Some eyes opened wide, others began to look around to the other players. A couple of mouths hung open and a couple of heads nodded yes. Their reactions were mixed.

"I didn't really want to be there at 6:00 in the morning. I was thinking, Oh, man! I have to be here this early? For what? But Coach came in like it was midday, with a real spring in his step. The intensity in his eyes was amazing. And that first statement really woke me up. It was like coffee. I made eye contact with him. His emotion, his passion, just went through my eyes, down through my head, and straight to my heart. I said to myself, I believe him and I'm going to do it."

—Chris Duhon

"When we first came into the locker room, it was our lowest point of the season. We were all losing hope. But Coach came in and gave us hope. That's what we needed."

—Nick Horvath

"Coach created a whole new attitude."

—Reggie Love

"When the coach said it, I believed it. I had no doubts."

—Jason Williams

"When he told us, I bit into it half-heartedly. I wanted to see if it would work. But it meant a lot the way he came in. We were all down and he was upbeat. That picked us all up."

—Casey Sanders

"I raised my eyebrows. Wait a minute, I thought, Carlos is out and he's promising us we'll win the national championship if we believe? All right! This is where it starts. But it was not instant belief. I wanted to know more."

—Mike Dunleavy

Then I outlined what we were going to do. "Casey is going to start, but we're going to make a change," I began. "Chris is going to start instead of Nate. It's not because you're playing poorly right now, Nate. We have to change our style. We're going to go quick. Nate, you coming off the bench will help us. It's not going to affect your playing time. You're going to play just as much. What do you think?"

"*Whatever you need, Coach,*" Nate responded.

"Okay. Jason, you're not covering the ball to begin with. Chris is going to do that. Is that a problem for you?"

"*No,*" said Jason.

"Guys," I concluded, "we are not going to use the loss of Carlos as an excuse. We have enough players on this team to be successful. Nobody feels sorry for us. People want us to fall flat on our faces. Well, we're not going to do it. We're Duke. And we're going to live up to our tradition of excellence. Okay, let's get our butts moving."

At times, when things aren't going well, it's not what a leader says, it's how a leader looks that matters. When I went into that locker room, I wanted to be upbeat. I wanted to project confidence. When people are emotional like they were, they don't necessarily hear. But they do see, they always see. And they always feel. If they saw me being strong, it could put them in a position of hearing what I said.

The other key point of this meeting is that I told them as a group. I wanted to put everything out on the table all at once in front of everybody. I did not want to have private meetings beforehand—like I could have done with Nate, for instance. Rather, I wanted to see true emotion in their faces, true feelings. And I wanted the other players to see them, too. That would tell me what they really believed at that moment.

Basically, I needed to know right away. This situation was too critical and too urgent to mess around with. Besides, there were too many things that had to be implemented immediately. It was a *major* strategy change. If I did see something negative, I was prepared to ask: "Do you have a problem with that? Why?" And we would have discussed it in front of the entire group. We were going to get to the truth and have everything right out in the open immediately.

All the players reacted well. But I was especially proud of Nate. I could see in his eyes and in his face that he was okay with everything—at least for that moment.

As the players were warming up and stretching before practice, Johnny came up to me and expressed his reservations again about starting Duhon in place of Nate. Usually when he says something to me along these lines, I do what he advises without hesitation. His insights are invaluable, and he is almost always right. But this time, I didn't budge. "Johnny, it's got to be done. I appreciate what you're saying and I always want you to tell me your feelings. But it's got to be done."

The players expected a practice of loose ball drills, taking charges, and generally beating each other up. But I surprised them again. "We're going to go to an up-tempo style, fellas," I said. "We're going to scrimmage in four-minute segments—just like the game is played with TV timeouts every four minutes. I want us to sprint for four minutes. Then we're going to get that TV timeout. Then we rest for two minutes. Then we sprint for four minutes again. Do you think you can do that?"

"*Yeah, yeah, we can do that,*" Shane answered.

"Good. After the first segment, I'll sub Nate for Dunleavy, and Reggie for Casey. You're going to get tired, but I want you to play through the tired. Okay, let's go."

We practiced three four-minute sessions that way, and then I gave them a rest. The kids were tired, very tired. All that sprinting left them huffing and puffing. But I knew they'd get used to it because they were in such great shape—because of our early-season emphasis on conditioning. The problem, I felt, wasn't that they weren't ready physically; it was that they weren't yet ready mentally. "Don't look at it like we're going to beat somebody for a whole game," I told them. "Look at it like we're going to beat them for four minutes. It's like a kid who takes smaller bites. You get the whole meal in, but you don't have to digest it all at once. Don't forget: It's four minutes, four minutes, four minutes."

* * * * *

After the 6:00 A.M. practice, Shane Battier and Mike Dunleavy went back to their apartment and began to think about what had just happened.

"Are we going to be able to do this?" wondered Mike.

"I don't know," Shane responded. *"I don't think everybody's head is really in this."*

"But Coach promised us. He promised us. If we believe and follow him, we'll be playing in the national championship game."

"If the other guys come around, we can do it. I tell you one thing, though, I think we've got a good shot at beating Carolina."

"You really think so?"

"Yeah. We are going to go in there and surprise everyone. They'll be shocked at this kind of speed."

Meanwhile, on the other side of campus, Jason Williams had tracked down Carlos Boozer, who could not be at the morning meeting because he was getting more detailed x-rays.

"What happened?" asked Carlos as soon as he saw his teammate.

"Coach was really upbeat. He said we weren't going to use losing you as an excuse. We're going to get better. We're going to North Carolina and we're going to beat them. You know what else he said?"

"Go on. . . ."

"He said if we believed in him and did everything he asked us to do, we'd win the national championship."

"Oh, man. Oh, man."

* * * * *

Over the course of a long season, a team can get worn down. And that might have happened to us if Carlos had not been hurt. But this new style revived us and made us fresh again. As a matter of fact, we went back to a training camp atmosphere just like we had had in the preseason. There was a new system to implement, so we went to two-a-day, shorter practices instead of one long one in the afternoon. We got them up at 6:00 A.M. and we practiced for an hour. Then we brought them back at 3:00 for another hour.

That afternoon, we repeated the four-minute drills. We also began to discuss and work on other more detailed strategies—some X's and O's, if you will.

The first thing we did was turn a negative into a positive. When Carlos was in the game, he took up a lot of space inside. Now that he was out, we could fill up that space by letting Jason drive to the basket more. Then we decided to bring our big men out on the perimeter and use them as screeners.

"Shane, do you like to dance?" I asked.

"*Yeah, I like to dance.*"

"Do you like to dance alone or with somebody?"

"*With somebody, I guess.*"

"Okay, you have a screening partner—just like a dance partner. Casey, Reggie, and Matt, you belong to Shane. You're going to screen for Shane when he has the ball and when he doesn't have the ball. After you screen for him, look to see if he or someone else has taken a shot. If they have, go to the boards. If not, take time to look around—and go get him again. Find your dance partner. I want you guys to run! Run like crazy. Tire out the guy who's defending you. Just keep running. It will have a big impact on the game. Shane, we're going to run motion offense and we're going to dance. So when you're on the floor, find your partner."

Wojo took charge of these drills, and I mean to tell you, Shane loved it. He was continually yelling out: "*Come over here, partner! Come over here!*"

We also found that the low post was so open, it created the opportunity for Shane to drive to the basket more. With him now able to do that, I reasoned he was going to get fouled more—which could only help us because he was a high-percentage free throw shooter.

Another side-impact of this strategy was that it would take the other team's biggest defensive rebounder away from the basket because he'd have to go out to cover our big guys. Well, when he did that, we would end up getting more offensive rebounds, which, in turn, would give us more chances to score. So we coached the rebounders to get a running start as a shot was being taken. That way they'd get a step on the defense and be able to get a tip-in. Nate James was particularly adept at doing this. This whole idea was beautiful basketball. It was beautiful.

Starting Chris Duhon also gave more confidence to Jason Williams. Chris, who is a tireless defender, would guard the ball handler when we were on defense. It's a lot of work to guard the opposing team's ball handler—turning his back, keeping him left, keeping him right, pressuring up on him, getting around screens. Jason did that most of the time when Carlos was in. Now it would be Chris's job. That would free up Jason to concentrate more on scoring. It played to both guys' strengths—Duhon on defense, Williams on offense. I knew it was going to work. I knew it.

On defense, we employed trapping schemes at the top of the key—something we rarely ever did. This was something that North Carolina would never expect us to do. We had Duhon and Battier come out and trap the guy with the ball. That would push the opposing team's offense farther away from the basket. If we were successful, they'd be five or six feet farther out. A side bar to this strategy was that it would also take away the other team's vision into the low post. And that meant we wouldn't get in as much foul trouble because the ball wasn't going to go inside as often.

Trapping would also create longer passes, slower passes, longer shots—and it would bring the shot clock into play more because it would take longer to get off a good shot. These strategies were smart, they made sense, and, once the guys saw that they could work, our team would gain greater confidence. It would also be great fun for them. And that's what basketball should be all about.

As a matter of fact, our entire new strategy was going to be a lot of fun. The four-minute sprint was not only up-tempo, it was run-and-gun to a certain extent. The players were allowed the freedom to make plays on their own. They were allowed to play with abandon, to shoot when they had a good shot, to rebound and shoot again. If we were going to go fast, there really wasn't any time to be calling set plays. Essentially, we set them free. And when they got used to it, I knew they were going to have a blast out there on the court.

*   *   *   *   *

All that first day, I was keeping a close eye on everybody. But two guys especially had my attention—Nate James and Chris Duhon. In this crisis situation, Nate, a fifth-year senior, was being asked to give up his starting position just before his last regular-season game. Even though I had the greatest faith in Nate, I knew that was a lot to ask of anybody. It had to impact him. And the whole thing had the potential to blow up if he handled it poorly. On the other end of this deal was an 18-year-old freshman who had been deferring to the older guys all year. I also knew that Chris really loved Nate and looked up to him. How both guys handled this situation concerned me greatly.

"I was worried about how Nate would react. From the beginning, he was there for me every game. We would basically have the same defensive assignment. He'd tell me what to do. He'd help me. Nate was a fifth-year senior. He's given Coach everything he had. You would think that Coach should have loyalty to him. But in this crucial situation, he was putting a freshman in front of him. Nate seemed to be in a funk all day. He really didn't talk to me, and it kind of had me worried."

—Chris Duhon

"Whatever Coach tells me, I believe. And I want what is best for the team. But at that moment, I was taken aback. Sometimes things can be the best for the team and it still affects you. Well, it did affect me. I went home that night and thought, Whew, man! It's going downhill. I'm not playing that well. I only have a month left. I just lost my spot. I don't know how this is going to affect my future. It just rocked me.

"Then I started thinking about my teammates. I knew it would affect Chris

if I came in angry and resentful. He wouldn't play as well as I knew he was capable of playing. I also realized that, because my teammates and I were so close, it really didn't make any difference whether I came off the bench or not. So I thought, Hey, man, you do only have a month to go. Is it going to be a bad month or a good month? I was thinking about my teammates. That's what got me over the hump. That's what got me over feeling sorry for myself."

—Nate James

At the next morning's practice, Nate came in with a different attitude. I could tell by the look on his face that something was different. During warm-ups and stretching, I saw him pull Duhon over to the side.

"*Listen, Chris,*" said Nate, "*you have a big responsibility. I'm going to be right behind you backing you up. Early on in the year, you were passing the ball a lot, not taking your own shots. You were taking care of us because we were the seniors. Now it's time for you to step up and take your own shots—and for me to take care of you. Get out there and play, man. Don't worry about me. You're going to do well and I'm going to do well. Everything's going to be all right.*"

"It wasn't Coach who told me not to worry about Nate. It was Nate. His saying that to me made everything a lot smoother for me. I wasn't worried whether he was going to perform well or whether he was going to give his all. Now I knew it. I wasn't worried about how he felt anymore. Now, I was ready to move on to the Next Play. And later that day in practice, Nate was attacking all of us on defense—making us better."

—Chris Duhon

* * * * *

After about a half-hour of practice that morning, I could tell the team was not mentally prepared for the major change I was asking them to undertake. They appeared tired and not all on the same page. I could tell they weren't sure if all the work they were putting in was going to pay off. In reality, they got caught up in the process, not the goal. And winners cannot get caught up in the process.

They were working pretty hard, but it wasn't enough. The belief wasn't there and their hearts weren't in it. There wasn't the passion that comes with conviction. I could see that. I could feel it. They were not yet where they needed to be. They hadn't crossed that threshold of becoming something special.

So I just stopped the practice and called them all together. I didn't yell, but my eyes were moist and I was emotional. "The biggest thing you can do to hurt me is not believe me," I said. "You don't believe what I'm saying. So just get out of here right now. And this afternoon, don't come back unless you have total belief."

"Coach didn't get angry and he didn't yell. It was like he was going to cry. Really, he was like a disappointed father."

—Dahntay Jones

Right after I asked them to leave practice, the team went back into the locker room and had a closed-door meeting among themselves. It started out with Shane really getting mad. At first, he was so mad he couldn't talk—so he kicked the wall, the bathroom door, a wastebasket. Then he found the words and he just exploded:

"With this kind of attitude, we can lose the next three games easy," he said. *"You guys will be here next year. But I don't have a next year. This is it for Nate, J.D., Ryan, and me. We're going to fight this adversity. And if we don't fight together, you'll have to fight me—and you'll have to fight them. We are not going to let the season die. It's too important. We've put too much into it. We're not going to make excuses and go out like this. We're just not going to do it."*

Then Nate and J.D. spoke up.

"Everybody has to come together and go hard," said Nate. *"You know what Coach expects. Why aren't you giving it your all?"*

"Do you guys realize Coach promised us we'd win the national

championship if we did what he asked?" J.D. reminded them. *"Why wouldn't we do that? Why wouldn't we follow him? If we're going to be a great team, we've got to stick together, work hard, and do what Coach wants us to do."*

Then Matt Christensen surprised everybody by standing up and saying a few words. Matt almost never spoke at team meetings. A quiet guy by nature, he usually said things to the guys one-on-one, in private. Now, he picked up his chair and moved it to the center of the locker room. Then, still standing, he rested one foot on the chair and spoke softly: *"I experienced this before,"* he said. *"Remember, I sat out a couple of years while on my Mormon mission. It was the season when Coach hurt his back. I remember that Chris Collins hurt his ankle real bad. But he still played on it. He was the heart of our team. He inspired us all. That was a team that only went 18–13. And as much as everybody thought we had a disappointing season, it was really a great success for us. It was great because we believed in each other. When the going got tough, every guy on that team could look behind his back and one of us would be there. I don't have that same feeling with this team. And I want to know what you're going to do about it!"*

"We had a lot of team meetings this year, but they were mostly b.s.—just pick-'em-up talk. But this team meeting was very different. It was the best we ever had. It wasn't rah, rah. It wasn't corn. Everybody was just talking among each other—getting everything out in the open. There was a genuine feeling afterwards. We all knew where we stood. We all knew what it would take. We decided to do what Coach asked of us. And we all decided to go out there and get the job done."

—Nate James

"We had always been together as a team. But I felt there was always something missing. After that meeting, though, we started spending more time together off the court. We went out to dinner that night as a group. We

worked on relationships with each other. Things began to jell. I think that's when we really started to totally become a fist."

—*Chris Duhon*

When the team meeting ended, the three captains of the team, Shane, Nate, and J.D., went out for breakfast. They wanted to talk things over and determine how they could better lead the team. But Shane also wanted to get a message across to Nate. "*You're so unbelievably valuable to the team, we can't win without you,*" he told Nate. "*You've been our rock this year. Whenever I had any doubts—and believe me, I had them— I've gone to you. You cannot stop giving back to us right now—because* now is when we need it most. We need you, Nate. We need you.*"*

*   *   *   *   *

I walked onto the court that afternoon while the guys were stretching. I didn't say anything at that point because it was time for them to say something to me through their actions. But as soon as they took the court, I could tell there was a difference. The way they interacted, the way they played, the look in their eyes. I could just tell they had gotten over feeling sorry for them-selves. After three four-minute drills, I brought them together. "Now, that's what I'm looking for," I said. "That's the way it should be. That's what I want. Wait a minute! Hold it! This isn't about what *I* want. This is about what *we* want. That's what was missing this morning. This morning *I* wanted something, *we* did-n't. This afternoon, *we* wanted it. Do you guys understand?"

"*We understand, Coach. We understand.*"

"Okay, then. We're going to be really good. Really good."

*   *   *   *   *

The last practice before the North Carolina game went extremely well. The players accepted direction—and they worked with great enthusiasm and passion. One of the big things we focused on was the play of our big men.

Motion offense is much more taxing on the big guys than on the guards and perimeter players. They always have to be ready to block out, screen, shape-up, or shoot. They have to think, they have to read, and they have to adjust to the players on the floor. In order to find their place in the offense, then, they have to know not only their own position, but two or three other positions as well. We took some of the pressure off them by not asking them to do things that they were not used to doing. In other words, we asked them to play to their strengths.

Reggie Love was so fast, for instance, that he could wear out other big men by forcing them to run up and down the court. But Reggie wouldn't get tired because he could run all day.

"Can you do that Reggie? Can you run?" I asked him.

"*Sure, Coach. I love to run.*"

Matt Christensen, on the other hand, had bad knees and could not run well. So his job was to screen for his dance partner, block out, and rebound.

"Can you do that, Matt?"

"*Absolutely, Coach.*"

Casey Sanders would start in place of Carlos and get most of the playing time. But we did not ask him to be Carlos or do what Carlos did. At that point, it was not about how Carlos was wired, it was about how *Casey* was wired. So we just asked him to do what we knew he could do.

> *"In practice, Coach told me to play to my strengths—screen for Shane, box out and rebound every possession, play hard and be enthusiastic, and move up and down the floor as fast as I could. 'Sometimes, you're going to sprint ahead and you're going to get a lay-up,' he said. So I'd sprint down the court in practice, I'd get ahead of the other players, my teammates would see me, they'd pass me the ball, and I'd get a lay-up. That's what we worked on in practice."*
>
> *—Casey Sanders*

We did not ask Reggie, Matt, and Casey to perform miracles. "Run your own race," I told them. "Don't run anybody else's race."

I believe many people would naturally think that if all you're asking someone to do is something that they're good at, then you really don't have to worry about them. You can leave them alone and everything will be just fine. But the rest of our team did not take anything for granted. They rallied around our three big guys to provide them more support than you could imagine.

Ryan Caldbeck hung out a lot with Matt—worked with him in practice, gave him encouragement, and kept his morale up. Shane met with Reggie frequently to discuss game strategy, on-court positioning, and the ins and outs of motion offense. But the way the team rallied around Casey Sanders was the biggest story of all.

Casey had come late to the game of basketball. He had played poorly when he went in for Boozer in the North Carolina A&T game. And he had a tendency to get nervous. The guys knew all these things—so they stepped forward to help and support their teammate. Early on, Andre Buckner saw that Casey was worried and went out of his way to boost his confidence and calm him down. Every day in practice, Andre would say something positive. And later, when we got into the tournament, he'd go over the scouting report in detail with Casey before each game. Mike Dunleavy, who roomed with Casey on the road, spent a lot of time joking with Casey as well as riding him, because he knew how his roommate was capable of playing. So Mike pushed him to a higher level of achievement—and tried to do it with a smile and a wry wit.

Nick Horvath spent the most time with Casey. They had built a close relationship when, back in mid-January, we put the two of them on a four-a-week workout schedule. Because they shared an apartment, Nick drove Casey to and from practice every single day. Back then, Casey was frustrated that he wasn't playing more—and when he did get his big chance in the North Carolina A&T game, he played poorly.

"Don't worry about it," Nick said to him at the time. *"We'll lift. We'll get big. We'll just keep going at it every day, and I'll guarantee you by the end of the season, you'll be in there and making a differ-*

ence." And when Carlos broke his foot, Nick looked at Casey and said, "*Now is the time, buddy. Now is the time.*"

> "*Casey started to get really nervous. I told him to relax. 'Just go out there and play your game. Don't try to put the pressure of the whole world on your shoulders.' In simply talking to him every day after practice, I started to notice his confidence level pick up, until finally, he was totally at ease out there on the court.*"
>
> *—Nick Horvath*

The relationship Nick and Casey had developed paid off for the team in a big way. If that had not occurred, then after Carlos went down, Nick's voice would have become just one of the many voices encouraging Casey. But now, Nick's voice became key. It was like a radio station that Casey had preset on his car radio. He punched the button and Nick was there—a soothing voice, a friendly voice, a comfortable voice. And it made all the difference in the world to Casey Sanders.

When Nick was working with Casey back in mid-January, he believed he would play again this season. But Nick's bone bruise never did heal properly. In fact, it developed into a stress fracture that caused him continual pain and mental anguish. He wanted to come back, but he couldn't. Finally, he had to apply for a medical red shirt—which would allow him to maintain another year of eligibility. At this point in the season, Nick could have become a distraction. He could have gone into a "poor me" syndrome and gone looking for sympathy. But he was a man. He accepted what happened to him and he dealt with it. Not only that, he went out of his way to help his friend and teammate. He was unselfish, not jealous, and he showed incredible empathy.

> "*I was part of the team, and this was the best way I could help the team. Now it was Casey's chance. So I focused on getting him ready to play.*"
>
> *—Nick Horvath*

The other guy who could have felt sorry for himself was Carlos—who had broken his foot just when he had found himself, just when he was playing his best basketball. X-rays had confirmed that he had suffered a clean break in the third metatarsal of his right foot. There was a chance he could be back for the last part of the NCAA tournament—if we lasted that long. But neither our trainer, Dave Engelhardt, nor any of the doctors made any promises to him.

In spite of that, Carlos showed up at every practice in a cast and on crutches. When Johnny, Wojo, and Chris were working with Casey on the court, Carlos stood on the sidelines and cheered Casey on. And during breaks in the action, he talked privately with Casey about all aspects of his game. Over the next month of the season, Carlos would be one of Casey's biggest supporters.

> *"Casey had to do well if our team was going to be successful. So I kept telling him to go out there and give it his all. 'Don't be scared; don't be worried about making mistakes. Just go out there and play your heart out. I'll be there for you on the sidelines.' "*
>
> *—Carlos Boozer*

*   *   *   *   *

As we prepared for the UNC game, I walked into our team film session as confident as I could be.

"I've been watching tape of UNC and here's what we're going to do. They will not be able to handle our up-tempo style. Plus, if we really focus on the traps at the top of the key with Battier and Duhon, they will become frustrated. All we have to do is control the pace of the game. Be quick, shoot threes, trap, rebound, and press. If we don't let them control tempo, we'll win. But we can't be tired, guys. We can't be tired. As soon as you feel tired, look into the eyes of your opponents. You'll see that they are more tired than you are."

"When Coach said that, my mind flashed back to the Princeton game when he said we should control the pace of the game. It was ironic. He said that in the first game of the season, and now that we're preparing for the last game of the regular season, he says it again."

—*Mike Dunleavy*

After I reviewed the film and showed the team what I'd found, I turned on the lights and smiled at all the guys. "I'm telling you, there is no way they can beat us. No way. We're going to kill them." Then we went out onto the court, and I began to set the tone for the upcoming game.

"First, no one is allowed to say they're tired," I told the players. "How can you be tired, anyway? You're only going to be playing in four-minute spurts. Then you get a two-minute rest. Don't forget that two-minute rest. You're not allowed to say you're tired. You're not allowed to look tired. You're not allowed to lean over and grab your shorts. Your character in this drama never gets tired. That is the role you play. And you guys on the bench, you're just like the trainer in the corner of a boxing match when the fighter comes to the corner during breaks in the rounds. Your role is to tell them they are not tired—over and over and over again. Tired is not allowed."

The second thing we did during that practice was to implement a new drill that focused on our other primary strategy—the three-point shot. We gathered all of our three-point shooters—Shane, Jason, Chris, Mike, and Nate; then we assigned them each rebounders—J.D., Dahntay, Andre, Ryan, and Andy. We put them all on the court at the same time and then set the game clock at five minutes. "Okay, guys," I said, "Let's see how many threes you can hit before the clock runs out."

The first few times we did it, the guys hit 150 and then 160 baskets. "Come on," said Chris Collins, "you guys can do better than that!" Then Chris assigned 160 as our opponent's score, which gave the guys something to beat. When we ran the drill again, they hit 200 baskets.

It was an interesting drill for a number of reasons. The guys were all working together—both rebounders and shooters. No one was afraid of missing shots—which enhanced the No Fear Zone. If one or two of the guys were not hitting, they could see that the others were. So they saw that it might take only one guy getting hot to make the difference in a ball game. At times, there would be streaks where three or four balls would go through the basket in the same second. It was kind of awesome. It was inspiring. And it was fun.

Most important, though, was the fact that our guys got to see the ball going through the hoop a lot. In the Army, it would be like an artillery officer firing on the practice target so the soldiers could see the explosions before they went into battle. This drill allowed the players to view the visual impact of their scoring like nothing I'd ever tried before. And that's what I wanted. I wanted them to visualize everything from seeing a single ball going through a basket to winning the national championship.

*   *   *   *   *

When the sun rose on March 4, 2001, it marked the dawning of a new season for us. This was the day we played North Carolina. This was the day we put our new system into effect. I felt like a new man. We felt like a new team.

Our Senior Day loss to Maryland seemed like it had occurred last year—but it had been only five days ago. In that time, Virginia had beaten UNC, so we were still only one game behind in the ACC regular-season standings. That was a real break for us, because now we had hope. Now we really had something to fight for—a share of the regular season title. If we won, it would be our fifth straight—and no team had ever done that before.

But we were a heavy underdog going into the game. Nobody on the outside knew what our team had been through in the last five days. As far as they were concerned, we were still hobbled, broken, left for dead. They thought the only choice we had was to replace Carlos Boozer with Casey Sanders—and in their minds, that meant we didn't match up man-for-man. Everybody expected us to lose—and lose big. Even many of our own fans didn't think we had a chance.

The toughest thing about playing this game was that we had to venture into enemy territory. Nine miles down the road to Chapel Hill might as well have been 9,000 miles away from home. The mood in the Dean E. Smith Dome wasn't as hostile as the one we had encountered at Maryland's Cole Field House. But the crowd was hungry, they were overconfident, and they smelled blood. It was also Senior Day at UNC, and everybody in the arena not only hoped we would lose, they expected us to lose. It was one of the few times I can remember going into a gym where that was the case.

The feeling in our locker room was a combination of both apprehension and confidence. In a way, it was like our first game of the year. We were coming out of a training camp atmosphere with a new system. And we were all anxious to see if it would work in a game situation.

> *"It was almost like Christmas Day when you get a new bike but there's snow on the ground outside and you can't ride it. You want to ride that new bike so bad. Well, we wanted to try out this new system that bad."*
>
> *—Shane Battier*

I could tell that Casey and Reggie were nervous. But I also saw Nick with his arm around Casey, talking to him quietly. And I saw Shane giving Reggie a pep talk. Even with all the anxiety and apprehension, I really believed everybody felt we were going to win this game. There was a quiet confidence in that locker room.

When we came out on the court, the fans booed me and they booed our team. But our guys had an upbeat look on their faces. A few were even smiling.

During the introductions, Casey Sanders was introduced first, then Shane Battier, and then Mike Dunleavy. In the moment before Chris Duhon and Jason Williams were introduced, they hit each other's fists and said in unison, *"Guards win championships."*

"I'll never forget the look on the face of UNC center Brendan Haywood [7' 0", 260 pounds] when Casey stepped into the jump-ball circle. He got this sarcastic smile on his face and started shaking his head. He was thinking, You have got to be kidding. You're starting this guy? Casey didn't even notice. He was preparing to sprint down the court after the jump. I looked over at Mike and we just smiled at each other. I could read his mind. We were both thinking, Haywood, you just don't know what's coming. You just don't know."

—Shane Battier

Duke at North Carolina
Dean E. Smith Dome, Chapel Hill, North Carolina

March 4, 2001—With their star big man, Carlos Boozer, sitting on the sidelines in a cast, Duke invaded Chapel Hill and turned their basketball game with the Tar Heels into a track meet. While the Blue Devils raced up the court on each offensive possession, Shane Battier turned into a one-man zone by trapping any Tar Heel who ventured near the top of the circle. Less than three minutes into the game. Mike Dunleavy grabbed a defensive rebound and made a bullet pass out to Chris Duhon. Duhon, who saw that Casey Sanders (Carlos Boozer's replacement) had sprinted downcourt ahead of everybody else, hit Sanders for a lay-up. On UNC's next possession, Sanders blocked a lay-up attempt by Brendan Haywood and the Duke bench erupted in cheers. . . .

"After four minutes, we were leading, and the whole place was shocked. Even we were a bit shocked. We didn't know it was going to work that well. But we all thought, You know what? We've got something here."

—Shane Battier

"In the huddle after that first timeout, Coach kept telling us to 'Fight! Fight!' and we all had the look of warriors in our eyes. And then I said, 'Are you guys tired?' They all said, 'No, we're not tired.' 'Neither am I,' I said. But Carolina was out of breath and we saw that. We gained energy from our opponents' exhaustion."

—Jason Williams

"After about three or four times down the court, the look on Haywood's face changed. He was huffing and puffing, bending over, grabbing his shorts. It got to the point where he wasn't even making it over half-court."

–Mike Dunleavy

"After I made that lay-up and then blocked Haywood's shot, I looked over at the bench and everybody was going nuts. I focused in on Carlos and Nick, and they just made me feel great. We'd been working on this in practice all week, and now I saw that it worked in a game situation. After that, I wasn't nervous anymore. After that, I finally believed Coach K when he said we were going to win the national championship."

–Casey Sanders

. . . The lead seesawed for the rest of the first half until Duke finally managed to take a two-point lead, 42–40, into the locker room at intermission. . .

Two times in the first half, something happened to both the game clock and the shot clock. Both times, I stopped action and called it to the attention of the officials. Both times, I was right—but the crowd really got on me. So when the buzzer sounded the end of the half, I stopped at the scorer's table on my way to the locker room and pointed at the clock official and asked, "Should we get the clock set?" I didn't really have a purpose in doing that, except that I knew if I lingered at the scorer's table for a moment, it was going to get the crowd in an uproar. And sure enough, everybody started yelling: "Oohhhh! Boooo!"

When I went into the locker room, I told the guys: "I just wanted you to know that I did that purposely. I wanted to see if the crowd still wanted to beat us that bad. And they do." The guys thought that was cool.

. . . With three minutes gone in the second half, Duke was leading, when Joseph Forte stole the ball on defense and had a breakaway lay-up. But Shane Battier, in one of the great defensive plays of the season, came out of nowhere and blocked Forte's shot from behind. Mike Dunleavy grabbed the ball, and Duke immediately went down the court and hit a quick three-point shot. That seemed to turn the tide of the game in favor of the Blue Devils. With 11:54 left in the second half, Duke had surged to a 15-point lead, 72–57, when North Carolina coach Matt Doherty benched center Brendan Haywood and power forward Kris Lang in favor of a smaller lineup in an attempt to keep pace with the Blue Devils. . . .

> *"When that happened, I just smiled and thought, Well, they're playing right into our hands, now. We took their best weapons out of the game. It's over. We won."*
>
> *–Nate James*

. . . But it was too little, too late, as Duke cruised to a share of its fifth straight ACC regular-season title. Jason Williams (33 points) and Shane Battier (25) combined for 58 points in the win. Battier also added 11 rebounds, and Williams added nine assists. Mike Dunleavy had 16 points, and Chris Duhon, 15. The North Carolina home crowd, shocked at how Duke's breakneck pace stifled their Tar Heels, conceded defeat as they began to filter out of the stadium with four minutes left in the game.

Final Score: Duke 95, North Carolina 85
Overall Record: 26–4 **ACC:** 13–3

This victory against North Carolina was one of the most memorable moments of my basketball career. A scant five days earlier, our season looked like it had ended. But instead of letting the loss of Carlos Boozer destroy our morale, we actually used that event as a rallying point. We became a deeper team—both mentally and physically.

When I had walked into the Duke locker room at 6:00 that Thursday morning after the Maryland game and promised my team that we'd win the national championship if they believed in me—I wasn't totally sure we could do it, largely because I wasn't sure if all of them would come around to believing in themselves. It took awhile for that to happen. Jason and Chris believed almost immediately. Mike Dunleavy had to see what we were going to do in practice before he believed. And Casey Sanders didn't believe until he made that lay-up at the beginning of the game.

It was a good example of what I believe coaching really is. Coaching is not just giving a Knute Rockne fire-'em-up speech. It takes time, patience, commitment, and passion to pull a team together to play like these guys did. And it takes one more thing—it takes great kids. It takes, for example, a Carlos Boozer, who, after being hurt and possibly knocked out for the season, showed up on the sidelines as his replacement's biggest cheerleader.

I'm telling you, I've been in sports my whole life. When a player gets hurt, there's a part of him that doesn't want the guy who replaced him to do well. Most won't admit it, but jealousy and envy almost always come into play. The player feels those emotions, and as much as he may try to overcome them, they are almost never totally absent. But I was watching Carlos Boozer closely the entire week. And as God is my witness, there was no jealousy in him, whatsoever. His support of Casey was unconditional. And I know that had a huge impact on Casey's performance. I know it.

In the locker room after the game, everybody was hugging each other. After I hugged Carlos and Casey, I tapped both of them on their chests with my fist. In Casey's instance, he had been playing back-up ball for a year and a half, and when his moment came, he seized the opportunity and stepped forward. But the real key to Casey's success was not his one-on-one battle with Brendan Haywood, it was his five-point play. During that entire week, he communicated, he trusted, he was collectively responsible, he cared, and he took pride in his performance.

When I tapped my two guys on their chests, it was by instinct. But, I was really trying to tell them that they played with their hearts and they were part of a fist today. And if you think Carlos didn't play in that game against North Carolina, you're wrong. Carlos was as much a part of that victory as anybody else on our team.

For the rest of the season, in the locker room after the team prayer, before they took the court, I would put my hand on the chest of each player. It was just a small physical thing, but it allowed me to symbolically touch their hearts—and to let them know I was there for them, I believed in them, and we were in this together.

Following his 500th win, Mike Krzyzewski is greeted by the Cameron Crazies and honored by the naming of "Coach K Court" on November 17, 2000.

Coach K makes a point to senior captain Shane Battier.

Sophomore Jason Williams directs the Blue Devils on the court.

Sophomore Carlos Boozer grabs a rebound on the way to being named MVP of the Preseason NIT.

Duke students camp out in Krzyzewskiville prior to a home basketball game.

Three former guards make up Coach K's dynamic coaching staff (from left to right): Chris Collins '96, Steve Wojciechowski '98, Coach K, and Johnny Dawkins '86.

Sophomore Mike Dunleavy skies (below) in the Duke/North Carolina game, the greatest rivalry in college basketball.

Battier blocks Juan Dixon's shot (left) during the "Miracle Minute" at Maryland's Cole Field House in one of the greatest comebacks in Duke basketball history, a 98–96 overtime win after being down 10 with 54 seconds to go in regulation.

Casey Sanders, starting against North Carolina for an injured Carlos Boozer, helps lead Duke to a 95–81 win and a share of its fifth straight ACC regular-season title.

Injured starter Carlos Boozer (fifth from right) watches from the bench with his teammates at the ACC tournament in Atlanta.

Senior Nate James (left), the only player in ACC history to play on five conference championship teams, celebrates the 2001 ACC tournament championship.

Battier is immortalized at Duke (above) by becoming the 10th player in school history to have his jersey retired.

Battier talks in a team huddle as Duke readies for action at the 2001 NCAA Final Four in Minneapolis.

Carlos Boozer (12 points and 12 rebounds) gets back in form as he starts the second half of the championship game against Arizona.

Williams slams home two of his 23 points during the largest comeback in NCAA Final Four history—a 95–84 thriller over ACC foe Maryland, in which the Blue Devils erased a 22-point first-half deficit.

Freshman Chris Duhon's signature move, the Giant Killer (left), floats in over Arizona's Loren Woods. James is fouled (right) while scoring a key reverse lay-up in the title game's final stretch.

Dunleavy hits one of three straight three-pointers during a 45-second flurry in the second half against Arizona, finishing with a team-high 21 points and earning All–Final Four honors.

Duke celebrates its third national championship in 11 years (left)—an 82–72 win over Arizona. Coach K stands with All-America guard Jason Williams (right), who had declared his intention of returning to Duke to complete his degree. Duke's championship vision becomes a reality (below) as they watch their "One Shining Moment" video on the big screen in the Metrodome.

ACC Tournament

Every year, by design, our last regular-season game has been against North Carolina—either at home or away. And every year, to get refreshed, we have taken a day off after that game. But not this year.

We all wanted to get back to work as fast as we could because our new style of play was not only exciting, it was great fun. Normally, it's tough to get a team invigorated at the end of the season, just prior to entering March Madness. But when we beat North Carolina so decisively—after talking about our new strategy and working on it in practice—everyone really understood we had a real shot at winning the national championship. And that goes to that old teaching maxim I like to utilize: You hear, you forget. You see, you remember. You do, you understand. So the next day, the entire team turned its attention to our conference's upcoming tournament.

The Atlantic Coast Conference tournament is the granddaddy of all basketball tournaments. It started a tradition in 1953 that has since been copied by other conferences across the nation. Usually, the tournament is held in Greensboro or Charlotte, but this year we were going to Atlanta to play in front of more than 40,000 people in the Georgia Dome. I was really proud to be a member of the ACC, because the people who planned the tournament created what was to be a fabulous environment in which to play. It was going to simulate the Final Four in nearly every way. People were scarfing up tickets left and right, and it was anticipated that in the four days of the tournament, there were going to be more than 200,000 people in attendance. Now that is a big-time event!

The media was making a big deal about North Carolina and Duke fighting it out for the Number 1 seed in the East region of the NCAA tournament. But, to tell the truth, I gave it very little thought. Rather, I was focused on three major concerns during our practice sessions. First, the ACC tournament would be an endurance race. Due to a tiebreaker with North Carolina, we were seeded Number 2, and our schedule called for three games in three days—if we won the first two, of course. That would be a tough challenge, but we were determined to win this event because the victor would be crowned the "official" 2001 champion of the ACC. Second, I was concerned that our players might view the UNC game as a one-time thing. There was a very real danger of a letdown, and I did not want us to fall flat on our faces. And third, we had to reinforce our new system so that it could carry us all the way to the national championship.

Also that week, I spent quite a bit of time evaluating the strength of our team as we entered postseason play. Nick Horvath would definitely be unavailable for the rest of the year—as would Andre Sweet, whose mid-term grades had not improved sufficiently to be removed from academic probation. Carlos Boozer would miss the ACC tournament but had a very real chance of returning for the later stages of the NCAA tournament—but he would really have to apply himself to make it happen.

The final diagnosis of Carlos's foot was a clean break of the third metatarsal in the right foot, which was exactly the same injury Bobby Hurley had suffered in 1992. Bobby was out for three weeks and made it back in time for us to go on to win the national championship. Though Carlos is much larger than Bobby (who was a guard), I figured there was a good chance he could make it back, too—even though his foot had to bear more weight than Bobby's. And Dave Engelhardt agreed, although he was more cautious. "We'll just have to take it week by week and see if there's any bone growth as we go," said Dave. "He could make it back. It's possible."

When we sat down with Carlos and reviewed the diagnosis and the possibilities with him, he was determined to do all he could to make it back for the Final Four.

"Listen, Carlos," I said, "When you come back, you will have to adjust to our new style, rather than our adjusting to you. You'll have to be faster. You'll have to train harder. When you come back, you'll have to run the court much faster."

"*Don't worry, Coach,*" he replied. "*I'll do that.*"

The only other player I had any real concern about was Reggie Love, who was participating in spring football practices as well as playing and practicing with us. I was afraid he might either wear himself out or that he might be a little down because he had not played much in the Carolina game. So I pulled him aside the day before we left for Atlanta and told him not to worry about playing only a few minutes against UNC. "With three games in three days, I guarantee you will see a lot more playing time," I said.

"*I'm okay, Coach,*" he said. "*But the football coach wants me to stay behind and fly down on the day of our game so I can go to football practice.*"

The Duke football program doesn't mind if one of their guys plays basketball, as long as he plays and doesn't sit on the bench. In this case, they thought Reggie was not going to play. So later that day, we assured them that Reggie would play, and they had no problem letting him travel with the team.

*   *   *   *   *

When we arrived in Atlanta and checked into our hotel, I was told that Bobby Hurley was in town for an ACC Legends luncheon— so I tracked him down and asked him to spend a little time with Carlos. "Would you talk to him about your mind-set back then," I asked Bobby, "about how you believed you were going to be back, the things you did to get back, and the fact that you *did* make it back in three weeks?"

"Sure, Coach," said Bobby, as I knew he would. "I'll take care of it."

> *"Bobby Hurley was really great. He came to practice with his family and encouraged me to get on the Stairmaster and start pumping away at it. But he also cautioned me not to do too much, too soon. He said he watched me during the UNC game and advised me to get a seat belt to keep me from jumping around all over the place. He said I should keep the enthusiasm, but not make my injury worse. All in all, Bobby gave me a lot of encouragement. After talking to him, I knew I could make it back before the NCAA tournament ended."*
>
> *—Carlos Boozer*

*   *   *   *   *

On our bus ride over to the stadium to play NC State, Jeff La Mere came up to me with a concerned look on his face. "Coach," he said, "We have a problem."

"What's that?"

"We forgot our white uniforms and our game warm-ups. They're back in Durham. All we have with us are our black uniforms."

In the tournament, a team has to wear white if they are a higher seed. For this game, we were the Number 2 seed playing the Number 7 seed.

"Well, let's go through our options," I said to Jeff. "We don't have time to get our warm-ups down here. Is there a store we can stop at—a big sporting goods store?"

"I know they sell shirts at the concession stands," replied Jeff. "We can buy some there. Hopefully, they'll have enough big sizes."

"Okay, let's do that," I said.

So when we got to the Georgia Dome, Jeff and the managers went to the concession stands and I went straight to Fred

Barakat, ACC tournament director, and explained the situation. He said if I could work it out with Herb Sendek, the NC State head coach, everything would be okay. I knew NC State had both black uniforms and red uniforms, and I was hoping they had brought their red ones. But if State had brought along only their black uniforms, we were going be in trouble. I met with Herb right away and explained the situation to him.

"Well, we brought our red uniforms," he said.

"We have to wear our black uniforms, Herb. Is that a problem?"

Herb Sendek is a class guy. He was really great about the whole situation. He simply said, "Not at all Mike—not a problem."

Next, I had to go into the locker room and deal with this enormous distraction. Our routine was being broken because the guys couldn't go through their normal pregame process. That might not sound like a big deal to some people, but athletes have rituals—individual rituals, team rituals, superstitions. I didn't know what all the rituals were, but I did know one thing. Whatever rituals our players had, they weren't happening tonight!

I was also concerned about our managers. They made a huge mistake and they felt terrible about it. It was one of those, "I thought you packed them"; "Well, I thought you packed them." And our managers never, I mean *never* make mistakes. Not only that, they would dive on land mines and grenades for the team. So I saw this situation as a chance to be collectively responsible for them.

In the locker room in front of everybody—players and managers, alike—I addressed the situation. "Look, this is what's happened," I explained. "We forgot the white uniforms and the warm-ups. Notice I didn't say the *managers* forgot, I said *we* forgot. We're all responsible for this situation. Just like with a mistake on the court, when it happens, we're not going to jump down someone's throat and blame that person. There's no room for blame on this team. We are collectively responsible."

I paused a moment and took note of everyone's reaction. They didn't flinch and all eyes were on me. "This is not going to be an excuse," I continued. "When you guys go out on the court, I don't want you to be goofy about it. Or if something doesn't go quite your way, I don't want you to say, 'Geez, if I only had my shooting shirt,' or whatever. Forget it! We're not going to do that. Don't even think about it. We're going to do the best we can with this situation and we're not going to lay any blame. And I don't want the managers to be walking around worrying about having made a mistake. Let's get on to the Next Play. We'll get the white uniforms and the warm-ups here by tomorrow. But right now, let's take care of tonight. Does anybody have anything to say?"

"*No excuses,*" said Shane.

"Okay guys," I said. "We bought these T-shirts at the concession stands, and you can wear them for the warm-up." I saw some of the guys start to smile and could tell they wanted to laugh, so I joked about it a little bit. "And you know what?" I said as I held one up. "They're not bad. Maybe we should throw out our regular shooting shirts and start using these?"

That made everyone laugh.

So the guys put on these shirts and went out onto the court. I must admit, though, that some of them looked kind of funny, because the shirts either seemed to hang loose because they were too large or ride up their backs because they were too small.

> *"I felt a little naked out there. We just had this little T-shirt and it didn't fit too well. It was certainly different, I can tell you that."*
>
> —*Mike Dunleavy*

Mickie had come to the arena with our daughter Debbie and grandson, Joey—and was unaware of the uniform snafu. When the players took the court in shorts and their ill-fitting shirts, her jaw dropped.

What's this, she wondered, some sort of motivational thing?

North Carolina State vs. Duke
The Georgia Dome, Atlanta, Georgia

March 9, 2001—Third-ranked Duke forgot their home uniforms but didn't miss a beat, as sophomore Jason Williams scored 10 of his 19 points during a

15–0 first-half run. NC State surprised Duke with a smaller lineup to combat their opponent's speed. It worked for approximately 11 minutes. The Blue Devils missed 14 of their first 18 shots, including 1-for-8 from three-point range. Down 19–16, Coach Mike Krzyzewski then inserted freshman Reggie Love into the lineup in place of Casey Sanders. Love, a wide receiver on Duke's football squad, sparked his team over the next six minutes with four points, two steals, several traps, and blocked shots. Six minutes later, when Love exited for the bench, the Blue Devils had a 31–19 lead with 5:30 remaining in the half. . . .

> *"At one point, Reggie made this incredible slam dunk, and I was so happy for him I almost knocked him over on our way back down the court. It was like we were back in summer school, racing up and down the court at Cameron. I just felt so good for him."*
>
> *—Chris Duhon*

. . . Chris Duhon, making only his second career start, paced Duke early by scoring nine of his team's first 12 points. On the night, Duhon scored 14 points and hauled in six rebounds. Shane Battier added 16 points and Nate James, 13.

Final Score: Duke 86, North Carolina State 61
Overall Record: 27–4

After beating NC State, we had less than a day to prepare for our third match-up of the season with Maryland. Now ranked Number 11 in the nation, they were one of the hottest teams around—having won six in a row by an average margin of 19.5 points per game.

It had been only two weeks prior that we had lost to Maryland on Senior Day. Now, we had to beat them without Carlos. But I was confident that our new up-tempo, three-point shot strategy would keep us in the game. And I believed we were not going to be playing any team in the NCAA tournament that was better than Maryland—so if we could stay with them and come out on top, I knew we'd be in a position to go all the way.

My main focus before the game was to keep our players loose and upbeat. So when we went out to eat after the NC State game, I joked and kidded around with everybody in an effort to set the tone.

Andy Borman and J.D. Simpson started to ride Mike Dunleavy about his free throw shooting prowess. Mike went right along with them and said, "Hey, if something comes up and I get to shoot two free throws down the stretch to win a close game, you guys will be scared to death that I'll miss them, won't you?" Then they all started laughing.

Maryland vs. Duke

The Georgia Dome, Atlanta, Georgia

March 10, 2001—Eleventh-ranked Maryland stormed into the Georgia Dome in front of 40,000 people and jumped off to a big lead over Duke. The Terrapins led 10–0 four minutes into the first half. They were hot, and Duke was ice cold, having missed their first 11 attempts. But Coach Mike Krzyzewski, declining to call a timeout, sent Nate James in off the bench, and he promptly hit a three-point shot to stop the bleeding. A minute later, the game's first TV timeout was called, with Maryland leading 12–5. Two minutes later, the score was knotted at 12. . . .

When they jumped off to a 10–0 lead, I was worried, but rather than call a timeout, I wanted to show my players I had confidence in them. I didn't want to rescue them. They needed to rescue themselves. Then, at the TV break, I pulled the guys together in the huddle.

"A lot of coaches would have called a timeout with their team down 10–0," I said. "Do you know why I didn't? Because I believe in you. I believed you could work it out. Just to let you know, that was me showing confidence in you."

. . . Seven minutes into the game, Coach Mike Krzyzewski subbed for Mike Dunleavy who, up to that point, was having a bad game. He had air-balled two shots, missed several key rebounds, and had one of his shots blocked. . . .

"When Coach pulled me out, I thought, Oh, man, this is not going to be good. So I go sit down and he was waiting for me. But instead of ripping into me, he said, 'Just calm down. You're a great player, and you're going to go back in there, do great, and help us out. Now just settle down and be the player we both know you are.'"

—Mike Dunleavy

. . . Duke center Casey Sanders also started the game poorly, but at a TV timeout with 3:40 left in the half and the score tied 33–33, Duke assistant coach Steve Wojciechowski had an animated talk with the 6' 11" sophomore about his play. Sanders responded by scoring Duke's next five points to give the Blue Devils a 38–35 lead with 2:30 left in the first half. But Maryland surged back to seize the lead 45–42 at halftime. . . .

> *"Wojo told me I was playing like Katie. Katie is a nickname the guys had given me for when I don't play as tough as I can. When he said that, it got me going."*
>
> —*Casey Sanders*

. . . Duke came out on fire in the second half—hitting five consecutive three-point shots (two from Williams, two from Battier, and one from Dunleavy). The Blue Devils converted those shots into a 19–2 run, which gave them a 61–47 lead with just over 15 minutes left in the game. They still had a seven-point lead with 4:30 remaining, before Maryland put on a run of their own—finally going ahead, 78–77, with 2:22 left on the clock. Duke came right back and took the lead, 79–78, on a Mike Dunleavy running shot at the basket. Then, with one minute left and Duke ahead 80–78, Casey Sanders got back in the action by blocking Terence Morris's baseline lay-up attempt. Duke ran some time off the clock, and the final 22 seconds of the game were furious. After a change of possession, Maryland's Danny Miller was fouled going to the basket, but he missed his first free throw. . . .

After Miller missed his first shot, Mike Dunleavy motioned to me that he wanted to take it out of bounds. Normally, Shane inbounds the ball, but in that situation, Mike wanted to get the ball into Shane's hands so he could be fouled and take the crucial free throws. At that moment, my mind flashed back three months to the Stanford game we lost, in which Mike had missed two important free throws at the end of the game. After he returned to campus, he had to live with people calling him a choke artist. Now, in this game, in almost the exact same situation, he didn't want to take the foul shots. He wanted to let his roommate take them. Normally, Mike craved the ball in big moments like that. Well, I did not want him to lose that quality. So I pointed at him and said: "No! I want you to take the shots. I want you."

. . . Miller made his second free throw to pull the Terrapins within one, 80–79. Shane Battier inbounded the ball, and Maryland fouled Mike Dunleavy with 16.5 seconds left in the game. Dunleavy then calmly swished both free throws to give the Blue Devils a three-point lead at 82–79. . . .

"I wanted to win this game and knew that Shane was a great free throw shooter. But Coach looked at me and said, 'No!' I was really shocked at first. What's he thinking about? I wondered. But then I thought to myself that I was going to have to make these free throws because Coach was really putting himself on the line for me. I was not so confident, at first, but Coach gave me the confidence I needed by believing in me. Sure enough, I got fouled. When I went up to the line, I looked over at the bench and saw Andy and J.D. looking really nervous. I just kind of smiled and winked at them. Then I sank both shots. I knew I was going to make them. There was no doubt."

—Mike Dunleavy

. . . Maryland guard Steve Blake then beat a path down the court and sank a long three-pointer to tie the score at 82 with eight seconds remaining. Rather than call a timeout, Duke's Jason Williams drove the entire length of the floor and raced in for a lay-up that bounced off the front of the rim. But Nate James and Casey Sanders closed in for the tip-in. It appeared that both got a hand on the ball. James, however, was higher in the air and received credit for the two points that put Duke in front 84–82 with 1.3 seconds to go. . . .

"As soon as Jason started to penetrate, I said to myself, I'm gonna get a tap-in. I knew their big guys were going to fly in and make a difficult shot for him. So I focused on the ball, went up, and tapped it in."

—Nate James

. . . Out of timeouts, Maryland quickly inbounded the ball to Juan Dixon, who launched a half-court shot that hit the rim and bounced away—ending the contest. For the game, Maryland out-rebounded Duke, 51–30, but Duke made 12 of 33 three-point shots. Shane Battier played all 40 minutes and scored 20 points. Williams added 19, Dunleavy 15, and James 14. With the victory, the Blue Devils earned the right to face Number 1 seed North Carolina in the ACC championship final.

Final Score: Duke 84, Maryland 82
Overall Record: 28–4

Immediately after the game ended, Shane Battier grabbed Juan Dixon by the shoulders and said, "*You're a great player—one of the best I've ever faced. See you at the Final Four.*"

Dixon then walked over to me and shook my hand. "Good game, Coach," he said. "I'll see you in the Final Four."

Nate James and Casey Sanders were interviewed together about who exactly got that last-second tip-in. "*I got the tip,*" said Casey, "*Nate was over my back. My hand was first, then he kind of pushed it into the basket. It doesn't really matter, though. The fact that we won the game is the biggest thing.*"

"What about it, Nate?" asked the reporter.

"*I think Casey was in the area,*" responded Nate as he and Casey both started laughing. "*You have to give Casey credit. If he wants a little piece of the pie, that's okay with me.*"

As I walked down the tunnel toward the locker room, I kept marveling at how closely this game resembled our Stanford game in the last minute. In both games, Dunleavy had made a big shot to keep us in it. Then, just a few seconds later, he was on the line for two key free throws. Jason then ran the entire length of the court and missed the lay-up, and Nate James tipped it in. In the Stanford game, Nate's tip-in was just a second too late. But in this game, Jason had eight seconds instead of 3.6 seconds to bring it down the court. So Nate had that extra second he needed to get the basket.

In the locker room after the game, there was a lot of excitement. Everybody was really happy because they knew they had just played in a great game. At that point, I took Mike Dunleavy to the coaches' locker room, where it was just the two of us.

"Pretty damn good free throw shooting," I said.

"*Thanks, Coach. Thanks for believing in me.*"

"Mike, when you're on the line, you're shooting *our* free throws, not *your* free throws. And there's nobody I would rather have shooting *our* free throws than you."

*   *   *   *   *

Now we turned our attention to our archrival, the North Carolina Tar Heels, who had defeated Georgia Tech, 70–63, in the other semifinal game. The winner of this game would not only be the 2001 ACC champions but also would likely receive the Number 1 seed in the East region of the NCAA tournament—to be played in Greensboro, N.C., just 45 minutes from Duke. It would essentially be a home court advantage for the first week of the tournament.

Duke vs. North Carolina
The Georgia Dome, Atlanta, Georgia

March 11, 2001—Third-ranked Duke decisively defeated sixth-ranked North Carolina for the second time in eight days to earn its third consecutive ACC tournament crown. The victory marked Shane Battier's 69th ACC win (out of a possible 76)—setting the record for most wins by one player. It was also Coach Mike Krzyzewski's 600th victory as a college coach. The game started out close, as the two teams changed leads several times. But then, Duke's vaunted defense took over. Forcing North Carolina turnover after turnover, the Blue Devils went on a 19–1 run that broke the game wide open. After that, the Tar Heels seemed lifeless, as Duke cruised to a 50–30 halftime lead. . . .

> *"After that run, I looked at their facial expressions and they acted like they didn't want to play anymore. The competitiveness wasn't there. They started bickering with one another and just waiting for the time to expire so they could go home."*
>
> *—Nate James*

. . . With 13:00 remaining in the second half, and Duke leading 62–38, Jason Williams came down on another player's foot under the UNC basket and began writhing in pain on the floor. The crowd suddenly fell to a whisper and Williams could be heard to cry out in pain, "Oh, my dear God." . . .

Dave Engelhardt rushed out to Jason, and I followed close behind.
    "Is it your ankle?" I asked him.

"*Oh, yeah,*" he said, obviously in pain.

"Did you step on somebody's foot."

"*Yeah.*"

"That's good, J. That kind of injury huts like crazy—but it's probably not broken."

Dave and I tried to settle Jason down, as he seemed emotionally distraught. While Dave looked him in the eye and talked, I rubbed the back of his neck. "Just take it easy," I said.

"Okay, Jason," said Dave, "we're going to get up together. I want you to put a little weight on it as we walk off. Okay, let's go."

Dave was on one side and I was on the other. As we began to lift Jason up, I said, "I got you, Jason. I got you." And I continued to talk to him and give him encouragement as we walked over to the bench, until Andre Buckner came over and took my place. After that, I don't think Dahntay Jones left Jason's side while he was on the bench.

> "*When I looked at Jason on the floor and saw the look in the eyes of my teammates, I felt this knot in my stomach. Then I knew it was time to play.*"
> —*Chris Duhon*

. . . Williams did not play for the rest of the game. After the injury, freshman Chris Duhon stepped up and ran the team with seasoned precision, as Duke's lead never fell below 20 points. Mike Dunleavy led the Blue Devils with a career-high 24 points and 13 rebounds. Shane Battier also had a double-double, with 20 points and 13 rebounds. Jason Williams had 15 points before he left the game, and Nate James added 10. In what was the second largest margin of victory in 48 ACC finals, Duke forced 20 turnovers, had 12 steals, and held North Carolina to 29.2 percent shooting from the floor. After the game, Tar Heel standout Joseph Forte lauded the Duke effort. "You want to play them because you're a competitor, but you can't play them like this," said Forte. "They're a team. They're a true team. They have two great players but they're a team. We need to play somebody other than Duke."

Final Score: Duke 79, North Carolina 53
Overall Record: 29–4

Our victories in the ACC tournament were an incredible team effort. Everyone contributed. Everyone stepped forward when he needed to do so—Reggie Love and Chris Duhon in the NC State game; in the Maryland game, Mike Dunleavy's foul shots, Casey Sanders' five straight points, Nate James' tip-in at the end; Chris Duhon running the show so ably when Jason went down in the North Carolina game; Mike Dunleavy's game-high 24 points; and Jason Williams and Shane Battier, our two pillars, with stellar performances in all three games.

Battier, Williams, and Dunleavy were named first-team all-tournament choices. Nate James made second-team all-tournament. Shane was named the most valuable player of the tournament, and after the game, he stated, "*I came back to Duke for three reasons: a degree, a national championship, and maturity. I have a hunch that my last game as a Blue Devil will end up in tears. Hopefully, they'll be tears of joy.*"

In my mind, that was the statement of a champion. And with their amazing team effort, all of our players were champions that day. Every single one of them.

NCAA Tournament
East Region

Upon our return home from Atlanta, we found out that the ACC had placed six teams in the NCAA tournament—North Carolina, Maryland, Virginia, Wake Forest, Georgia Tech, and Duke. And for the third straight year, we were selected to be the Number 1 seed in the East region.

The media made a big deal out of that placement, but all through the conference tournament, we weren't playing for seeding so much as we were playing to win. And it's a good thing, too, because when we closely analyzed the brackets, we felt that the toughest road to the national championship was through the East region. We saw right away that we had the potential to play Missouri, UCLA, Kentucky, Southern Cal, or Boston College. All these teams matched up well against us, and I knew we were not going to out-athlete any of them. Johnny Dawkins even mentioned to me that he believed it was a tougher road for us than we had had in 1999, when we lost to UConn in the championship final.

I was intrigued that the cities we would be playing in, if we kept winning, were the very same cities that we had gone to in winning our second national championship in 1992—Greensboro, Philadelphia, and Minneapolis. Maybe it was a good omen.

Being in Greensboro for the first round this year, I believed, was definitely going to help us. After our devastating defeat on Senior Day, we had played four games in eight days and had two-a-day practices. Not having to do all that extra preparation for travel was a blessing. I thought it would also help to have a lot of Duke fans in the crowd.

On a more personal note, I was glad we were going to be in Greensboro, because my daughter Debbie would be able to attend. Being eight and one-half months pregnant prevented her from flying anywhere too far away. She and Joey, my 15-month-old grandson, ended up staying with Mickie and me in the two-bedroom suite we occupied at our hotel. Debbie's presence on the road scared the heck out of our trainer, Dave Engelhardt. I saw him reading a midwife book on how to deliver a baby and I told him, "Look, I'll be damned if my grandchild is going to be delivered by you, Engelhardt. We're going to the nearest hospital!"

Not having to travel also allowed us to get more treatments for Jason Williams's ankle, which x-rays had shown was not broken but only sprained. Still, Jason was in a lot of pain, and we were very concerned about his ability to play in the first round—especially since his replacement, Chris Duhon, would be playing in his very first NCAA tournament.

Having four days to rest was going to be of help, but Jason would not play in the first couple of practices, which brought up another concern. Earlier in the season, he had allowed his ankle injuries to become something of a distraction. He didn't practice as much, so he got a little bit out of shape. And then, in thinking too much about his ankle, he had made 10 turnovers in our loss to Virginia. So we talked to Jason about that previous situation in an effort to remind him of how it had negatively affected his play.

"It won't be a problem, Coach," he said. "I always want to be on the court and I'll make sure I'm out there for the Monmouth game. I'll be ready, I'll be in shape, and I'll be mentally prepared. I want to play."

We also got some good news about Carlos. The x-rays taken after the ACC tournament indicated good bone growth in his foot. He was now able to do some treadmill work and should be cleared to practice in a week. Dave Engelhardt told me if Carlos kept healing at that rate, he might be able to play in the tournament's Sweet 16 round in Philadelphia.

Overall, I felt our team was doing very well. Despite the fact that we had shot only 37.9 percent from the field in the tournament, we had continued to win with our new up-tempo strategy. It was apparent that the first UNC win was not just a one-time thing.

Confidence comes from doing, and this team's confidence was soaring. As I always say, with confidence comes courage—which meant that we were becoming more courageous as well. We had confidence, we had courage, and we were getting better. So going into the tournament, I was feeling optimistic about our chances. There was genuine belief on our team that we could win it all—and that belief was deepened when the national polls were released, ranking Duke Number 1 in the country for the third consecutive year going into the NCAA tournament. In that same week, Shane Battier was named Co-ACC Player of the Year, AP All-America, Academic All-America, and Naismith Award winner as National Player of the Year.

*   *   *   *   *

Our first opponent in Greensboro was 16th-seeded Monmouth College out of West Long Branch, New Jersey. Head Coach Dave Calloway and I had worked together in the past for CBS, and one of their assistant coaches, Ronnie Krayl, was a long-time friend of mine. He and I had played together on the All-Army and Armed Forces All-Star teams from 1969–1971. His son, to whom I'd been sending Duke basketball stuff all his life, was now playing on their basketball team. I knew we were a much stronger team than Monmouth, and if there was a team in the tournament that we could out-athlete, this was the one.

In reviewing the scouting report for Monmouth, I started something I would continue to do for the entire tournament. I began writing on the reports, over and over again, *30–4, 30–4, 30–4*. That would be our record if we were to win the next game. It was a small motivational thing for me personally, but it became my mantra. Seeing it on paper made it visual for me. And soon, I would be saying it to myself on a regular basis—especially if, during a game situation, things weren't going exactly the way I wanted them to go.

Before the Monmouth game, I wrote our four-team bracket up on the board in the locker room. And as the guys went out on the court, I filled *DUKE* in on the empty line for this game.

"Okay, guys, this is the real thing," I said. "Let's go out there and set the tone for the rest of the tournament."

Monmouth vs. Duke
Greensboro Coliseum, Greensboro, North Carolina

March 15, 2001—Top-seeded Duke took out 16th-seeded Monmouth in the opening round of the East region of the NCAA tournament in an awesome offensive shooting display. Monmouth students didn't help their cause when, as the Blue Devils were warming up, they started chanting, "Overrated! Overrated!". . .

> *"I hate that cheer."*
>
> —*Jason Williams*

. . . Sophomore Jason Williams quickly nailed three three-pointers, and before Monmouth knew what hit them, the Blue Devils had an 11–0 lead, then 16–1. Williams was 7-for-9 from the field in the first 14 minutes of the game, as the Blue Devils opened additional leads of 31–12, and 46–20. All Duke players saw action as Williams and the other starters were taken out by Coach Mike Krzyzewski when the lead soared to 43 points with 14:27 left in the second half. In addition to Williams's 22 points in 20 minutes, senior Shane Battier scored 21 points and pulled down 10 rebounds for a double-double. In this game, both Battier and Williams set new Duke records for three-pointers made in a season. Battier took his total to 114, and Williams to 115—breaking Trajan Langdon's old mark of 112. In all, Duke connected on 18-for-38 three-point field goals—the second most in an NCAA tournament game and the most in an East region contest.

Final Score: Duke 95, Monmouth 52
Overall Record: 30–4

*   *   *   *   *

"Carlos, how does that happen?" I asked.

"*I don't know, Coach,*" replied Carlos.

I was reviewing videotape of our upcoming opponent, Missouri, and words would intermittently appear on the screen. I think it had something to do with the hearing-impaired function on the television. But because our staff used an array of clips from different games, it appeared very haphazardly.

"Hey, there they are again!" I said. "Carlos, how does that happen?"

"*Beats me, Coach.*"

Every time some words came up, I'd interrupt my analysis of Missouri's game strategy and mention it again. And each time, the players would chuckle a little bit more, because Carlos, who is quiet by nature, was getting frustrated.

"Carlos, how does that happen?"

"*Coach, I don't know how the hell it happens!*" Carlos finally snapped back. And this time the entire team howled with laughter.

"Carlos, you should know the answer to simple little questions like this," I said. "So by the time we get to the Final Four, you've got to have the answer."

Now Carlos was shaking his head and laughing with everybody else.

I made light of this little situation and singled out Carlos because I wanted to keep him included. His broken foot was healing on schedule, and physically, I thought he was going to be fine. Mentally, though, I did not want him to feel left out; he was still a big part of our team. So, when Carlos laughed, I definitely knew he felt included. My request of him also had a subtle message because, by the Final Four, I wanted Carlos to have an answer for us on the court.

*   *   *   *   *

We had only one day to get ready for Missouri. But even if it had been a week, I don't think I would have been mentally prepared. Missouri's head coach was Quin Snyder. I had recruited Quin when he was in high school. He had played at Duke, had been on three Final Four teams, and had graduated in 1989. Then he had become my assistant coach and stayed through the 1999 season, before he had accepted the head coaching job at Missouri. Quin was not only my friend, he was part of our family. He'd actually spent most of his adult life with us at Duke. He's a good coach, his own man—and I'm proud of him. But I sure wasn't looking forward to coaching against him. Why would anyone want to coach against someone he loves? It wasn't by choice that I was in this situation. It was the luck of the draw.

The thing I was most concerned about was maintaining our friendship in that type of competition. Because at this level in the NCAA tournament, a loss ends the season. And that hurts the most. I didn't want whatever happened in the 40 minutes of that game to ruin our relationship.

I also found myself concerned about Quin. After all, not only had he coached at Duke and knew Shane and Nate very well, but he had also worn the uniform, and he had been the captain of his team. What was *he* going through?

Earlier in the week, when I found out we were in the same bracket, I called Quin to chat about it. We congratulated each other, of course. But then I tried to ease his mind a little bit.

"You know, if we play each other," I said, "the press will ask you how it feels to coach a game against Duke. I don't want you to feel obliged to talk about me. Just talk about your team, because they deserve that. I know how you feel about me, and you do not have to say so on television. Let's not let that be Greensboro. Let's let our teams be Greensboro." I was trying to let Quin off the hook, and I believe he appreciated it. But who was going to let me off the hook?

The night before the game, I called my staff together for a brief meeting in my hotel room.

"This is not a good situation for me," I told the guys. "I'm definitely distracted about having to coach against Quin. Just make sure we're doing this the right way," I said in reference to our coaching strategy. "I may be off my game. I'm going to try not to be. But I need your help. If you see something that needs to be done, don't hesitate to take action. Be bold."

Although I didn't say it outright to the staff, I was concerned about these emotions preventing me from coaching our team as intensely as I should. Overall, Johnny, Chris, and Wojo were very understanding.

After the meeting ended and the guys went back to their rooms, I decided to watch some more tape of Missouri. Usually, after preparing the team, my duty is to get a good night's sleep before a game. But this night, I couldn't sleep. I would watch some tape, then get up and pace back and forth, watch some tape, and then pace.

At about midnight, there was a knock at my door. It was Wojo.

"Coach, I need to talk to you," he said.

So we sat down for a few minutes.

"Quin will be all right," Wojo told me. "Our duty is with our team. I know you're very worried about Quin, but we also have a responsibility to these kids: Shane, Nate, Jason, Mike, Chris, Carlos, Casey—all the guys. These are *your* guys. Don't worry about Quin, he'll be okay. And don't worry about yourself, I'll be there for you, and so will Chris and Johnny."

It was quite a remarkable thing I was hearing from my 24-year-old assistant, because after all, it was Wojo who had replaced Quin. I could see his eyes were teary. He was emotional, and I knew he was speaking from his heart. And the truth is that Wojo got through to me. I was so worried about Quin that I really wasn't thinking about the kids on my own team. Wojo was absolutely right. It took courage for him to tell me that and I appreciated it so much.

In just about every game this year, there had been at least one person we concentrated on to help get prepared for the game. In this instance, that person was me. And all three assistant coaches really came through.

Johnny Dawkins and Chris Collins stepped forward and were much more demonstrative and vocal in practice, during the scouting report review, in the shoot-around, and on the bench during the game. Johnny, in particular, really believed we had a chance to win this whole thing. He had been denied in the championship game twice before—once as a player in 1986 and once as a coach in the 1999 loss to UConn. He was not going to be denied in 2001.

*   *   *   *   *

Before the game, my mind drifted back to 1989 and Quin's senior speech at our year-end awards banquet. In that set of remarks, which was one of the finest a Duke player has ever given, Quin had emphasized the word friend as one of the most important standards he had learned at Duke. Now here he was as a head coach in his own right and about to take me on as an equal. I was so proud of him.

While the players were warming up, Quin and I met on the sidelines. We had a handshake and a hug.

"Quin, I said, "no matter what happens, I'll always be your friend. And I'll always be there to help you."

"Thanks, Coach," he responded, "Thanks."

When the ball went up, I was ready to coach my players. I *had* to be ready because Missouri had a great team, and I knew Quin was going to fight like crazy. I expected nothing less.

Missouri vs. Duke
Greensboro Coliseum, Greensboro, North Carolina

March 17, 2001—Missouri surprised Duke by starting a small lineup to combat the Blue Devils' breakneck speed. Duke built a 15-point first-half lead before the ninth-seeded Tigers closed to within six at the intermission. Duke freshman Chris Duhon was hit by an elbow and suffered a minor concussion during the first half. . . .

"I got an elbow and felt dizzy during the game, but I just kept playing. I remember most of what happened during the game, but after I hugged Coach Snyder, I don't remember anything."

—Chris Duhon

. . . In the second half, Missouri managed to close the game to one point, 63–62, before the Blue Devils got hot and scored on 13 of their next 14 possessions, including six straight, to build the lead back to double figures with 7:49 remaining. Missouri, coached by former Duke player and assistant coach Quin Snyder, could not get closer than eight, despite hitting 11 of 21 three-point shots. For the first time in 35 games, a Duke opponent made more three-pointers than the Blue Devils during a game. Missouri finished 11-for-21, while Duke was 9-for-26. Jason Williams, still nursing a sore left ankle, scored 31 points with nine assists. Shane Battier had 27 points and 11 rebounds for his third straight double-double. He led his team at the free throw line, hitting 12 of 13. For the game, the Blue Devils sank 21 of 25. With the victory, Duke advanced to the Sweet 16 for the 12th time since 1986.

Final Score: Duke 94, Missouri 81
Overall Record: 31–4

In the locker room immediately following the game, I grabbed a marker and wrote *DUKE* in the championship space on the four-team bracket. "Congratulations, guys," I said. "We won that tournament—and next week, we'll play in another one." Of course, I was referring to the fact that we had advanced to the Sweet 16 and were now headed to Philadelphia. Our first opponent would be the UCLA Bruins, and we would be playing in the First Union Center, home of the Philadelphia 76ers—the very place we had played perhaps our best game of the season against Temple back in December.

It's at the Sweet 16 level of the NCAA tournament that the media really starts to get in gear. And right after our victory over Missouri, there were two big stories that were being touted.

First, by making 27 three-point shots in Greensboro, Duke had broken the national record for most converted three-pointers in a season. Arkansas had set the record in 1995 with 361 threes in 39 games. We had 377 in 35 games and were still not through playing. We were averaging more than 10 successful three-point shots per game and were hitting nearly 40 percent of our attempts. A number of writers pointed out that back in the mid-1980s, when the three-point shot was introduced to college basketball, I was a vocal opponent—and how ironic it was that Duke was now contending for a national title with those kind of three-point shot statistics. I don't know how ironic it was. All I knew was that the game had changed, and if I didn't adapt and change right along with it, I would not be a successful basketball coach. I think that's what leaders have to do—change and adapt to the times.

A Philadelphia paper was touting the second story. They did a six-page spread on a possible Duke-Kentucky rematch of the famous 1992 East Regional final that had also been played in Philadelphia. That was the game in which Christian Laettner's shot at the buzzer in overtime won it for us and allowed us to move on to the Final Four. Some have called it the greatest game ever played in college basketball. Kentucky was going to play USC in the other game of our bracket. If they won, and if we could get by UCLA, then Kentucky and Duke would be playing each other again. This story could have been a distraction to me, but it really wasn't. And it really didn't impact the players much, although I didn't want to take any chances.

"I don't know how this could distract you guys too much," I told the team. "Heck, you all were only eight, nine, or 10 years old when that game was played. C'mon. If the press asks you anything about it, I'd advise you to say something like, *"Oh, yeah. Coach mentioned it and showed us a picture of the team."*

* * * * *

This week Carlos Boozer was given the green light to return to practice, and we believed he would probably get in some light playing time in the upcoming games. Despite his dedicated workouts on the stationary bike and Stairmaster, Carlos still had a long way to go before he returned to top playing shape. In addition, I was steadfast in my conviction that he would have to adjust to the way we were now playing—not the other way around.

I was concerned about the new dynamic Carlos's return might create. He had been out for six games and we'd won them all. Now he would be back—and whenever somebody comes back, people's thinking changes. So now I was trying to anticipate how it might impact us by having another low-post presence in the game.

The most important thing I did was spend some extra time with Casey, Matt, and Reggie. I wanted them to fully understand what Carlos's returning to the team would mean to them personally. To Reggie and Matt, I said, "It will probably impact you guys first. Casey will still be starting, but I'll probably sub Carlos first. I don't know how Carlos is going to play. I hope he'll do well. But I don't want you guys to check out on us. He could break his foot again. He might not be ready to play. And he's certainly not in the condition to play big minutes."

I was also quite concerned about Casey possibly having a little bit of a letdown. So I kept a close eye on him in practice. And at one point, I had to blast him in front of the whole team.

> "I knew Carlos was coming around and I was getting a little set in my position. I started the morning practice a little slow. As we started to set up the defense, there was a question in my mind about what I should do, but I didn't ask because I was afraid I'd sound silly. Well, I was supposed to open up on help-side defense, but I hugged my man and didn't open up. Shane said, 'Come on, Case, you need to get going.' Then all my other teammates started to yell at me. That kind of shocked me. But they really thought I was starting to get complacent. Then I made the same mistake again and Coach really got on me. 'Oh, have you had enough?' he asked. 'Just because Carlos is suiting up, you don't have to play now? C'mon, let's go!' Coach was right, I needed to get my act together."
>
> — *Casey Sanders*

I didn't say anything at first for two reasons: I wanted to see if his teammates would speak up, and I also wanted to see if he would work himself out of it. The other guys did speak up, but when I saw Casey wasn't going to come around, I blasted him because we didn't have time to mess around.

I don't normally yell at a player—but when I do, they all know it's something serious. And I did yell at Casey. Coaching is all about changing limits—and changing is not easy. People make mistakes as a result of change. I try to create an atmosphere in which it's okay to make mistakes of commission—not omission. Casey's mistake at that point was one of omission. He just didn't do what he was supposed to do. He wasn't playing at the level he needed to play at. I had to get on him at that point. Our guys would never allow a player on our team to be complacent.

*   *   *   *   *

Chris and Wojo handled the scouting report for UCLA together. As a matter of fact, they had stayed behind in Greensboro to take notes and critique the UCLA–Utah State game, which immediately followed our win over Missouri. At our review session, they pointed out that UCLA's point guard Earl Watson was top-notch—"one of the best in the country," said Collins. And Dan Gadzuric, their big man, was "almost seven feet tall," according to Wojo, "and he was playing great going into our game."

"Great scouting report, guys," I said. "But you never know when people are watching you as you perform your jobs."

Then I turned on a clip of game tape from the UCLA–Utah State game in which the camera had panned the audience during a time-out. And there we saw our two assistant coaches whooping it up. Wojo had a big wad of pizza in his mouth, and Chris was laughing. It looked like they were partying.

The players broke up when they saw that, and when the laughter began to subside, I said, "We always wondered what your scouting technique was, guys. Now we know."

Johnny Dawkins got a big kick out of that.

*   *   *   *   *

When the team arrived in Philadelphia, we felt we were in familiar territory. We practiced at the 76ers' training facility again. We ate at the same restaurant the night before the game. Each player was given a new set of brackets for this four-team tournament. And I reminded them how great we had played against Temple in the First Union Center the last time we were here.

The night before the game, I was feeling very good about the team and the upcoming game. I really thought we were ready to play.

"After dinner, I mentioned to Shane that I felt if we could get past these two games, we were going to win the whole thing. But we had to get over this hump, because the Sweet 16 was where we lost to Florida last year. And there was no way I was going to let us lose this game to UCLA. Back in the hotel room, I read part of my journal from last year. I wanted to remember how I felt after losing the Florida game. I wanted to remind myself that only a few days after we lost that game, I had gone into the gym and begun working out all the time. And I wanted to read again the vow I had made to myself that we were going to get past the Sweet 16 this year—no matter what. Then I wrote one entry into my journal. 'Tomorrow night,' I wrote, 'I will not be writing about a loss!!!'"

—*Jason Williams*

* * * * *

Once I had made it through the Missouri game, with the emotional issue of having to deal with Quin and all that, I felt like a 20-pound weight had been lifted off my back. Now I was fresh and ready to go. It was a good thing, too, because the UCLA game didn't get started until 10:30 at night, and I could tell that the players were not as ready as they should have been. It turned out that this would be one of the hardest games for me to coach all year. I would have to use extraordinary measures to get them to play well enough to win this game.

UCLA vs. Duke
First Union Center, Philadelphia, Pennsylvania

March 22, 2001—Top-ranked Duke survived a scare from Number 15 UCLA in the Sweet 16 round of the NCAA tournament. UCLA sent a message to Duke in the very first minute of play, when Mike Dunleavy crashed to the floor after a driving lay-up. Dazed and holding his shoulder, Dunleavy was escorted to the bench by the Duke trainer and Coach Mike Krzyzewski. The tone had been set for what turned out to be a very physical first half. . . .

For the rest of the game, Mike could not lift his arm above his head. He would play fairly well on defense, but he could not extend his arm to shoot the ball. At the time, we were worried he might have a pinched nerve.

. . . A lackluster Duke started the game 0-for-6 from the floor. But UCLA was worse—only managing to score one basket in the first seven minutes. . . .

At the 17:47 mark, I put Carlos Boozer in the game. He not only provided us with an inside physical presence that we had not had for three weeks, but also he blocked a shot, grabbed a rebound, and scored a basket. We were behind 2–0 when Carlos went in and, over the next several minutes, we ran off 12 straight points to take a 12–2 lead. Carlos was back—and the impact on the entire team was obvious.

. . . Both teams were playing so poorly that the score was only 15–11 (Duke ahead) when a timeout was called with 7:51 remaining in the first half. . . .

"32–4," I kept murmuring to myself. "32–4." I didn't know what was wrong with our guys, but they were way out there in left field. They had that lobotomy look on their faces. During this timeout, I grabbed a couple of them by the shoulders. "Look at me!" I said. "Look at me! Where *are* you tonight? Where *are* you? We're playing scared. Why? Don't you know that if we do not do the job tonight, that's it? None of you have the look in your eyes like, This is it!"

I had no idea what was causing this lackluster performance. Maybe it was the late start or the day spent waiting for the tip-off. Maybe they were nervous because this was the same point in the tournament where we lost last year. Maybe it was because Dunleavy got hurt. Maybe it was because it was Boozer's first game in a long time, and roles had changed a bit. Maybe that made Casey and Reggie nervous. Maybe it made Carlos nervous.

I was searching for an answer because I had to snap them out of it fast. This was definitely the worst we had played the entire year. If it were practice, I would have kicked them out. But this was worse than a bad practice. At every timeout, I was pleading with them to get their heads in the game. Thank goodness, UCLA was playing poorly, or we would have been blown out.

. . . Things weren't much better when UCLA called a timeout with 2:23 remaining and Duke holding a seven-point lead, 26–19. . . .

At this point, Shane was saving us with his individual performance. But even though we were ahead by seven, we were still playing horribly as a team. So when they got to the bench, I gathered them together.

"We got here because we're good!" I said. Then I pointed at one player and said, "You're good!" then another, "You're good!" I said the same to each player. "C'mon, you guys. You're good! Show it on the court, will you?"

. . . Both teams began to hit some shots in the last minute of the half, and when the clock finally ticked down to 0.00, Duke carried a 33–26 lead into the locker room. . . .

At halftime, I was so frustrated with my team that I just put a big *20* on the board. "We have 20 minutes," I said. "The next 20 minutes determine your entire year. How can you not be excited? How can you not be emotional? Where *are* you tonight? I'm going nuts trying to coach you guys tonight! Where *are* you?"

Then I appealed to them in another way. I thought maybe referring to "moms" would reach them and bring them back from wherever they were.

"Fellas, before every game, I pull out my mom's rosary," I said. "I keep it in my coat pocket by my heart. I say a rosary and I offer each game for her—not to win, but to do my best and to lead with my heart.

"What about you guys? Can you not play with heart? Can you not play like you're playing for your mom or for your families? If you can't play for yourselves tonight, can you play for someone else you care about? Can you understand how important this is?"

I felt like I was in the emergency room using the heart pads— Poompf! Poompf! C'mon! C'mon! Come back to life!—I was very animated because it's so tough to get enthusiasm from a group when there hasn't been any all night. It's like trying to get blood out of a rock. It happens on every team, but you sure don't want it to happen in the Sweet 16.

. . . In the second half, Duke ran the lead up to 12 before UCLA made a 9–0 run to trim it to three. Then Jason Williams went on a spectacular run all by himself. Over a six-minute stretch, he scored 19 straight points for Duke. Every time UCLA crept close, Williams did something to stretch out the lead again—whether it was a three-point bomb or a driving lay-up. . . .

One of the key plays in Jason's run was a pass from Mike Dunleavy. At the 14:30 mark of the game, Carlos fed a pass out to Mike who was wide open. But rather than take the shot, he passed to get it to Jason in the corner. And Jason drained a three-pointer.

> *"I was open, but I wasn't 100 percent physically. My arm hurt. I knew Jason was hot, so I got the ball over to him as fast as I could. He nailed that shot and I felt great."*
>
> —*Mike Dunleavy*

That was a perfect example of both unselfishness and collective responsibility. Mike made the extra pass. He gave up a good shot for a great shot. That three-pointer was just as much Mike's as it was Jason's.

. . . When Shane Battier completed a three-point play with just over three minutes left in the game, UCLA could not catch up. And over the last 1:29, Duke went 8-for-8 from the free throw line to shut the door. Battier and Williams combined for 58 points out of Duke's total of 76. Williams finished with a career-high 34 points as the Blue Devils advanced to a regional final game for the 10th time in 16 years. This game also marked the return of Carlos Boozer, who played 22 minutes and finished with two points and six rebounds.

Final Score: Duke 76, UCLA 63
Overall Record: 32–4

We were beat up after the UCLA game, and my primary concern was with our overall health. When an athlete suffers an injury like Mike Dunleavy suffered, he can sometimes play through it, but the next day it can become extremely painful. We really were going to need him against USC—who had soundly defeated Kentucky in the other semifinal game. It was already 1:00 A.M., and we were still in the arena. So my immediate thought was, Let's get back to the hotel, get some food, get Mike some treatment, and get some sleep.

I was also worried about Carlos. He had played 22 minutes against UCLA, and even though he only scored two points, he gave us a lot of bulk underneath the basket—something we were going to need for the rest of the tournament. But we knew Carlos wasn't yet 100 percent. How was *he* going to feel the next morning? He might be sore. Was *he* going to be able to play against USC?

And then there was Chris Duhon to think about. Chris got cracked in the head during the Missouri game. He seemed okay now, yet he did not score a basket against UCLA.

For most of the year, we had averaged five players in double figures. That was one of the keys to our success. If one person had not been shooting well, another guy or two would pick up the slack. But now, all of a sudden, we had become a two-man scoring team. Jason and Shane had 58 of our 76 points against UCLA. That's 76 percent of our total coming from only two players. That's too much.

Then there was the problem that we had played very poorly as a team against UCLA. Usually, a good team won't play two games like that in a row. And this game against USC was a big, big game. I've always felt that the regional championship game is the toughest game for a team to win—because it means a trip to the Final Four. And for coaches and players, that is *the thing*—the promised land, Mecca—and you have a chance to win the ultimate prize, the national championship.

When we got back to the hotel, we grabbed a sandwich and then met as a staff until about 6:00 in the morning. At that meeting, we watched about seven USC games and noticed that on defense they had a tendency to double-team the player who had the hot hand.

Johnny Dawkins knew USC's head coach, Henry Bibby, and he realized that coming from a pro mind-set, Bibby would, in all likelihood, try to take Jason and Shane out of the game. If USC double-teamed both of them, then there were going to be one or two of our players left unguarded. We knew that's what they were going to do, because they had played that way all year long.

So the question now was, How do we counteract that strategy and score anyway? Well, we all felt that Chris Duhon was going to be the guy they would leave open, because he had not made a single basket against UCLA. He had been 0-for-2 on field goals, had been 0-for-2 on three-point shots, and had gone 4-for-7 from the free throw line for a total of four points. It became clear to us that Duhon was going to have to step up in this game. And that meant we had to get him off his habit of deferring on offense.

We had another problem with that strategy, though. USC was a very athletic team, and they had a terrific point guard in Brandon Granville. In order to take him out of the game, we had to put Chris Duhon on him—which would lend toward Chris not shooting as much.

So, in our minds, Chris Duhon's defense on Granville was going to be a key to the game. But Chris Duhon's offensive shooting was also going to be a key to the game, because USC was not going to guard him. We had to start working on Chris to get him ready. And we really had only one day to do it.

*   *   *   *   *

The next morning, Mike Dunleavy woke up feeling better than we had anticipated. He still hurt a little bit, but he didn't complain at all. It looked like he was a go for the game. Carlos also woke up strong. No aches, no pains, and his foot felt fine. It seemed that all the hard work he had done to get back was now paying off in a big way. I was ecstatic with Carlos's performance against UCLA. He hadn't played in a month, he wasn't 100 percent, yet—and he still gave us 22 strong minutes. I was so proud of him.

At breakfast, we showed Duke's uplifting 1992 championship

video, "One Shining Moment." And when it finished, I said to the team: "Don't forget—this is *our* moment. We win this game and we're going to the Final Four. Right now, this is *our* moment."

Johnny and Chris immediately began talking to Duhon and showing him tape of previous USC games.

"You're going to have wide open shots during this game," said Chris Collins, "You need to start getting into the frame of mind to shoot the ball when that happens."

"You also have to do a good job guarding Granville," said Johnny. "Don't let him get the ball back. Pressure him. Turn his back. We're counting on you, Chris. This will be your big night."

> *"They told me that I was going to make big shots against USC. At first, I didn't believe them. But when we watched USC on tape, I could see they were going to try and take Jason and Shane out of the game."*
>
> *—Chris Duhon*

* * * * *

We arrived at the First Union Center two hours before game time to give our guys plenty of time to prepare. USC decided not to take advantage of early shooting, so we had the entire court to ourselves. We went through our normal warm-up drills, and when free shooting started up, Chris Duhon went over to Wojo and asked if he would feed passes to him so he could concentrate on his shooting.

I'll never forget seeing Wojo, in his suit and tie, under the other basket spotting Chris Duhon threes. They must have been over there for half an hour—just the two of them. It was a beautiful sight.

USC vs. Duke
First Union Center, Philadelphia, Pennsylvania

March 24, 2001—Duke out-dueled a tough USC team to win its ninth regional championship in 10 attempts under Coach Mike Krzyzewski and another trip to college basketball's Final Four. The story of the first half was the combined shooting of Shane Battier and Jason Williams, who totaled 33 of Duke's 43 points. The Blue Devils hit on 10 of its first 15 shots from the field and took a five-point lead, 43–38, into the locker room at the intermission. . . .

At halftime, we were up by five, but we should have been up by 11 or 12. We had a chance for an early knockout, but USC wouldn't go down. They showed us that they were going to fight to the end. I was also interested that they were not double-teaming anybody—which was good for us, because it allowed Shane and Jason to score a lot. After conferring with the staff, we felt that it would be a close game and that Coach Bibby would probably order the double-team in the second half.

"Okay, listen up, guys," I said to the players. "This team is *not* going to go away. So we'd better be ready in the second half. We should beat them, because we're better. But USC is a great team. If we let up for even one exchange, they're going to score, or get a steal, or do something else to beat us. So you can't let up—not even for one exchange."

Then I looked directly at Chris Duhon and said, "You've got to be on top of your game defensively and shoot when you're open. *Shoot when you're open!*"

. . . In the second half, the Trojans went to a roving man-to-man defense that focused on Shane Battier and Jason Williams but, at times, left other Blue Devils open. . . .

Chris Duhon took his first three-point shot during the first minute of the second half and missed. After that, he seemed tentative. He was only 1-for-3 in the first half, with his lone basket coming on a fast-break lay-up. We were all encouraging him from the bench. Then, during the first TV timeout at the 14:41 mark, Wojo pulled Chris aside. "Listen, Chris, *now* is the time," Wojo told him. "It's now or never. Just let it loose."

. . . With 14:10 left in the second half, Chris Duhon brought the ball down the court and passed it over to Shane Battier. Battier dumped it inside to Carlos Boozer, who immediately kicked it out to the top of the key where Chris Duhon was standing all alone. Duhon, standing a couple of steps behind the three-point arc, shot and made it, boosting the Duke lead from six points to nine, at 54–45. . . .

> *"As Carlos passed me the ball, I could hear somebody from the USC bench yelling, 'He can't shoot! He can't shoot!' I looked to my right over at Mike Dunleavy, but he was covered. Then I heard Wojo yell, 'Shoot!' so I did. After I hit that first one, I felt a lot of confidence flowing through my body. Then I stopped thinking and just played on instinct."*
>
> *—Chris Duhon*

. . . The freshman would hit similar three-point shots twice more in the second half—all as USC was building momentum. The second one came with 5:17 left, on an inbounds pass from Jason Williams. That pushed the lead to 11 points. The final Duhon bomb came at the 3:01 mark, when Jason Williams found him wide open on the right wing. That shot put Duke ahead by 11 points, 75–64, and the Blue Devils cruised the rest of the way. Jason Williams led all scorers with 28 points, followed by Shane Battier, who recorded his fifth straight double-double with 20 points and 10 rebounds. Duhon finished with 13 points, while Mike Dunleavy scored 11. With the win, Head Coach Mike Krzyzewski takes Duke to Minneapolis for his ninth Final Four.

Final Score: Duke 79, USC 69
Overall Record: 33–4

> *"As soon as the game ended, I went straight over to Chris Duhon and gave him a big hug. 'We're going to the Final Four,' I said. 'Savor this. A lot of people would pay a lot of money to trade places with you.'"*
>
> *—Shane Battier*

> *"I went up to Chris, put my arm around him, and said, 'Thank you. Let's do it again!'"*
>
> *—Mike Dunleavy*

> *"It really didn't hit me until after the game and Coach K came up and*

embraced me. He told me that I hit some big shots. I thought a minute and replied, 'Hey, I did!' It was kind of amazing. I thank God for giving me the opportunity to make them."

—*Chris Duhon*

Jason Williams was named the most valuable player of the East region—and he really deserved it. But the award could just as easily have gone to the other pillar of our team, Shane Battier, who recorded a double-double against both UCLA and USC. Even though we had won both games largely because of those two guys, I was pleased with our team's overall improvement after that gut-wrenching first half against UCLA.

After his injury, Mike Dunleavy had reared back and played a terrific defensive game against USC. He never offered one excuse about his shoulder—not one. Chris Duhon not only came out of his scoring slump to help us win the game but also played terrific defense against Granville, who scored only one point the entire game and committed four turnovers. And Carlos Boozer was back. He had given us over 20 minutes in both games, and I just knew that with another week's preparation, he'd be playing and scoring just like he was before he was injured.

I was proud of everybody. But I was particularly proud of Casey, Matt, and Reggie, who had filled in for Carlos and made it possible for us to go to the Final Four. In the eight games since Carlos broke his foot, those three guys combined for more points and rebounds than the three of them had produced in the previous 29. They were absolutely unbelievable. I still do not completely understand why they were not more nervous. They simply played like champions. And now, that's exactly what they were—champions of the East region of the NCAA tournament.

In the locker room, before everybody showered and dressed, I told the guys they should go back out on the court and try to see their families. Parents and loved ones can't get anywhere near the locker room after an NCAA tournament game, and since we were going straight to the airport from the arena, I knew the parents wouldn't get to see their sons. "Fellas," I said, "I want you to go back out on the court and see your families for a few minutes. They've come a long way to support us. Give your moms and dads a hug. And tell them we're going to Minneapolis."

*   *   *   *   *

When we finally boarded the bus to go to the airport, our driver, James Alexander, was blaring the Bee Gees song "Stayin' Alive"—which was a theme song of sorts for us during the tournament. When I got on, all the guys were yelling, "*Dance, Coach! Come on, dance!*" But two years before, after we won the East Regional, I had done a little dance on the bus and then we lost in the national championship game.

"No," I said, "I've learned my lesson."

Then there was a collective groan from the team.

"All right, all right, I'll tell you what," I said, "I'll dance when we win the national championship."

The Final Four

On Monday, March 26, 2001, my daughter Debbie went into the hospital for the scheduled delivery of her second child. She had planned to have the baby between the East Regional final and the Final Four because Mickie and I would be home. I don't know why, exactly, but she had been very confident we would be going to Minneapolis.

Our entire family was waiting in a room on the maternity ward when Mickie, who had witnessed the cesarean delivery, came in to tell us the good news. "Michael Giovanni Savarino just came into the world," she said. "He's eight pounds, 14 ounces." Debbie and her husband, Peter, had named their baby after me. I couldn't have been more proud.

After I saw Debbie and met Michael, I headed back to my office to tell our team the good news and to begin preparing for the Final Four. The guys on the staff and team were very happy about the arrival of the newest Blue Devil—and Dave Engelhardt was relieved to put away his midwife book. The birth of a grandson really helped me keep things in perspective. It made me realize that no matter what happened in Minneapolis, I was a lucky man.

I also couldn't help but think back to 1999, when we played in the Final Four. It was only two years ago, but it felt like an eternity. We had a completely different team that year. The only common denominators were Shane and Nate. And the truth was that if you only looked at physical talent, the 1999 team was stronger—and they had *lost* in the championship game. But I had high hopes, because this team was a much closer group of kids. They had played more like a true fist than any other team I'd ever coached—and they were still improving. My hope was that they would peak and be playing their best basketball of the year in the Final Four.

> *"Our team was very different from the 1999 team. This team had been sculpted by adversity. We came together and fought hard to get to this point. We were on a mission. And we'd worked a lot harder than the '99 team to make it to the Final Four."*
>
> *—Shane Battier*

The most glorious day in college basketball is that last Saturday when four regional winners converge in a single city—all with grand visions of becoming the national champions. Joining Duke were three terrific teams with three great coaches: 1997 national champion Arizona, led by Lute Olson; defending national champion Michigan State and Tom Izzo; and Maryland, making its first trip to the Final Four and coached by Gary Williams. And wouldn't you know it, by the luck of the draw, the two ACC schools had to play each other in the semifinals.

In my 26 years of coaching, I couldn't remember playing any team four times in one season. I thought about what Juan Dixon had said to me after the ACC semifinal. "See you in the Final Four," he had said. I guess it was meant to be, but psychologically speaking, Maryland was not a good opponent for us to play. We had won two of the three previous contests—but just barely. And Maryland had beaten us in the second game when Carlos broke his foot. I had no idea what would happen this time. But I was pretty certain of one thing: The Terrapins were not going to be nervous playing against us. Even though they'd be excited about playing in their first Final Four, they would be playing a familiar opponent. And I felt sure they'd have a serious revenge factor after our victory over them in the ACC tournament.

* * * * *

Almost every week during the season, we picked out a guy who was our top priority for the upcoming game. This week it was Nate James, who had played very poorly in the regional finals. He had scored two points against UCLA and four against USC. He had only six points in Philadelphia! The guy who made that fabulous tip-in to beat Maryland in the ACC semifinal game was nowhere to be found. It was like *our* Nate was being held hostage somewhere and somebody else was in his body.

At our first staff meeting back, I addressed the issue. "We're not going to win the national championship," I said, "unless we have Nate playing like the warrior he has always been. I'm not going to let him finish his career like this. So, I'm going to kick him out of the first practice. I'm going to put the pads on his heart and just shock him emotionally."

At our first team meeting on Monday afternoon, we gave each player a Final Four bracket and an itinerary that took them from our trip up to Minnesota, through the semifinal game, the championship game, the return to Duke, and the official welcoming home ceremony. We wanted them to think beyond the first game and to visualize winning it all. Then we talked to them about potential distractions. "When you make the Final Four, all of a sudden you hear from cousins you never knew you had—and they all want tickets. But you have to be a little bit selfish this week. You should keep your immediate family and your best friends close. But don't over-commit or spread yourselves too thin. I want you to remember that this is *our* moment. This is *our* time. Let's picture ourselves as champions."

As the players headed out to the court to stretch and warm up for practice, I went into my office and tried to work myself into a lather so that I would be angry when I kicked Nate out of practice. But that day, Nate didn't give me an opportunity to follow through. Afterward, Johnny, Chris, and Wojo gave me a look as if to say, Well, Nate's still here.

"Okay, okay," I said. "I'm not getting soft. He just didn't give me a reason to do it."

"Yeah, he had a great practice," said Johnny.

"Tell you what," I said, "for tomorrow, let's put together about 10 or 15 clips of the Southern Cal game. Focus on individuals, both good and bad. But make sure there's a couple in there of Nate playing awful. That will give me a chance to shock him like I want to. Afterwards, though, I'd like you to get with Nate and show him a tape of all the good stuff he's done throughout the year. Show him that Clemson game, when he carried us on his shoulders—and some clips of him pumping his chest. Remind him of the player he has been over the last five years. Remind him that he's our warrior, our rock."

*   *   *   *   *

In the locker room the next day, I reviewed the USC tapes with the team and coaches. First I showed some clips of Jason—both good and bad. Then I got to Nate. In the first clip, he was shown just wandering around the court. "What's wrong with you, Nate?" I said. "It looks like you don't care." And the second one exposed something he *should* have done—a mistake of omission. "Look! Here you're not going to the boards," I said in an irritated tone of voice. Then I just stopped the tape and looked at him. Everybody else was silent.

"I can't believe . . . I can't believe that you, who has given us everything, has stopped giving. I can't believe you're not going to finish this journey with us. And you know what? We can't do it without you.

"You're just not the same person we have come to know, Nate. You've been a warrior. You've been the best offensive rebounder on our team. We've always been able to count on you for defense, too. And now, you're going to let us down? Now—when we're playing in the Final Four?

"Well, I'm not going to allow you to play like that. And you know what, I don't want you to come to Minneapolis with us. Just stay here. I'm not going to have you there and play the way you played in Philadelphia. That's not who you are. If the *real* Nate James wants to come, I'll take him. But I'm not taking the guy on this tape."

Those were pretty harsh words to speak to a veteran ballplayer, especially in front of the whole team. But I knew Nate could take it—and at that point, I knew he needed it. "Okay," I said to the team, "I can't bare to watch any more tape. Get out on the court."

At practice, Nate played with a new intensity and a new abandon. I had gotten through.

*   *   *   *   *

The next afternoon, we all received a real treat when legendary UCLA basketball coach, John Wooden, spoke to our team. Coach Wooden was in town for the McDonald's All-Star game, which Duke hosted at Cameron Indoor Stadium. I invited him to our team meeting in the locker room and, if he wished, to stick around for our film session. He said some very nice things about me, about the program, and about teaching.

"Having John Wooden, who won 10 NCAA championships, in our locker room prior to the Final Four was awesome. He was very soft-spoken. He complimented our team play and told us that this could be a very special time in our lives. He didn't speak long, but just the fact he was there was exciting. He complimented Coach K and then stayed for the tape of Maryland. I kept looking over at him and he would often smile. I think he really enjoyed being in a locker room again with players. As we all left to go out to practice, he shook our hands and wished us well. Coach Wooden was a real gentleman."

—Mike Dunleavy

*   *   *   *   *

Out on the court, we primarily practiced end-of-game situations, such as: Duke 78, Visitors 74, and one minute left in the game; Duke 36, Visitors 28, and one minute left in the half; Duke 80, Visitors 80, and six seconds left in the game. My main goal was to get the players accustomed to thinking while they were on the court. I wanted them keenly aware of what was going on in the game at all times.

When the Blue team won one of those situations, Battier really got angry.

"*We can't have this!*" he screamed. I was really glad for his outburst, because it showed me just how much he really wanted to win. Shane had lost in his sophomore year and was denied again last year. This time, he really wanted that championship ring.

* * * * *

Having played Southern Cal on a Saturday, we had a full week to prepare for the Maryland game. And it really came in handy for Boozer. Carlos had played over 20 minutes against both UCLA and USC, but he did not jump very well. Our goal at this point was to get him ready to score. And since the doctors were telling us that his foot was all healed, I believed we needed to focus on building Carlos's confidence level so that he believed his foot would be just fine if he went all out.

"How can we create some confidence for him?" I asked Wojo. "Can we be creative and do some things that will let him feel more comfortable in exploding off that foot?"

Later that day, Steve invented a special drill just for Carlos, in which the big man would grab a ball, extend himself toward the basket, and dunk it—no dribbling, and only one step off his previously injured right foot. Carlos and Wojo worked on the "Boozer drill" over and over and over again, just the two of them. And the more they did it, the more you could see Carlos's confidence build. He would explode toward the basket, dunk it, and then land on his feet.

"How's the foot, Carlos?" Wojo would ask.

"*Not bad,*" he'd respond.

"Carlos will be ready for Maryland," Wojo told me a few days later.

* * * * *

At practice the day before we left for Minneapolis, I gave each player a photograph of our 1992 national championship celebration in which the guys were holding up the trophy. Only there was a twist to this picture. I had asked our staff to superimpose our current players' heads on the bodies of the players on the '92 squad—and write down at the bottom, *2001 NATIONAL CHAMPIONS*.

"Put this in your notebooks," I said. "And once in a while—on the plane ride up to Minnesota, before you go to sleep at night— take it out and look at it. I want you to think of yourselves holding up that championship trophy on Monday night." The players chuckled and grinned at each other when they looked at the picture. It was a little humorous to see their heads on other players' bodies. But I was also very serious. "You guys know I believe in visualizing our dreams," I said. "Well, this is our moment. And remember, only one team can have this moment. Not many teams ever get the opportunity to make it happen. You have that chance. So don't be nervous. Be excited."

I had two primary goals in getting them to focus on this picture. First, of course, I wanted them to think about their moment, because visualization can be a great motivator. But I was also attempting to get them to think of the Final Four as a new and separate journey from the rest of the season.

They had beaten UNC to win a share of the regular-season conference championship. They had won the ACC tournament. They had won the East Regional and were going to the Final Four. In Minneapolis, they would be adored, praised, and pampered. So there could be a tendency to wonder how it could get any better. And the truth is, somewhere along the line, any human being could say, "That's good enough. We did great." Then they could rationalize and relax. But my goal as head coach was to lead these guys to the big prize. So I had to inspire my team to perform at the highest possible level.

In addition to getting my team ready, I also had to prepare myself. Much was made about me going for a third national championship. And it really *was* a little bit of a hump to get over. I already had two, and there could have been a tendency to rationalize that they might be enough. Visualization also played a part in motivating myself, although not like you might expect. I could *not* visualize myself cutting down the victory net. But I *could* visualize Mike Dunleavy doing it—or Jason Williams holding up the championship trophy. I reminded myself, also, that this was Shane's time. He deserved to win it. We were in Shane Battier's car and this was his ride to the national championship. By visualizing the players and coaches winning it all, I needed no other motivation.

*   *   *   *   *

After a light morning workout, we all flew up to Minneapolis on Thursday afternoon. But before we left, the managers passed out small, hand-embroidered patches that were personalized for each of the players. In turn, the guys put them in their gym bags and carried them to the Final Four. Each patch had a heart on it—and was thoughtfully made by Jonathan Patton, our young friend from Duke Children's Hospital.

Also on the trip, Mickie handed me a note from Debbie. I had gone over to the hospital every day since the baby had been born, and I had seen her earlier that morning. But I still missed my oldest daughter very much. She had always traveled with me before—especially when we went to the Final Four. "Dad, I'll be with you," Debbie's note read. "I'll be watching on TV with Joey and Michael. I'll be thinking of you and I'll be with you in spirit. Win the whole thing."

Debbie's note and Jonathan's patches served as reminders to all of us that life is more than a basketball game—and that we should count our many blessings.

*   *   *   *   *

That first evening at the Final Four, the head coaches are required to attend a special program put on by the NCAA. The only problem that I had with it was that it separated me from my team and prevented us from going to dinner together. All year, I had tried to avoid anything that broke our routine.

On Friday, we went to the Hubert H. Humphrey Metrodome and practiced for 50 minutes in front of 30,000 people. It was a good time to get the team accustomed to the environment. And even though there were a lot of people in the stands, we had a very intense practice. At the Final Four, teams are allowed only one 50-minute practice on-site the day before the game—and then a shoot-around on game day. If you arrive in town too early, you have to find some place else to practice. One reason we traveled on Thursday instead of Wednesday was because I'd rather practice on our home court than in a strange place.

After the workout, we went to eat at a downtown restaurant recommended by Nick Horvath and Dave Engelhardt, both of whom had grown up in Minneapolis. The players could order whatever they wanted. There were no restrictions on food—except that they couldn't get three orders of steak and lobster. We *did* have a budget. Several of our former coaches also joined us, including Jay Bilas, David Henderson, Quin Snyder, Tim O'Toole, Chuck Swenson, and Mike Brey. It was a way of staying connected with former players and coaches—and being a family.

After dinner, we held a team meeting in my room back at the hotel, in which my main goal was to keep the players motivated. I began by reminding them that they had won every tournament they had been in this year: The Preseason NIT, the ACC tournament, the Greensboro tournament, and the Philadelphia tournament. "Now, let's win the Minneapolis tournament," I said.

Then I read a letter from an old friend of mine, Colonel Ishmon Burks. He was an officer at West Point when I was coaching there, and now he was Commissioner of the Kentucky State Police:

I spend most of my day thinking about "force multipliers." Those are the things that make you and the organization better without any increase in manpower or dollars. "Force multipliers"—like superb leadership on the floor, preparation and planning, enthusiastic optimism, tough training, and truly caring for soldiers—can make a difference. I also believe that when force multipliers are present, courageous acts take place. I have found, in many ways, we are not equal. The great equalizer is courage. Evaluate the courage and the will of the opposition. Take nothing for granted. Go Duke.

"That's interesting, isn't it?" I said to the team after reading the letter. "The five points we've been talking about—communication, trust, collective responsibility, caring, and pride—are force multipliers, aren't they? They don't cost money. They only cost the commitment and time it takes to make your group a fist. As a result of force multipliers, then, you are more apt to have courage—both individually and collectively. Well, fellas, I want you to think about tomorrow—and about having *courage* tomorrow."

Next we showed the team video of Duke's 1992 national championship victory. After it finished, I said: "Wasn't that great, guys?" Then I held up a video that our staff had put together especially for this moment. "But this tape is even more appropriate," I said.

Every year, at the Final Four, CBS puts clips of the championship team's performance to the song "One Shining Moment"—and shows it to conclude their television broadcast. It's the national anthem of college basketball, and every kid's dream is to appear in that video. I wanted the kids to visualize themselves standing on the podium watching "One Shining Moment" after they had won the championship game. So I had Jeff La Mere and Johnny Moore, the producer of our television show, put together our own personalized version of that highlight tape with great plays from the season. That's what I was holding in my hand. "As you watch this," I said, "I want you to think about this Final Four being our moment."

THE MUSIC STARTS
> *Shane leading a huddle before a game*
> *Nate dunking the ball*
> *Jason making a three-point shot*
> *Shane slapping Jason's hand*
> *Carlos dunking the ball*
> *Mike hitting a three-pointer*

THE LYRICS BEGIN
The ball is tipped.
> *Casey making a tip-in at the ACC tournament*

There you are.

Jason dribbling the ball
You're running for your life.
Jason driving toward the basket and dunking the ball
You're a shooting star.
Chris making a lay-up
Shane winking and smiling at Duhon
All those years,
Nate making a lay-up
No one knows just how hard you worked.
Jason and Nate high-fiving and pounding their chests together
But now it shows.
Jason feeding Carlos on an alley-oop and Carlos dunking the ball
Shane blocking a lay-up attempt
That one shining moment
Shane blocking another lay-up
You reached deep inside.
Jason stealing the ball in the "Miracle Minute" against Maryland
In one shining moment,
Then Jason hitting the three-point shot that cut the lead to five
You knew you were alive.
Jason driving against UCLA and rolling a ball off the rim,
Feel the beat of your heart,
Then Shane following up with the dunk
The wind in your face,
Mike hitting the floor after going for a rebound
It's more than a contest.
Shane diving for a loose ball
It's more than a race.
Matt and Chris bumping each other's chest
Casey blocking a shot under the basket
Nate feeding Jason on a fast-break lay-up
Mike feeding Shane on a fast-break lay-up
Jason making two daredevil lay-ups
Nate helping Jason up off the floor
Shane making a driving lay-up, hitting the floor, and being helped
up and embraced by Matt

And when it's done,

Carlos taking one step toward the basket and dunking the ball through the hoop

Win or lose,

Mike dunking the ball on a breakaway lay-up

You always did your best.

Just before halftime of the first Maryland game, Jason taking the long pass from Mike and laying it in the basket just as the buzzer sounded

'Cause inside you knew,

Chris making the "giant killer" shot in the last second of the Wake Forest game

Wojo and Coach K on the sidelines jumping in the air with both arms raised

That one shining moment, you reached for the stars.

Jason embracing Chris

Shane making a lay-up

One shining moment you knew . . .

Shane making a driving two-handed dunk

Carlos on the sidelines, in civilian clothes, roaring his approval

One shining moment you were willing to try.

Shane making that incredible block of Joseph Forte's lay-up attempt from behind

One shining moment you knew . . .

Shane blocking a shot from the front

Nate making a lay-up and beating his chest

Chris diving for a loose ball and Carlos coming in to grab it

One shining moment.

Mike feeding Jason on a fast-break lay-up

Nate's last-second tip-in against Maryland in the ACC tournament semifinal

Shane yelling his approval

Andy Borman embracing Casey Sanders

The entire team holding the ACC tournament championship trophy over their heads

THE MUSIC ENDS

When the video concluded, there was complete silence—no talk, no cheering. But their eyes told the story. They were moved. The impact of that video went beyond what I normally try to reach with a motivational technique.

"Okay," I said after a long pause. "Everybody get a good night's sleep. And think about being courageous and about this being our moment." Normally, they'd walk out of the room joking and jostling around. But this time, there was not a sound. They now understood what a huge moment this was.

*   *   *   *   *

Nobody said much in the locker room before the national semifinal game. Everybody was walking around with a quiet confidence. We simply knew that we were going to win this game.

There was no quiet confidence out in the crowd, however—especially among members of my family. Joining Mickie and Jamie behind the Duke bench were my daughter Lindy and her fiancé, Steve Frasher, who had flown in from Los Angeles. Also there were my brother, Bill, and his wife, Pat, who had traveled from Chicago. This was the first time Debbie had not been with the family, and they were all concerned that her absence might be some sort of jinx. So they went through all their rituals and traditions. As they always do, Bill and Pat brought along a cup of Sprite for Mickie and a bag of peppermints. The mints had to be passed out at certain key points in the game. And everybody had to sit in a specific order.

Anticipation in the arena was mounting. Forty-six thousand people had just watched Arizona defeat Michigan State and were now clamoring for the game that would determine whether Duke or Maryland would be the second team in Monday night's championship game.

National Semifinal Game
Maryland vs. Duke
Hubert H. Humphrey Metrodome, Minneapolis, Minnesota

March 31, 2001—Duke trailed by as many as 22 points in the first half, before cutting the deficit to an 11-points at halftime. Maryland got off to a rapid start in its fourth meeting of the year with the Duke Blue Devils. While Duke was missing 12 of its first 16 shots, Maryland was hot—going 5-for-6 from beyond the three-point arc. . . .

After the first two minutes, Maryland was leading 7–0. We had been playing very poorly overall, and after that seventh point, Jason walked the ball down the court and held out his hand to call a set play.

At the 16-minute mark, we were down by five and Jason signaled for another set play. This particular play calls for five passes so we can move the ball around and take a bit of time off the clock. What the heck is he doing, I wondered. We never call that play at the beginning of the ball game. We were supposed to be running the ball up and down the court. I was really getting frustrated. But Jason was just nervous—and he called that same play three times in the first eight minutes of the ball game.

The third time he called it, I started saying to myself, "34–4. 34–4." I was beginning to have some doubts whether or not we were going to win this thing. So I tried to put a lid on those doubts by thinking about something positive. Johnny Dawkins heard me and looked at me kind of funny. "Johnny, that's important for me," I said to him. "I am not going nuts."

"I know, Coach," he replied with a smile "I know you're okay."

. . . Maryland continued to shoot well and deny Duke their outside shooting, until Coach Mike Krzyzewski called an apparent desperation timeout only nine seconds before a scheduled TV timeout. At that point, the Terrapins were leading 23–10 with just over 12 minutes to go in the first half. But by the next TV timeout at the 7:55 mark, Maryland had extended its lead to 17 points, 34–17. During that break, Duke senior and the consensus national player of the year, Shane Battier, was the image of frustration as he hurled a half-full cup of water to the floor. . . .

"I was embarrassed. We had played so great the whole year. Now we're at the Final Four, and we're getting killed by Maryland, of all teams. I couldn't believe it. I wasn't going to go down without a huge fight. So I started yelling at our guys. 'We better get our rears in gear,' I said. 'This is the Final Four. We need to fight them—I mean literally fight them. We're not playing hard enough or smart enough right now. Let's get out there and fight!'"

—Shane Battier

Everybody was a little uptight and a little scared. After all, at that point, it looked like we were going to get blown out in the Final Four. But I kept thinking there was still a lot of time left in the game. I also didn't feel the need to jump all over the players, because they were already doing a good job of that themselves.

"Look, fellas," I said, "we're playing as bad as we can—and they are playing as well as they can. This is not going to last the full 40 minutes. Just go out and play ball. We're losing by 20 points. What are you afraid of—that we'll lose by 40? Why don't we just settle down and do the things that got us here, okay?

"Don't look at it like we have to beat them all at once. Let's take it in segments. Remember, we used that strategy at North Carolina. And I don't want any more set plays called. Follow your instincts. Be the players I know you are. That's what got us here, and that's what will get us out of this hole."

I think I actually smiled during that huddle. Sometimes instead of cursing and screaming, a smile or a laugh is what we need. In this case, I noticed that the guys started to relax. They went back onto the court with a new attitude.

"Our bench was real active during this game. We kept cheering for our guys to get back in the game. We reminded them that we had been in this situation before. We'd beaten Maryland with the "Miracle Minute," and we'd come back from a 10–0 deficit in the ACC semifinal game. We knew we could do it again."

—Dahntay Jones

... Two minutes after the timeout, Maryland's lead went to 22 points, 39–17, on Steve Blake's three-point shot. However, Nate James immediately responded with a three-pointer of his own, and Duke seemed to get back into their rhythm. The Blue Devils managed to cut the lead to eight points with less than a minute left in the half. But a Duke turnover and a Juan Dixon three-point bomb just before the buzzer pushed Maryland's lead to 49–38 at the intermission. During the first half, Duke was only 2-for-12 from beyond the three-point arc, while Maryland shot 55 percent from the field. ...

In the locker room at halftime, I was really angry that we had allowed Juan Dixon to hit a three. That was a heck of a punch to take. Just when we had clawed our way back into the game and cut the lead to single digits—we committed a turnover and Dixon hit a big one that said to us, You're not back in it. It gave them the psychological advantage of a double-digit lead at halftime.

At another time in my career, I would have blasted my team. But we made a significant comeback, and we were playing much better, so I bit my tongue. "Okay, forget about the three," I said. "Forget about it. It's not a good thing, but we've done so many good things we shouldn't worry about it. Right now, we're only 11 down after having been down by 22. That's good."

There was a part of me that couldn't believe those were the words coming out of my mouth. I mean, I was *very* angry. But I did not show my team anger. I didn't want to shake them up in a negative way. Basically, I tried to focus on the fact that we cut the lead in half. I tried to focus on the glass being half-full. The key was to ease the nervousness of the team, because I was pretty sure no team had ever come back from this kind of deficit in the Final Four.

While our staff was meeting in another part of the locker room, the players got some drinks and talked about the game. Then, when we all got together, one of our managers handed me a statistic that I shared with everybody. "Remember, we were playing the game in four-minute segments?" I said. "Well, let's see how we did. Looks like we lost the first three four-minute segments, but won the fourth and the fifth. That's good. So, listen up, guys. We still have plenty of time. Do you remember the first Virginia game? Do you remember that one word that was plastered all over the locker room before that game?

"*ATTACK. ATTACK,*" they said.

"That's right—ATTACK. I want you guys to go out there and just have one thing in mind this second half—ATTACK!"

The other key thing we had to do in the second half was to stop Juan Dixon. He had burned us for 16 points in the first 20 minutes, and we just could not afford to let him keep doing it. Somebody had to step forward and accept this challenge. But who was it going to be? When

I mentioned what I wanted, Nate James simply said, "*I got him.*"

"Okay, Nate," I responded. "Just stop Dixon. Just stop him!"

> "*I knew I was the one to do it. I had to dig down and deny Dixon the ball or get a hand in his face when he did shoot. When he had the ball, I concentrated on his left hand, because it usually tipped off whether he was going to shoot, pass, or drive. I also felt I could take advantage of my three-inch height difference over him.*"
>
> —*Nate James*

The last thing I said to the team as they went back out on the court was: "Let's go out there and follow our instincts. Let's find our heart. Let's be men. Let's be the team that got us here all year. And let's play defense."

THE FIST. "*One, two, three—Win!*"

... Duke scored on five of its first six possessions of the second half, and after a Chris Duhon three-pointer from the right wing, the Blue Devils cut Maryland's lead to four points. The Terrapins built it back up to eight, but Duke fought back to get within two at the 12 minute mark. After Maryland scored five unanswered points to push the lead back to seven, Shane Battier hit a three-point bomb that reversed the momentum. Then he led his team in a sprint back down the floor as if to signal to Maryland that Duke had more energy left. ...

Shane's three-point shot was one of the turning points of the game. We were down by seven, and things were starting to go Maryland's way. Then, all of a sudden, he drains this long shot that said to everybody, We're going to win this! Now we were down by only four—and the momentum had shifted back our way. It was a downright arrogant shot at a time when a player would normally be tentative. It was Larry Bird–like. It was huge.

... With 6:52 left, Jason Williams gave Duke the lead for the first time, 73–72, by making his first three-point shot of the game. Up to that point, Williams had been 0-for-9 from beyond the arc. ...

Jason's three-point shot to give us the lead was one of the great plays of our season. In that moment, in what was perhaps his toughest shooting game of the year, Jason had the courage to go for it. I believe you win championships when your best players have the freedom and the courage to take those kinds of shots.

. . . Duke took the lead for good at 78–77 when Carlos Boozer knocked down two free throws with 4:43 to go. A minute later, there was a violent collision between Chris Duhon and Steve Blake as they went for an errant pass. Both players hit the floor. Blake got up first and was escorted to the bench, but Duhon was apparently knocked unconscious when the back of his head slammed into the floor. Duke trainer Dave Engelhardt and head coach Mike Krzyzewski knelt on either side of the freshman. While the trainer examined Duhon, Krzyzewski held his player's right hand and rubbed his shoulder. After a few minutes, Duke players Andy Borman and Andre Buckner assisted the trainer in helping their teammate stand up. But Duhon's feet barely touched the floor as he was carried toward the sidelines. Duhon had been called for a foul on the play, and Terrapin Drew Nicholas took Steve Blake's free throws and made them both. Maryland had cut the lead to 80–79, but Duke would never trail in the game again. . . .

As Chris was being helped through the portal to the locker room, I did something I've never done before. I looked up into the stands, saw Mickie, and motioned for her to have Chris Duhon's mom come down. Usually, I wouldn't do that, because the parents might be too emotional to handle such a situation. But Vivian Harper is a very strong woman—and she is also very good for Chris. They have an amazing relationship.

She came down out of the stands and went to her son. By then Chris was leaning up against a wall and seemed to be recovering. Vivian asked Dave Engelhardt if Chris was all right. "I think he's coming around," responded Engelhardt. "What do you think?"

"Let me look at him," said Vivian—who then took her son's face in her hands and looked into his eyes. "Chris, are you all right?" she asked.

Duhon looked into his mother's eyes and said, "*Mom, I'm okay. I want to go back out there.*"

Then Vivian turned to Dave Engelhardt and said she felt it was okay to take Chris back to the sidelines.

With only 43 seconds remaining, and with us leading 91–84, I put Duhon back into the game. Normally, I would not have done that, but this was an unusual circumstance. I knew we were going to be playing for the national championship on Monday night, and I did not want Chris's last impression to be to be one of being carried off the court. Rather, I wanted him to have the more positive thought of having come back to finish the game. I felt he would have a much better chance of going on to the Next Play with that as his base. It was a small thing, but I knew it could be a help in getting him over a potential psychological barrier.

> *"After I got back in the game, Jason was at the free throw line, and I was standing behind him next to Steve Blake. Just before Jason took his second shot, Blake leaned over to me and said, 'I knocked you out.' I looked up at the scoreboard, which showed us leading 91–84, and there were only 22 seconds left in the game. Then I looked over at Blake and said, 'Actually, I knocked you out.'"*
>
> —*Chris Duhon*

. . . Duke scored 57 points in the second half. After being down 22 in the first half, the Blue Devils outscored Maryland 78–45 and ended up winning the game by 11 points. Shane Battier led all scorers with 25. Carlos Boozer played 25 minutes and scored 19. Jason Williams, despite a poor performance in the first half, ended up with 23. Nate James chipped in nine points and also limited Maryland star Juan Dixon to only three points in the second half. Said Dixon after the game, "He made me work hard. He's a great defender. Duke is fortunate to have Nate James." Maryland coach Gary Williams came right to the point afterwards. "Nobody is 22 points better than Duke," he said of the biggest comeback in an NCAA tournament semifinal game. The Blue Devils now advance to play Arizona Monday night in the national championship game.

Final Score: Duke 95, Maryland 68
Overall Record: 34–4

When the final buzzer sounded, there was not a lot of celebrating. We shook hands with the Maryland players and coaches and walked off the court. Everybody knew we had just won a tough game against a great team. But there was more work to be done.

> *"We still had one more game to play. Our mission was to win the national championship."*
>
> —*Shane Battier*

In the crowd, Mickie, Jamie, Bill, Pat, and Lindy were ecstatic at the victory. Steve, who was just learning the game of basketball, watched in amazement as we came back from a 22-point deficit and ended up winning by 11. "Okay," he said to Lindy, "we're going to church tomorrow to give thanks for divine intervention."

In the locker room, I went over and congratulated Nate and Carlos. The two guys we had focused on all week really came through. Nate had nine rebounds and nine points—which was 150 percent better than he had done in two games in Philadelphia. Not only that, he had shut down Juan Dixon in the second half—allowing him only a single three-point shot. Nate was absolutely awesome. In many ways, we owed that victory to him. Carlos also played very well. In coming off the bench for the third consecutive game, he scored 19 points by converting 7-for-8 attempts. In the previous two games, he had scored only three points and attempted just four shots. It looked like our big man was back—in a big way.

*   *   *   *   *

Now it was time to turn our attention to our seventh national championship game in my 21 seasons at Duke. Our opponent, Arizona, had thrashed Michigan State in the first semifinal game. In fact, Arizona's average margin of victory in the tournament so far was over 16 points. To me, they looked like an NBA team—perhaps the best we would face all year. The Wildcats had started the season ranked Number 1 in the nation but dropped after a few early losses. Then they had come back and were now ranked Number 2. There was, however, a much bigger story to Arizona's journey to the national championship game.

Lute Olson had lost his wife, Bobbi, to cancer in early January. He left the team for awhile—and that's when the team plummeted in the national polls. But when Lute returned, the Wildcats started to pick it up and were now playing their best basketball of the year. The media really hyped this story, and when they combined it with the fact that Lute and Bobbi had grown up in Minnesota, there was no doubt that the Arizona Wildcats were the sentimental favorites. There were huge billboards all over town that simply said: FOUR BOBBI. And although we wanted to win, nobody wanted to be the team that ended Arizona's amazing season.

That really put Mickie and me in an odd situation. We had known Bobbi. She was a wonderful person. And I was concerned for Lute. And, at the same time, we didn't want Duke perceived as the heavy in this situation. Heck, if I didn't have to coach against him, I would have been rooting for Lute, too. However, I began to think of my players—and that helped me get in the right frame of mind. Wojo had taught me that lesson when we played Missouri. Right now, I had to do everything I could to win this game—for them.

Once again, the staff and I stayed up all night reviewing film and planning a game strategy. I was particularly concerned about our team's ability to get past a big victory in a short period of time. We had had some problems with that scenario earlier this year. After our thrilling "Miracle Minute" win over Maryland, we followed up with a loss against North Carolina four days later. And after our last-second win at Wake Forest, we lost to Maryland three days later in Cameron. Now, we had only one day to get over this incredible victory. Back then, I made a big deal about it to our players and coaches. Now, I was hopeful we had learned from those experiences and would be able to put it behind us. Our Next Play philosophy was crucial in this instance, because our next game was for the national championship. It can't get any more serious that that.

In our review of the game, it became obvious just how poorly Mike Dunleavy had played. Actually, he had not scored well in the entire tournament—having been only 6-for-19 from the field. I felt certain that Lute Olson was going to concentrate on shutting down Jason and Shane offensively. That meant someone was going to have some open shots. Chris Duhon and Nate James were now playing well. That left only Dunleavy.

"We need to isolate all of Mike's minutes," I said to the staff. "Clip them out, make a separate tape, and let's show it to him. Mike is going to be the key guy in the championship game. We've got to get him ready." Then I turned to Chris Collins. "Chris, Sunday is going to be crazy for me with all the media requirements," I said. "Will you get with him and show him the tape? Show him where he wasn't tough, where he was tentative, and where he was trying to finesse it too much?"

"I'll do it." said Chris. "He'll be ready."

"Great. And Wojo, you get with Boozer and show him tapes of the Wake Forest game. Remind him of how he played before he was hurt. And tell him he needs to play that way in the championship game."

"Will do," said Wojo.

At that meeting, we also came up with a simple game strategy to beat Arizona. They had five terrific players and ran plays for each one. So our plan was to use team defense to stop them rather than defend them one-on-one. Because Loren Woods played predominantly at the high post, we decided to put Shane on him. That way, Shane could be a defender in almost every defensive play. He could help defend against the drivers and also come down and double Wright when he got the ball in the low post.

The first order of business on Sunday was to make sure that Chris Duhon was okay. He woke up with a headache and a big knot on his head—so we decided that he should not participate in practice. Fortunately, he felt better as the day went on. The second order of business was to get our team a new locker room. The one we had been in for the Maryland game was extremely small. And, I believe, because we had played in the second game and had to wait around in there, it could have been a contributing factor to our guys being nervous out on the court. It was such a confined area, and there was not a lot of room to walk around. So I requested a change and we were given the same locker room we had had when we won the national championship in 1992.

During our feedback session, we did not even show the players the first eight minutes of the ball game. I didn't want those negative images in their minds. We did, however, address the issue of why they were nervous. And Johnny Dawkins perhaps provided the best perspective. "You let the moment become bigger than your performance," Johnny told the players. "You can never let the game be bigger than you are—no matter what game you're playing. The guys who become the most successful are those who rise to the occasion. Whether it's in a pickup game or the NBA Finals, the guys who can maintain their performances are, inevitably, the champions. You should be ready to play tomorrow night just like you did in the regular season."

*   *   *   *   *

At Sunday afternoon's press conference with several of the players and me, one of the reporters referred to the fact that Duke's 1992 championship had gone through Greensboro, Philadelphia, and Minneapolis—just like this year. "Are you a karma guy?" the reporter asked me.

"A karma guy?" I repeated. "I'm a Polish guy. Is karma a sausage or what?"

"Okay, Coach," persisted the reporter. "Did you feel a sense of déjà vu, given the path to this national title game?"

"What's déjà vu and karma," I replied, "I'm an inner-city Chicago guy. We don't do karma stuff. I do know Karma, though. He played second base on my baseball team when I was growing up."

Although there were numerous questions for Duhon, Williams, Battier, and Dunleavy, who were with me at the press conference, I was mildly concerned that no one had asked a question of Casey Sanders. "Why isn't anyone asking him questions?" I said. "Casey has had an amazing month, and I think it's a sign of what he's going to do, not only Monday night, but in the future." After that somebody did ask a question of Casey. "Okay, Casey," I said, "This is your first question. I built you up. Don't give them any karma or anything like that. Just tell them like it is."

*   *   *   *   *

While I did media interviews for nearly two hours, Chris Collins spent time with Mike Dunleavy. After they watched the tape of the semifinal game and reviewed Mike's performance, the two of them just sat and talked. "You know," said Chris, "Arizona probably watched this game and is thinking, Well, if we have to leave somebody alone, it should be Dunleavy because he's not playing well."

"*Yeah, that's for sure,*" responded Mike.

"You grew up in a basketball family, and I know you always dreamed of playing in a championship game. When you played the game in your back yard, you always made the shot. More than that, though, you always *took* the shot. The last thing you ever want to do is look back on this moment and say you didn't play with the confidence and the aggressiveness that you always dreamed of.

"Mike, it's the national championship game. Play confident. This is the game you dreamed of your whole life. Leave everything out there on the court. Take your shots."

"*You're right,*" said Mike. "*I'm fine*"

*   *   *   *   *

In the locker room, prior to our Sunday practice, I went over to Mike Dunleavy, who had not played a good game against Maryland. In 24 minutes, he had scored only four points and pulled down just three rebounds. He was 2-for-8 from the field, he was 0-for-2 from three-point range, and he took no free throws at all. I put my fist on his heart and I said, "You're going to be great tomorrow night?"

"*I'm sorry I didn't play well against Maryland, Coach,*" he said.

"Forget about the Maryland game," I said. You're going to be great tomorrow night." Then we had a really good practice and went out for our team meal. After eating, we all came back to my hotel room for a brief meeting.

> *"The night before the championship game, the team met in Coach K's hotel room. Coach was in the middle of his final comments when Nate James's cell phone started ringing. Uh-oh, I thought, this is not what you want to do. Coach is old school and he just hates cell phones going off in the middle of press conferences and meetings. It was one of our unwritten rules all year: No cell phones in meetings. Coach could have blasted Nate, but he didn't. Instead, he brushed it off by making a joke.*
>
> *" 'What's that, Nate? Don't your girlfriends know you're in Minneapolis?'*
>
> *"Everybody laughed. But the truth is that some of that laughter was in relief. If he had jumped down Nate's throat, we might have been a little more uptight. Instead, it was no big deal. That's a good example of how Coach K adjusted to the situation, to the moment—all year long."*
>
> *—Mike Dunleavy*

*   *   *   *   *

On the bus ride from the hotel to the national championship game, I did something different and unusual. Normally, everyone keeps quiet on that ride. It's part of the ritual. And if somebody does say something, he will generally get the evil eye. Well, this was a nice bus that had television monitors in the ceilings. So we slipped our personal "One Shining Moment" video into the cassette recorder and played it—just like we had done the night before the Maryland game. Again, I was trying to condition the players to believe that *this* was going to be *their* moment. When the video ended, I addressed the team. "Fellas," I said, "tonight, at the end of the game, we will be standing up on the championship podium listening to this song."

That's all I said on the bus. That was enough.

*   *   *   *   *

In the locker room before the game, I addressed the entire team. "Okay, guys, this is it. This is the moment we've been waiting for all year. When you're out there tonight, I want you to be thinking about one thing. I want you to be thinking about THE FIST—about a five-point play."

As I spoke, I wrote *THE FIST* up on the board along with the five points.

"Point one, Communication: "We're going to talk to each other on the court. We're going to tell each other the truth, and we're going to get on one another if we need to.

"Point two, Trust: We are going to trust each other to make the right passes, to take the right shots, and to play the best defense. We are going to have confidence in each other.

"Point three, Collective Responsibility: We win and we lose together. This is *our* pass. This is *our* shot. These are *our* free throws.

"Point four, Caring: We care about one another. If something happens, we'll be there for each other.

"Point five, Pride: We are proud of each other and of our performances.

"One final thing," I said as I wrote *DUKE* in the last space on the last bracket of the season. "Our destination now is not just to play the game. It is to win the national championship."

THE FIST. "*One, two, three—Win!*"

Then we took the court for the last game of the year. There were 46,000 people in the Metrodome and millions more watching on television. After I watched Arizona warm up for a few minutes, I turned to Johnny Dawkins. "This team is very, very good," I said. "Even better than I expected. It's going to take a lot of courage to win this game."

> *"Just before we were introduced, Jason and I hit fists and said: 'Guards win championships!'"*
>
> —*Chris Duhon*

National Championship Game
Arizona vs. Duke
Hubert H. Humphrey Metrodome, Minneapolis, Minnesota

April 2, 2001—The Duke Blue Devils and the Arizona Wildcats squared off in the national championship game, but neither team could manage more than a five-point lead as they battled back and forth in the first half. Dominated by defense, both teams combined to shoot only 4-for-22 from beyond the three-point line—and the big men dominated the scoring. Arizona took the ball right to the basket—taking advantage of Loren Woods's five-inch height advantage over Shane Battier. At the 8:56 mark, Carlos Boozer made an impressive drop-step fake to score against Wildcat center Loren Woods and give the Blue Devils a three-point lead at 20–17. . . .

Carlos usually goes to the basket with his left hand. But on this particular play, he faked left and went right. Loren Woods was completely fooled. It was not only a great play, but Carlos had never made a move like that before. And to make a shot like that for the first time in the national championship game was unbelievable. I grabbed Johnny's leg and said: "Did you see that drop-step move! He's becoming a player." Then I looked down the bench. "Wojo, did you see that? Unbelievable!"

. . . Duke's biggest problem in the first half was the fact that their All-America point guard, Jason Williams, got into foul trouble. Williams was called for his second foul less than five minutes into the game. Coach Mike Krzyzewski immediately substituted Chris Duhon but allowed Williams to play another eight minutes on and off during the half. . . .

> *"[Jason] Gardner was crowding me. He was really low and made it look like I was pushing off on him. They called a couple of fouls like that. Their strategy was good and it worked. They took me out of my rhythm and tempo, and I wasn't hitting my shots."*
>
> *—Jason Williams*

. . . Duke carried a slim two-point lead into the locker room at halftime, as the Wildcats were called for goal-tending on a Jason Williams driving lay-up with six seconds left on the clock. . . .

At the half, I wrote a big *20* on the board. "Twenty minutes, guys,"

I said. "We're 20 minutes away from being national champions."

Then we went into our staff meeting, in which the main concern was guarding Loren Woods—who had just killed us in the first half. Our strategy going into the game had been to put Battier on Woods, because Woods normally plays out at the foul line. Besides, most people didn't dare to drive at Battier, because he was one of the great defensive players in college basketball. But Lute Olson is one helluva coach. He moved Woods inside and had him go straight at Battier. It was a brilliant strategy and it worked well. Now we had to make a countermove.

My immediate thought was to put a heavy body on Woods in the low post—and that would be Carlos. That would mean not starting Casey, though—and he was playing very well. But I had a gut feeling about Carlos. He had done something new, something I'd never seen before with that drop-step move. He had also made a great block on one of Woods's shots midway through the first half. It was clear to me that Carlos was really up for this game. So in the staff meeting, I announced I was going to start Boozer in the second half.

"Will that break our rhythm?" asked one of the coaches. "I mean the guys have been playing with Casey in there for a long time, now."

"We've got to do it," I said. "We'll have a better chance of winning if Carlos is in there. We've got to get him more minutes. We're not going to play tomorrow, so we might as well get him in there right away."

"What are we going to do about Casey?" asked Wojo.

Wojo was right. Here we are at halftime in the championship game, and I'm going to bench a player, even though he's playing well. So now I've got two things going on. First, Carlos—who might have been doing well in the opening half because there really wasn't a lot of pressure on him. But now we needed him to help us adjust to Arizona for the second half—and that would definitely involve added pressure. Second, Casey—who, as a starter, had been playing extremely well. In starting Carlos, we still needed Casey to play well in the second half. I didn't want him demoralized.

There was no time to mess around, so I addressed this issue in front of the entire team. While I was speaking, the five points of THE FIST that I had written on the board before the first half were still visible behind me. "Okay, guys, listen up," I said. "Casey, I'm going to start Carlos. Now you can't have a problem with this. You can't be asking yourself, 'Does this mean he doesn't believe in me?' We don't have time for that, son. Besides, you know that's not the case. I do believe in you. But this is best for the team. Now, are you okay with it?"

"*I'm okay, Coach.*"

"Are you sure?"

"*Yes, Coach, I'm okay with it.*"

"Carlos," I said, turning to my other big man, "did you see that Casey is okay with you starting?"

"*Yes, Coach.*"

"So it's okay for you to keep going. You don't have to worry about him, right?"

"*Right.*"

"And all you other guys, you don't have to worry about Casey either. Casey, do you want anybody to worry about you?"

"*No, I'm all right.*"

"Okay, everybody. Then let's concentrate on beating Arizona in the second half."

I made a big deal out of this little exchange because I wanted to remove all possible doubts in their minds so they could go out there and play on their instincts. And also, because when you pay attention to people's feelings like that, you are able to create and preserve the No Jealousy Zone.

There was no problem with Casey and there was no problem with Carlos. It sounds simple, but the fact is that this does not happen on most teams. I really believe the groundwork for that moment was set when Carlos broke his foot yet continued to support and help Casey over the last month. Now it was Casey's turn to support Carlos. To me, it was truly a remarkable thing.

"I was very surprised when Coach decided to start me in the second half. And I was especially relieved when he talked to both Casey and me about being okay with the move. Casey's my teammate, and it was important that he wasn't going to have a problem with it."

—Carlos Boozer

"Carlos played really well in the first half. That's the first time he started to look like the Carlos of old. When Coach made the change, it wasn't so much that I thought my time was up. Rather, I thought, My time's still here, but now I have Carlos with me. I didn't feel any dejection. I was ready to do whatever was best for our team."

—Casey Sanders

"Okay, guys, get together," I finally said. And everybody put their fists on top of mine and we said our last collective cheer of the year: "*One, two, three—Win!*"

On the way out to the court, Chris Collins encouraged Mike Dunleavy to step up and take his shots in the second half. "This is your moment, Mike," said Chris, "Now is the time! Now is the time!"

And the Blue team yelled their encouragement. "*Come on, guys. Let's go! Let's go!*"

"*Let's do it! Let's do it!*"

"*This is our time! This is our moment!*"

"*This is our time! This is our moment!*"

"All during that second half—during the last 20 minutes of our season— **Coach K's words and The Lessons of the Season** *would ring true in the players' minds, consciously and subconsciously."*

—Shane Battier

. . . The second half began at a quick pace as Shane Battier and Carlos Boozer both scored in the first minute. . . .

"We Will Set the Pace of the Game."

"Carlos, if you believe, you will be the player you want to be and the player we need you to be."

. . . But All-America Jason Williams continued to struggle with two missed three-point attempts and a turnover. At the 17:01 mark, and Duke up by three, 40–37, freshman Chris Duhon drove the ball toward the basket, and the entire Arizona defense converged on him. Duhon then kicked it back out to Mike Dunleavy, who was left standing all alone on the right wing. . . .

Up to this point, Mike only had three points in the game. Usually, I am sitting down during the game. But for some reason, I found myself standing, and by the time Mike got the ball, he was only a few feet from me. I could almost touch him. As he caught the ball several steps beyond the three-point line, I just yelled, "Shoot!" And Mike shot *our* basketball.

. . . Dunleavy, who had scored only three points in the first half, then launched a long bomb that swished through the basket to extend Duke's lead to six. . . .

> *"When I caught the ball, I was going to shoot. And then I heard Coach say, 'Shoot!' and I felt a surge of confidence. So I let it go and it went in."*
>
> *—Mike Dunleavy*

"With Confidence Comes Courage."

. . . Only 24 seconds later, Shane Battier found Dunleavy on the left wing and passed it to him, and Dunleavy tossed up another three-pointer that caught nothing but net. On the ensuing possession, Defensive Player of the Year Battier pulled off a brilliant double-handed block on an Arizona driving lay-up and then slapped the ball over to Chris Duhon. . . .

"We Will Play Great Defense. We Will Stop Other Teams."

. . . Duhon raced the ball down the court, drove toward the basket, and kicked it out to Jason Williams on the right wing. But Williams gave up an open shot and threw a bullet pass across court to Dunleavy—who then hit his third consecutive three-pointer. . . .

"Chris and I were talking and said to each other that we needed to get Mike the ball on the next play. Chris reversed the ball out to me. I had a shot, but all I could think of was, Get Mike Dunleavy the ball!—so I blasted it over to him. He shot it and made it."

—Jason Williams

"Talk! Talk to Each Other on the Court."

"Make That Extra Pass. Give Up a Good Shot for a Great Shot."

"I was holding up my hands and calling for the ball. Jason quickly got it over to me, and the ball just floated out of my hands. I knew it was going in before I shot it."

—Mike Dunleavy

"When You're Hot, You Have to Call for the Ball."

"Shooters Don't Stop Shooting, at Duke."

. . . Mike Dunleavy's nine points in a span of 46 seconds gave the Blue Devils their first double-digit lead at 49–39. It also served to momentarily deflate the Arizona players, whose shoulders noticeably drooped after the third shot and just before they called a timeout. As Dunleavy went to the Duke bench, he was mobbed by his teammates. Arizona, however, stormed back with nine unanswered points. The string was broken when Casey Sanders, out on the high post, stole a pass and hit Dunleavy for a fast-break lay-up. Dunleavy subsequently scored seven of Duke's next 12 points to push the Blue Devil lead back to 61–51 with 10 minutes left in the game. . . .

"Mike, don't finesse it. Go right at the guy and make that basket. It could make the difference between winning and losing a ball game."

. . . Less than a minute later, however, Jason Williams was called for his fourth personal foul and was taken out of the game by Coach Mike Krzyzewski. . . .

When Jason committed his fourth foul, I immediately subbed Nate for him. It was really a dumb foul that Jason had committed—dumb! He was really off his game and everybody knew it. When he sat down on the bench, Johnny Dawkins went over to talk to him—and then Dahntay Jones followed up.

> *"I told Jason that he needed to get his head back in the game. And then I gave him some encouragement. 'C'mon man, you're our floor leader. You're the man! You're the best! We need you!'"*
>
> —*Dahntay Jones*

"If One of Us Is Weak, the Rest of Us Will Make Us Strong. When You're Having a Bad Day, You Must Allow the Others to Step Up for You, or to Pat You on the Back and Say 'C'mon, Get With It,' or to Get in Your Face and Try to Snap You Out of It."

When Jason went to the bench, something happened to our team. I could see a new level of intensity in their eyes. I was worried about Jason not being in the game, but this was a kind of determination that a coach dreams about. I believe all the players felt they had to step up, now that Jason was out.

Arizona was playing great. They kept coming back. Four separate times, they cut the lead to three points. But every time we needed a play, one of our guys stepped forward. Duhon ran the team up and down the floor. Shane had three out-of-body experiences. Nate, Casey, Mike, and Carlos all made big plays. And when I finally put Jason back in the game, he, too, came through in the clutch.

For the last 10 minutes of the national championship game, we were five playing as one. We became a perfect fist—and it was absolutely one of the most beautiful things I have ever seen. If it were a movie, a higher level of music would have been playing at this point.

8:27   Casey Sanders screens for his dancing partner, Shane Battier, who hits a jump shot and is fouled. Battier converts the free throw for a three-point play play.

         Score: Duke 64, Arizona 52

"That Was *Our* Shot."

7:57   After committing a foul, Nate James throws a pass out of bounds, and there is a TV timeout.

At the timeout, I walked straight toward Nate and got in his face. I was worried that he had not gotten on to the Next Play. That foul was still bothering him, and he threw the ball away and caused a turnover. I had to stop the cycle of bad plays—so I immediately addressed the problem.

"Nate! C'mon!" I said. "What the hell are you doing? You've just made two bonehead plays. You're throwing away *our* ball! C'mon, snap out of it. Do you know what we're playing for? We have a chance to be national champions. Get out there and play. Win a championship for us—don't throw it away!"

> *"I expected Coach to blast me. We were in the trenches, and I had screwed up. I deserved it. But then I began to think about my teammates. I wanted to do better for them."*
>
> —Nate James

6:54   Carlos Boozer feeds Nate James for a reverse lay-up. James is fouled and converts the free throw for a three-point play. Up to that point, James had only three points in the game.

         Score: Duke 68, Arizona 59

"Go On to the Next Play."

5:23   Arizona cuts Duke's lead to three, on a Gilbert Arenas driving lay-up.

       Score: Duke 68, Arizona 65

4:59   With the shot clock running down, Chris Duhon drives to the basket, makes a giant-killer over Arizona center Loren Woods, and gets fouled. Duhon converts the free throw for a three-point play.

       Score: Duke 71, Arizona 65

"Chris, shoot! Shoot, will you? Chris! Will you shoot the ball?"

4:43   Arizona comes right back and cuts the Duke lead to three, on a Richard Jefferson three-point shot.

       Score: Duke 71, Arizona 68

4:26   Mike Dunleavy feeds Carlos Boozer for a lay-up that misses. But Shane Battier follows, with a two-handed dunk.

       Score: Duke 73, Arizona 68

"If Something Happens, We're There for Each Other."

3:57   Arizona responds with two free throws.

       Score: Duke 73, Arizona 70

3:39   Mike Dunleavy shoots a short jumper and misses. Shane Battier wedges in between three Arizona rebounders and makes a magnificent backhanded tip-in.

       Score: Duke 75, Arizona 70

"Be Innovative in What You Do. Be Creative."

"The Timetable Is Set for Shane to Be Our Leader."

3:03   Jason Williams calls a set play and loses the ball. Williams and Mike Mike Dunleavy dive on the floor for it.

"Jason, dive for that ball. It could make the difference between winning and losing a ball game."

2:48   Richard Jefferson hits a short jump shot for Arizona.

   Score: Duke 75, Arizona 72

2:31   Jason Williams drives and feeds Shane Battier under the basket. Battier makes a spectacular one-handed slam dunk.

   Score: Duke 77, Arizona 72

"We're Riding in Shane Battier's Car."

1:43   Shane Battier sets up a screen for Jason Williams, who hits a crucial three-point shot. Up to that point, Williams was only 1-for-10 from three-point range.

   Score: Duke 80, Arizona 72

"I was thinking about how poorly I played in the Virginia game earlier this year. Then, as I'm bringing the ball down the court, I look over at Coach and he gives me the sign for the LA set play. That's my play. I did a double-take. Me? I thought. Are you sure you want me? I just made a turnover. I'm not playing well. And you want me to take the shot right now at this crucial point in the game? But Coach gave me the sign again, and this time, he pointed straight at me to reinforce exactly what he wanted. That gave me a tremendous burst of energy, and I thought, Okay, I trust Coach. I can do it. And I'm not going to let my frustration show this time. I'm not going to let my teammates down. I'm going to care about them. I'm going to care about my performance. I'm going to get on to the Next Play. Then I took the shot and made it."

   —Jason Williams

"Trust and Caring, Guys. Don't Forget. Trust and Caring."

"The Three-Point Shot Has to Be Taken with Courage, Unselfishness, and Intelligence."

0:47   As Duke tries to take time off the clock, Jason Williams is fouled. Williams converts one free throw. Battier grabs the rebound on the second shot to maintain possession.

Score: Duke 81, Arizona 72

> *"After the foul was called, I pulled everybody together in the huddle and said, 'Right now, right here, this is our moment. It's never going to happen again. We will never be in this situation again. Don't let down. This is it!'"*
>
> *—Shane Battier*

"No Excuses."

0:41   Chris Duhon is fouled and makes the first of two free throws.

Score: Duke 82, Arizona 72

0:32   Arizona misses a desperation three-point attempt. Carlos Boozer grabs the rebound and swiftly gets it into the hands of Chris Duhon. With 20 seconds left on the clock, Arizona coach Lute Olson motions to his players to back off and let the clock run down. At that moment, the Duke players and coaches know they have won the game. . . .

Sometimes at the end of a game like this one, the opposing coach will try to ruin it for the other team. But knowing that there was no way Arizona could win it at this point, Lute Olson allowed our team to bask in the moment for the final twenty seconds. It was a classy thing for him to do.

On the sidelines, the players were all jumping in excitement, the staff started hugging each other, and I finally gave Johnny Dawkins that high five I had owed him since the Wake Forest game.

Out on the court, Chris Duhon began hopping up and down in anticipation He was bouncing the ball high, fast, and hard—probably to the beat of his heart.

"If You Believe in What I Say, If You Do Everything I Ask You to Do, We Will Win the National Championship."

Then, with three seconds left on the clock, Chris Duhon did an extraordinary thing. He handed the ball to Jason Williams. It was the last pass of the season.

"I felt the ball should be in Jason's hands at that moment, so I deferred to him. But I also knew it had always been a dream of his to win a national championship and throw the ball up in the air as the clock hit zero. When the buzzer sounded, Jason launched that ball and yelled, 'Yeah!' It was a great moment."

—Chris Duhon

. . . Duke had four players in double figures that night. Mike Dunleavy led all Duke scorers with 21 points and was named Most Valuable Player of the Championship Game. Shane Battier, who played all 40 minutes, scored 18 points and had 11 rebounds in what was his fifth double-double in the NCAA tournament. He was named Most Outstanding Player of the Final Four. Carlos Boozer also recorded a double-double with 12 points and 12 rebounds. Jason Williams scored 16 points, and Chris Duhon added nine. Shane Battier finished his career with 131 total victories—tying the NCAA record. With nine three-pointers, Duke had a total of 60 for the tournament—tying the record set by Arkansas in 1995. Duke also became the winningest team over a four-year period in NCAA history. Their record of 133–15 broke the record set by Kentucky from 1996–1999. With the victory, Duke's Mike Krzyzewski became only the fourth college coach to win three or more national championships, joining John Wooden (10), Adolph Rupp (four), and Bobby Knight (three).

Final Score: Duke 82, Arizona 72
Overall Record: 35–4

When the clock hit 0.00, Carlos just held his arms in the air and had an expression of tremendous satisfaction on his face. Shane sank down into a crouch for a private moment. Mike slowly walked over to Shane with his arms outstretched, and the two roommates embraced. Then all the players gravitated toward those two guys. Jason, Nate, Carlos, Chris, Casey, J.D., Matt, Andy, Andre, Ryan,

Nick, Dahntay, and Reggie—they were all there hugging each other. It was a beautiful sight.

I went over and shook hands with Lute and all the Arizona players. Then there were the individual hugs.

The senior, Battier, hugged the freshman, Duhon. "*I'm proud of you. I love you.*"

Casey Sanders hugged Nick Horvath. "*We did it, buddy. We did it.*"

Jason hugged Chris. "*Guards win championships. Guards win championships.*"

I hugged all the players, but Shane's was as extended and as heartfelt as any I'd ever had with a player. "Thanks, Shane," I said. "Thanks for letting me ride you to this moment. I love you."

My hugs with Shane, Nate, J.D., and Ryan were more than just about winning the national championship. It was the end of our journey together. We were happy and sad at the same time. The feeling is not easy to explain.

Then I found my wife, Mickie, and our two daughters, Lindy and Jamie, who had come down onto the court. We were hugging each other when Jamie handed me her cell phone. "It's Debbie," she said.

"Debbie, did you see us hug one another?" I asked her.

"Yes, Dad."

"You were in the middle of that hug."

"I love you, Dad," cried Debbie into the phone. "I'm so proud of you."

"I love you, too. Hug Joey and Michael for me."

Hats and T-shirts were passed out to the team—and the scene was joyous, as more family and friends joined us on the court in celebration. Then it was time to receive the championship trophy. And there's no better moment in sports than, at the end of the competition, to be up on the podium with your team and be handed that trophy. The sense of fulfillment, the closeness and camaraderie, the magic of sharing that moment simply cannot be described in words. I was overwhelmed.

After we cut down the nets and hugged some more, we passed around the championship trophy. Then an announcement was made over the P.A. system in the arena: "One minute to 'One Shining

Moment.' " CBS was going to end its television broadcast and the 2001 college basketball season with the unofficial national anthem. So I quickly gathered the team around.

"Okay, guys, let's back up on the platform," I said. "We want to watch 'One Shining Moment' together. Just like we did with our own tape. But this time, it will be the real thing. You envisioned it, you thought about it, and now it has happened. Let's go up there and enjoy the moment."

When the video began, there were thousands of people still in the stands and millions more watching at home. But in a beautiful sort of way, our team was all alone up there—bound together by the common experience of our season, enraptured by the realization of having achieved our dream.

As the players stood on the podium together—their faces turned up, watching the big screen—the look in their eyes was almost spiritual.

Our journey was now complete.

$$*\quad*\quad*\quad*\quad*$$

There were interviews and press commitments to do after the game. And when Mickie and I finally made it to the team bus for our trip back to the hotel, everybody was waiting for me.

I walked to the back of the bus—giving everybody high fives along the way. And then the guys started to yell.

"*Come on, Coach. Dance.*"

"*Yeah, Coach. You promised us you'd dance when we won the national championship.*"

So I took my coat off and handed it to my daughter just as our bus driver turned the Bee Gees music on.

"Watch carefully, Jamie," I said. "It's all in the rear end."

And, as everybody hooted and hollered, I kept my promise and did my John Travolta strut down the aisle.

"Ah, ah, ah, ah, stayin' alive, stayin' alive. Ah, ah, ah, ah, stayin' alive, stayin' alive. . . ."

Epilogue

We arrived back at our hotel to an absolute mob scene. Students, fans, family members, and friends were packed shoulder-to-shoulder in the lobby and screaming at the top of their lungs. Johnny, Chris, and Wojo led us off the bus as the Blue Devils band played the Duke fight song. It was like a parade. People were slapping us on the back, giving us high fives, cheering, and waving.

The first person who met me was Elton Brand. A star in his own right, now he had put himself in that mass of people with the specific intention of greeting us as we got off the bus. When Elton gave a big bear hug, I immediately thought back to that scene two years before, when Elton and his mom had visited me in my hospital room, and we talked about his turning pro.

"What are you doing down here, buddy?" I asked. "Go on up to the reception."

"I'll be there, Coach," he said. "But first, I want to see the guys as soon as they get off the bus."

Elton and William Avery (who was also at the Final Four) were both in their second season in the NBA. If they had stayed in college, this would have been their senior year. Also present was last year's senior captain, Chris Carrawell, who was a big part of our two-year journey. It was really great to see them all—and I believe our winning the national championship helped put closure to the entire 1999 experience.

During that celebration, J.D. Simpson, our walk-on and tri-captain, came up and shook my hand.

"*Coach, I want to thank you for everything,*" he said, "*but especially for coming through on your promise.*"

"Thanks, J.D.," I replied, "but what promise?"

"*Well, don't you remember? That morning—the first practice after we lost on Senior Day—you promised us that, if we believed, we would win the national championship. Well, we believed and it happened. So thanks.*"

I couldn't speak—so I just smiled and hugged J.D.

When we arrived back in North Carolina the next morning, our team bus was given a police escort from the airport to the university. All along the way, people pulled their cars over and waved. At key intersections, crowds were waiting for us with Duke flags, homemade signs, and enthusiastic cheers. Cameron Indoor Stadium was filled to capacity, and when we arrived, we were given a thunderous standing ovation. Debbie, her husband, Peter, and the boys, Joey and Michael, were there and joined us in the celebration. The crowd wasn't satisfied with only a few remarks from the captains and head coach. They also called for each of the coaches and players to step up to the microphone and say a few words. It was a wonderful thing to have happen.

Actually, the entire season was wonderful. We won the preseason NIT. We tied for the ACC regular-season title. We won the ACC tournament. We won the East Regional of the NCAA tournament. We won the national championship. And we finished ranked Number 1 in the nation.

At the beginning of the season, sports analysts were saying that Duke's reliance on the three-point shot would be our downfall. But it turned out to be one of the reasons we succeeded. Over the course of the year, we took 1,057 three-pointers—450 more than our opponents and 72 more than anyone had ever shot before. We made 407 of those attempts for a 38.5 percent success rate. Because of the three-point shot, we were never out of a game— even when we were down by 22 points in the national semifinal.

Our 701 assists for the year also set a new NCAA record. And that, I believe, says a great deal about the unselfishness of our players.

I'd never had a team quite like this one. The players were only 18–22 years old, but I never once heard, "How come I'm not playing?" or "How come Shane's getting all the shots?" or "Woe is me." As unbelievable as it may seem, there was no jealousy on this team.

Neither was there any fear. The players were not afraid to lose. They were not afraid to fail. They were not afraid to take that open shot when it was there. They were not afraid to show their hearts to each other. And they were not afraid to say they loved one another.

These special things were not developed overnight. Team success is not just about the leader giving a motivational speech and expecting everybody to perform. Team success—and leadership, itself—is about relationships. Individual relationships and group relationships. And it's a never-ending process. You have to constantly nurture, grow, and work at them. That's one reason our journey to the national championship lasted two full years. It takes time to build trust. Last year, when we lost in the Sweet 16, we essentially had the same players. But the relationships were not yet at the point they needed to be.

Team success is also about practicing proper values until they become daily habits. It's about learning from defeats. And it's about the players being inwardly stimulated to perform when they're out there on the court. A leader has to give his players the latitude and freedom to make their own plays.

When Carlos Boozer broke his foot in our last home game of the season, we could have put the guys in a cage with set plays and a zone defense. Instead, we set them free. The entire basketball world was saying that Duke would not win another game. In fact, we did not lose another game.

In the middle of that crisis—at that moment of truth—we reached down for something deeper, something we did not even realize was there. It was a deeper form of commitment, a deeper level of brotherhood. We became much closer because we all knew we needed each other more than we ever had before. As a result, we were able to turn adversity into triumph. I don't think we would have won it all if Carlos had not broken his foot. That single event propelled us to the national championship.

All season, it seemed like there was a different player who stepped forward in each game. Shane against Princeton. Nate at Clemson. Carlos at Wake Forest. Mike at North Carolina. Casey, Matt, and Reggie in the ACC tournament. Jason against UCLA. Chris against Southern Cal.

But in the last 20 minutes of the championship game against Arizona—almost as if preordained—they all stepped forward:

Mike scored nine points in 46 seconds.

Carlos shut down Loren Woods and grabbed key rebounds.

Casey screened for his dancing partner.

Shane made a three-point play.

Nate made a three-point play.

Chris made a three-point play.

Jason made a clutch three-point shot.

They made the extra pass. They dove for the loose ball. The guys on the bench rallied their teammates on the court. Everything jelled in that last half. THE FIST came together.

And it didn't happen because a scouting report helped us get to know Arizona. It happened because we got to know our own players. We got to know them as individuals and as people. In leading the entire team's race, we let each kid run his own race. We let them be who they were. We encouraged rather than berated them. Our philosophy was about loving them and caring about them. It was about singling them out rather than selling them out.

And ironically, by working as a team, the players achieved their own individual accolades:

Mike Dunleavy became a legend in the championship game.

Chris Duhon was named ACC Rookie of the Year.

Casey Sanders became a starter.

Carlos Boozer started out on his way to becoming another Karl Malone.

Shane Battier won National Player of the Year and was a top pick in the NBA draft.

Jason Williams was named to the first-team All-America squad and was recognized as the best point guard in America.

And **Nate James,** the man who stepped back so that his teammates could step up on that championship platform, was perhaps the biggest winner of all. When he walked off the court in Minneapolis, he was not only a champion in basketball—Nate James was a champion in life.

*   *   *   *   *

Two days after we won the national championship, I sat down with the team in our locker room for a few minutes.

"It feels good to be together again, doesn't it," I said. "Even for a day, I missed being with you."

Then I began talking about academics. We'd been on the road a great deal, and I knew it had been tough for them to keep up with all their studies. But now, they had to come back down to earth right away.

"Fellas, we only have three weeks left of school," I reminded them, "and one of those weeks is for final exams. So you all have to get busy. You're champions on the court—now be champions off the court."

Then I stood up at the blackboard and posed one of the most important questions of the year.

"Why did we win?" I asked.

"*We were really together,*" said Shane.

"*We cared for each other,*" said Jason.

As the players responded, I wrote their comments up on the board.

"*We trusted one another*" and "*We played harder*" were a couple of other comments. When somebody said, "*We respected each other,*" I wrote it on the board and made another comment.

"That's a very good point," I said. "We respected each other. But you know, we also respected everybody else—the students, the secretaries, the people who clean the locker room, our opponents. And as part of that respect, we didn't forget to say, 'please' and 'thank you.' "

I paused a minute and once again began to write on the board.

"All of the things you've said are true. And here are a couple of other things.

1. We communicated well.

2. We trusted one another.

3. You already said we cared.

4. There was collective responsibility. We won and we lost together, and...

5. There was great pride.

"*THE FIST!*" said one of the guys.

"Right," I said, "THE FIST. Because we were a closed fist and because of our five-point play, we became national champions.

"But, you know, sometimes when people have success, they feel like it's a license to be somebody different than who they really are. They feel they don't have to do these things anymore. That's dumb, isn't it? Why wouldn't you do them all the time?

"So, if any of you see any one of us forgetting to do these things, remind us, will you? Remind your teammates. Remind your coaches. Remind me.

"But most of all, I want you to remind yourselves.

"I hope you will not forget why we're sitting in this locker room feeling so good about ourselves right now.

"I hope you got something more out of this season than the national championship.

"I hope you got a road map for success—forever."

2001 National Champions

"I've always enjoyed the success of my teammates. I knew if each of us per-formed his job at a high level, we'd be successful. So whenever my team-mates did something really well, I always made sure they knew from me that I wasn't jealous but, rather, that I was happy for them. It was an easy thing for me to do because of the great guys we had on our team. 'Unselfish' was a key value for each individual player—and for our team as a whole this year."

—Shane Battier

"It goes back to THE FIST. *We did everything together. We had to think as one out there. It wasn't about what we were going to do a couple of months down the road, it was about what we were going to do right then and there. That entire season was our time, our moment."*

—Carlos Boozer

"The greatness of our season was not defined by winning the national championship. That was just the cherry on top of the cake. We were more than just a basketball team. We were like a family. It was so special, it's hard to put into words. When people ask me about the season, all I can do is smile."

—Andy Borman

This year, we all went through a lot of ups and downs. The toughest point was when Carlos got hurt. But Coach K pulled us all together. He gave us a new plan, a new way to win. He also asked us to trust him—which we did. And look at what happened. I already believed Coach K was a great leader, but winning the national championship this year proved it beyond any doubt.

—Andre Buckner

"Unlike any other team I've ever been part of, we loved each other so much that if somebody was doing the wrong thing or really wasn't work-ing as hard as he could, then every single player could step up and say,

'Listen, this needs to change in order for us to win.' In one of our team meetings, the only players who spoke were members of the Blue Team. We told the starters what we thought and they listened to us. To do that, it takes love.

—Ryan Caldbeck

Coach K understood that the team needed to be ready for any game situation, and when we played Arizona, we were as prepared as a team could be. It is a magical moment when a group of people who have been working together begin to function in a way that they are greater than the sum of their parts. That alone will be one of my biggest memories from my time at Duke.

—Matt Christensen

"The main thing about this championship was the part of the team that did not get the glory—the guys on the Blue team who sacrificed every day but didn't play much in the games. That meant so much to me."

—Chris Duhon

"It was a perfect year. Everybody contributed. Everybody stepped forward when he had to. Destiny, fate—call it what you want. I think it was meant to be."

—Mike Dunleavy

"We had wonderful leaders throughout our organization. That made the players look good and it made our team look good. So I didn't worry about what might have been. I made up my mind that I was going to support my team. That was my role."

—Nick Horvath

"Nobody's going to remember who started and who came off the bench. What they are going to remember is that it was a national championship team, and I was on it. As a team, we were together. We really loved each other. That's the reason we won it."

—Nate James

"Whatever our roles were, we performed them to the best of our abilities. It didn't matter who scored the points or whose name appeared in the papers. Everyone was happy to contribute. Everyone was willing to be coached. We were all willing to do whatever it took for us to succeed as a team."

—Reggie Love

"I sat back and watched how Coach K handled himself on and off the court. I saw for myself the type of person he is. It's a real learning experience just to play under him. Patience is a virtue. My turn is coming, and when it comes, I'm going to be ready for it."

—Dahntay Jones

"This year, we all knew that we needed each other—especially after Carlos got hurt. So, whenever Coach got on one of the guys in practice, the rest of us would go up to that player, give him a pat on the back, and say something comforting: 'It's okay.' 'Don't worry about it.' Winning the national championship was the end result of always knowing we were there for each other."

—Casey Sanders

"Coach K helped us reach our fullest capabilities. We had constant conditioning in the beginning of the year. And practices were always really tough. It's hard playing through six months of basketball every day. But he provided us with a passion and a heart for it when we were tired. Coach K just never got tired. He was really hungry. And that inspired all of us."

—J.D. Simpson

"The reason for our success began and ended with Coach K. I'd run through a brick wall for him. I love Coach K. He's my father away from my father."

—Jason Williams

"It was a wonderful thing to see. All the behind-the-scenes things we did to prepare the players for their moment. Give them credit. They saw the

opportunity, they stepped forward, and they all seized their moment in time. It was perfection."

—*Johnny Dawkins*

"We had guys who were willing to lead and we had guys who were willing to follow. It takes courage to do both. We also had a shared championship vision. Everybody was selfless in our pursuit of that common goal."

—*Steve Wojciechowski*

"Whether it was going into a big game, overcoming an injury, or playing in the NCAA tournament—everything we did, we did as a group. It was the togetherness we had as a unit that made us champions."

—*Chris Collins*

"Coach K created an environment that included a specific process. The closeness and the togetherness our team shared was part of that process. It made all the difference in the world."

—*Jeff La Mere*

"Coach K and Shane were major reasons for our success. It's very uncommon to have both a coach and a star player who are so unselfish. Those two leaders set the example."

—*Mike Schrage*

"I just tried to sing my own song for this year's performance and not worry about things. It made me healthier and helped me coach for the right reasons. I had the most incredible year that I've had with a group of kids. I can't stop smiling."

—*Mike Krzyzewski*

Acknowledgments

Larry Kirshbaum shared our vision for this book from the very beginning. His insight, enthusiasm, and expert editing were invaluable contributions. Bob Barnett was key in turning our idea into a reality. We also appreciate the backing and assistance of Rick Wolff, Dan Ambrosio, and Rob Urbach.

Johnny Dawkins, Steve Wojciechowski, Chris Collins, Jeff La Mere, Mike Schrage, Gerry Brown, Jon Jackson, Debbie Savarino, Lindy Frasher, Jamie Krzyzewski, and the Duke basketball team managers all gave freely of their time and contributed significantly to the content of the book. Mickie Krzyzewski and Mike Cragg participated in every step of the writing and editing process—and the extent of their contributions to the book simply cannot be measured.

We would especially like to thank the players on Duke's 2001 national championship team. They were extraordinarily open about their feelings and generous with their time when it came to helping us research this book. Their collective attitude was very similar to their selfless mind-set during the season—which is why they are now champions both on and off the court.

About the Authors

One of the leading ambassadors of college basketball, Mike Krzyzewski is Duke's all-time winningest coach. The 2000–2001 championship season marked his 21st season at the helm of the Blue Devils' program.

Coach K became just the 10th coach in NCAA history to attain his 500th career victory, in his 23rd season as a college head coach. The Chicago native began his coaching career at Army in 1975–1976 where he led the Cadets to an NIT appearance. He took over the Duke men's basketball program prior to the 1980–1981 season.

Coach K served as president of the National Association of Basketball Coaches (NABC) in 1998–1999 and is very much involved with several community groups, including the Duke Children's Hospital and nationally with the Jimmy V Foundation.

Entering the 2000–2001 season, Coach K was a six-time National Coach of the Year and five-time ACC Coach of the Year with a 50–14 alltime record in the NCAA tournament. Coach K has the most wins in the NCAA tournament among active coaches.

Donald T. Phillips is the author of nine books, including *Lincoln on Leadership*, *The Founding Fathers on Leadership*, and *Martin Luther King, Jr., on Leadership*. He co-authored Coach K's *Leading with the Heart* in 2000. He currently serves as the mayor of Fairview, Texas.